Style and Socialism

Style and Socialism

Modernity and Material Culture in Post-War Eastern Europe

**Edited by
Susan E. Reid and David Crowley**

BERG

Oxford • New York

First published in 2000 by
Berg
Editorial offices:
150 Cowley Road, Oxford, OX4 1JJ, UK
838 Broadway, Third Floor, New York, NY 10003-4812, USA

Berg is an imprint of Oxford International Publishers Ltd.

Library of Congress Cataloging-in-Publication Data
A catalogue record for this book is available from the Library of Congress.

British Library Cataloguing-in-Publication Data
A catalogue record for this book is available from the British Library.

ISBN 1 85973 234 8 (Cloth)
1 85973 239 9 (Paper)

Typeset by JS Typesetting, Wellingborough, Northants.
Printed in the United Kingdom by Biddles Ltd, Guildford and King's Lynn.

Contents

Contents

Preface

Catherine Cooke

For those of us working on the material culture of the Soviet bloc – my own field is architecture – these materialized manifestations of such societies always seemed more revealing and enduring descriptors of their attributes and tensions than the ephemera of properly 'political' analysis. So history has proved.

Kremlinologists and their East European equivalents looked upon us as lightweights who swam in the froth while they probed the depths. When decontextualized and purely stylistic accounts were the norm they could argue a case, but that era is past. In the post-modern world we understand the potency of the fragment as a diagnostic site for exploring the condition of a whole system. We realize that any attempt to rewrite the histories of these states, any building of new understandings, must begin precisely by digging some new boreholes into their daily lives and looking afresh at the elements, the strata, the tensions and pressures we find there. The essays assembled here are such fragments and boreholes.

Mountains of documentation were hoarded in these states and their so-called 'collapse' has opened the doors for precisely such probing. The richness of the research that is emerging across all fields of cultural history, of which only a small front is represented here, is reflected in the way academic conferences on Soviet-bloc issues have become dominated by panels and papers from these areas, whereas previously it was earnest debates on political and economic minutiae which held sway.

The pre-collapse situation in Soviet-bloc studies had its ironies. Most prominent, perhaps, was the assumption, deeply inconsistent with the Marxist materialism underlying the polities being studied, that we can understand a superstructure without reference to the technological and material base that actually structures it. Modern systems analysis is enough to show us, without recourse to Marxism, if preferred, that it is what we would call in the broadest sense 'the technologies' that make possible certain lines of communication, which pattern certain paradigms of thought, which open or foreclose certain practical options for every organization or individual. While economic and political analysis focused on the middle term, those two more telling predictors of a system's behaviour, the meta-narrative and the detail, were ignored. The result was a failure to see that the system was becoming so unstable in relation to the external environment, and so organically fragile in its cells and mechanisms, that a chance concatenation of events could produce total collapse with enormous rapidity.

Systems, however, are how artists think. As the Russian Naum Gabo wrote long ago, 'artists are like sponges: they soak up what is going on around them, and it works on them.' The weakness of most political analysts, who believe their subjects to be so 'real', is their inability to read the languages in which either high art or popular culture ooze out their descriptions of that reality when the sponges are squeezed. This key area of diagnostics is not available to them.

The results have been costly. The clever analysts failed to predict system failure and their knowledge base was also too crude for any useful contribution to building the new universe thereafter. Some of the countries whose history is examined in this collection have fared better in that process than others. Some, as essays here show, never lost their memories of another, bourgeois, world akin to that with which they must engage now. In others, like Russia, it was not just an ignorance of their cultural makeup that gave the hoards of Western economic and political advisors the Dutch courage to plunge in – and be rapidly ejected, with the same force as a body rejects a transplanted organ. It was even an arrogant supposition there was no such culture. A little more knowledge of the subtleties, the richness of discourse, the independent value systems; of the level of cultural and aesthetic education; of the rich capacity to discriminate and communicate through the languages of art, personal display, and all the rest of material culture – a little more knowledge of this would have produced a greater modesty in the aftermath of that Big Bang when Gorbachev fell and the Berlin Wall came down.

The era of Khrushchev and Brezhnev, on which most of these essays focus, was where it all started. It was the period of opening up from what art historian Igor Golomstock described in 1974, in the dissident journal *Kontinent*, as 'a cultural vacuum'. In discussing the exhibition of 'unofficial' Soviet art shown in Grenobles that year his theme was the urgency of seeing such works through appropriate contextual spectacles: not as attempts at 'aping' contemporary Western art but as a 'striving to restore the broken links of cultural continuity' within their own. Golomstock's nuancing of the issue of readings and meanings was a brave attempt, like everything in that journal, at opening up Soviet-bloc culture to the level of discussion that is normal to us, and the papers here, in their modest way, follow that lead.

Here the artefacts of painters, the car industry, the fashion industry, the languages of consumer goods, of cartoons, of advertising, reveal to us the tensions that were involved in emerging, as Alexander Solzhenitsyn put it, *From Under the Rubble*. As he wrote there in 1973, the coming-alive again, 'the transition from silence to free speech' was more difficult for individual human beings than the earlier process of closedown. The difficulty was worse when blasts of Western culture were being thrown at the Soviet bloc, particularly from the US, which their own traditions and imaginations had somehow also to mediate.

Reactions to this cultural onslaught seem all the more robust and intelligent when we read now, in parallel probings of Western archives, of the resources that US government agencies devoted in the post-war decades to taunting the Soviet-bloc populations with America's consumer goods and her oh-so-free abstract art. For a salutary context to *Style and Socialism* I would commend any reader to Walter Hixson's *Parting the Curtain: Propaganda, Culture and the Cold War, 1945–1961*, of 1997, and Frances Stonor Saunders' *Who Paid the Piper? The CIA and the Cultural Cold War*, of 1999. Their titles indicate the plot. There was a warfare of artefacts and images and, as I have said, its analysis and legacy are more revealing and enduring than the history of political ephemera. Certainly they are more useful to understanding the tensions and aspirations of these populations now, and perhaps explain something of how they now vote.

List of Contributors

Catherine Cooke is a lecturer in design in the technology faculty of the Open University, Milton Keynes. She trained as an architect at Cambridge and since 1969 her research has been concerned with Russian and Soviet architecture and city planning. Her major publications include *Russian Avant-garde: Theories of Art, Architecture and the City* (London: Academy Editions, 1995) and *Soviet Architectural Competitions 1920s–1930s* with Igor Kazus (London: Phaidon Press, 1992).

David Crowley is a tutor in the History of Design at the Royal College of Art, London. He is the author of various studies dealing with the history of design and material culture in Eastern Europe including, *National Style and Nation-state. Design in Poland from the Vernacular Revival* (Manchester: MUP, 1992). He is also co-author of *Graphic Design. Reproduction and Representation since 1800* (Manchester: MUP, 1996). He is a member of the editorial board of the *Journal of Design History*.

Iurii Gerchuk is a Moscow-based historian and critic of Russian and Soviet art and design. From 1962 to 1967 he was an editor of the central journal of decorative arts and design, *Dekorativnoe iskusstvo SSSR*. He is the author of numerous books and articles on the history of graphics and book design, Russian art and culture from the eighteenth century to the present, the theory of ornament, book art and typography, and the history of Russian architecture.

Katarzyna Murawska-Muthesius, formerly curator of the National Museum in Warsaw, is a freelance researcher, publishing in Polish and British journals. She is editor of *Europäische Malerei des Barock aus dem Nationalmuseum Warschau*, exhibition catalogue (Herzog Anton Ulrich Musuem Braunschweig, 1988); *Trionfo Barocco*, exhibition catalogue (Gorizia, 1990); *Przewodnik Muzeum Narodowe w Warszawie* (with Dorota Folga-Januszewska, 1998) and is editing the proceedings of *Borders*. '*Kunstgeographie' in space and time*, a conference held at the University of East Anglia, Norwich. She has published various articles on the visual culture of the Cold War period.

Mary Neuburger is an Assistant Professor of Modern East European History at the University of Texas at Austin. She received her Ph.D. at the University of

Washington, Seattle. She has published numerous articles relating to Balkan history dealing with issues of nationalism, gender, and material culture.

Piotr Piotrowski is professor of Art History at the Adam Mickiewicz University, Poznań. He is the author of numerous studies of the history of Polish twentieth century art including *Znaczenia modernizmu: w strone historii sztuki polskiej po 1945 roku* (Poznań: Dom Wydawniczy REBIS, 1999) and *Dekada: o syndromie lat siedemdziesiatych, kulturze artystycznej, krytyce, sztuce – wybiorczo i sub-iektywnie* (Poznań: Wydawn. Obserwator, 1991). He has been the curator of various exhibitions including *Odwilż: Sztuka ok. 1956 r.* held at the Muzeum Narodowe in Poznań in 1995.

Mark Pittaway is Lecturer in European Studies in the Faculty of Arts at the Open University. He works on the social history and popular culture of post-war Hungary and is currently completing a book on industrial labour in the country between 1945 and 1958.

Susan E. Reid is Senior Lecturer in History of Art at the University of Northumbria, Newcastle upon Tyne. She has published on a range of themes relating to Soviet and post-Soviet visual culture in *Slavic Review, Gender & History, Art Journal, Journal of Design History* and *Art History*, as well as chapters in the anthologies *Regime and Society in Twentieth-Century Russia* edited by Ian D. Thatcher (London and Basingstoke: Macmillan, 1999); *Art of the Soviets* edited by M. Cullerne Bown and B. Taylor (Manchester: Manchester University Press, 1993); and *Women and Stalinism* edited by M. Illič (London and Basingstoke: Macmillan, 2000).

Raymond G. Stokes is Reader in Economic and Social History at the University of Glasgow and was previously Associate Professor of History in the Department of Science and Technology Studies at Rensselaer Institute. He is the author of *Divide and Prosper: The Heirs of I.G. Farben under Allied Authority, 1945–1951* (Berkeley: University of California Press, 1988); *Opting for Oil* (Cambridge: CUP, 1994); and *Constructing Socialism: Technology and Change in East Germany, 1945–1990* (Baltimore, MD: John Hopkins University Press, 2000). Stokes is currently completing a co-authored case study of privatization in the former East Germany during the 1990s (with Rainer Karlsch) and continues research on the history of BASF between 1925 and 1952.

Mark Allen Svede, doctoral candidate at The Ohio State University, has written extensively on Latvian contemporary art and visual culture. Forthcoming publica-tions include an essay on performance artists for an anthology about dandyism in contemporary art to be published by New York University Press, a chapter about

Latvian artists for a survey of gay and lesbian art and a collection of essays about nonconformist art making in Soviet Latvia to be published by Rutgers University Press. His curatorial work ranges from film restoration projects to serving as the Latvian acquisitions advisor for the Norton and Nancy Dodge Collection of Nonconformist Art from the Soviet Union at the Jane Voorhees Zimmerli Museum at Rutgers University.

Style and Socialism: Modernity and Material Culture in Post-War Eastern Europe

David Crowley and *Susan E. Reid*

Figure 1.1 Fashion spread from *Moda*, a Polish fashion magazine, 1957.

In Spring 1957 *Moda* (Fashion), a Polish magazine, published a spread that depicted models dressed in fashions approximating those currently emanating each season from Paris couture houses. (Figure 1.1) The models flirt with the seated figure of a chimney sweep. As if to stress his working-class credentials, this grimy workman is shown reading a copy of *Głos Robotniczy* (The Workers's Voice). Juxtaposing the productive worker and the profligate consumer, these photographs playfully satirize the polarization of two figures in the political imagery which had been reproduced by all regimes within the Eastern bloc during the Stalin years. One year after Nikita Khrushchev's 'secret speech' denouncing his predecessors, and the ensuing unrest in Poland and Hungary, these figures from the 'official' repertoire appear to have acquired dramatically different meanings. In fact, the magazine itself, perfect-bound and printed in colour, could be taken as evidence of the 'new course' in Poland. Such publications also reproduced articles and images from the Western press, thereby offering an insight into lifestyles which had hitherto been condemned or ignored. At the same time, their bright colours and strikingly modern covers seemed to suggest – not only to their Polish readers but also to other members of the socialist fraternity who encountered these titles – a version of modernity that differed significantly from that imposed by Stalinism. Illustrated magazines from Poland and the other satellites were available at Russian news stands. As one of the contributors to this book, Iurii Gerchuk, testifies, they found a receptive audience there: 'Every decorative-painterly cover of the journal *Pol'sha* (Poland) behind a kiosk window seemed like a manifesto of new artistic possibilities. And for the "keepers" [of orthodoxy] the very word "Pol'sha" became an odious symbol of "modernism" infiltrating the country.'[1]

In the new climate of the Thaw, a moderate fashion-consciousness was tolerated and even promoted in Hungary and Poland and, by the late 1950s, was also beginning to be viewed more sympathetically in the USSR. Fashion shows, including foreign ones from East and West, were held regularly in the Soviet Union and annual meetings of fashion designers from the fraternal countries were convened.[2] Soviet magazines and newspapers with predominately female readerships gave regular coverage to issues of fashion and contemporary taste in interior decoration.[3] Soviet cultural theorists began to attend to the function of fashion in a socialist society and command economy in which the planned obsolescence and competition essential to a market economy had no role to play. The nature of the relation between style and the particular socio-economic formation that produced it was also addressed. In 1961 the design journal *Dekorativnoe iskusstvo SSSR* (Decorative Art of the USSR) – itself a phenomenon of the Thaw – published a reader's query: surely distinctions in the material base must engender corresponding differences in such superstructural forms as style? Why, then, had those in socialist societies continued to dress similarly to people in capitalist countries?[4]

The late 1950s and early 1960s in Eastern Europe and the Soviet Union were a period not only of political and cultural liberalization but of economic and social modernization. The self-conscious rejuvenation of the material world raised questions about the appropriate expression of socialist modernity in all fields of visual and material culture. Style, a notion that had been suspect under Stalin, became an urgent issue. What forms of dress, furniture and housing as well as fine art would provide a stimulating environment that could meet the needs of, and give shape to, modern, socialist life? What was the appropriate style for socialist modernity?[5] Fashion, in particular, had been anathematized under Stalin as an alien, capitalist phenomenon. Even in the Thaw, the Soviet press maintained that 'The endless change-over of fashion is ruinous for those who blindly follow it, and it is above all produced by the entrepreneur's chase after profit.'[6] Numerous articles advised both male and female readers that fashion was permissible up to a point, but if taken to extremes it remained a form of capitalist exploitation and kowtowing to Western consumerism. They admonished: 'It is better to be dressed slightly unfashionably than ridiculously'; and 'It is necessary to develop a sense of measure.'[7] Moreover, the official commitment to social equality, not least in the distribution of commonly produced wealth, would appear to be compromised by this kind of materialism. And even in those countries such as Poland where a more liberal line was taken on the question of fashion throughout the period, the fact that the objects of desire that such magazines reproduced were hardly available in the Soviet bloc risked arousing appetites which could not be satisfied. The appearance of choice in the realm of domestic consumption, as presented on the pages of new magazines like the Polish title, *Moda*, summoned up the spectre of 'positional consumption', that is the use of goods as markers of social distinction. How, as the reader cited above queried, would such products differ from those of bourgeois societies? As the editors responded, 'every epoch gives birth to its own style. Modernity, progress must find its own modern or contemporary style'.[8]

The essays in this volume set out to explore the material and visual world of the socialist bloc in two contiguous but, in many ways, contrasting periods: that of post-war Stalinism; and that of destalinization and relative cultural liberalization known as the Thaw. The two decades from the end of the 1940s to the late 1960s might be regarded as the high-water mark of communism in European history. Taking a variety of approaches, the essays examine the forms and uses of objects that made up the environment of socialist life, from everyday clothing and home furnishings to paintings on the walls of galleries. They demonstrate that the relationships of things and people were dynamic in ways peculiar to the political and cultural conditions of the bloc. They investigate the particular ways in which material objects came to represent the often divergent aspirations of regimes and peoples in the Soviet Union and Eastern Europe, and illuminate the interaction between official rhetoric and state command on the one hand, and the popular applications of its material products on the other: how the material realities of what has been described as 'real existing socialism' were appropriated and negotiated in everyday life. Thereby, they contribute to the ongoing critique of 'totalitarianism', a paradigm developed by Western political scientists at the height of the Cold War in the 1950s to explain and categorize Soviet-type systems. This concept stresses, among other characteristics, the determining role of the leader, a single party, and central, top-level decision making. Taking at face value the emphasis on production in the command economy rather than on the consumption and reception of things within those societies, and concentrating on ideological claims and counter-claims rather than on the material realities of everyday life, the totalitarian model affords little insight into the negotiations, adaptations and evasions conducted by people in their everyday lives. This model has been subjected to cogent critique by revisionist historians who have turned their attention to the complexities of relations between regimes and people and the lived experience of Stalinism, as well as to other areas hitherto foreclosed by the emphasis on political voluntarism.[9] Studies of culture – broadly defined to include the conditions of everyday life, popular opinion and unregulated behaviours – have an important contribution to make to this history, as exemplified by work on the Stalin period by Sheila Fitzpatrick, Sarah Davies, Stephen Kotkin, Jochen Hellbeck, Vadim Volkov and others.[10] Nevertheless, the totalitarian paradigm continues tacitly to structure many accounts of, for instance, the 'imposition' of socialist realism and other cultural norms both within the Soviet Union in the 1930s and in Eastern Europe during the post-war period.[11] While it would be naive to deny the pervasiveness of state control over all aspects of cultural production and mediation, or to ascribe to the subject peoples a degree of self-determination of which they were so brutally deprived, this model precludes examination of certain potentially fruitful lines of inquiry. In this respect, two key themes warrant more detailed investigation in this introduction: first, the interaction and exchange between the states of the Eastern bloc during the periods of post-war Stalinism and destaliniza-tion when the relatively uneven distribution of attributes of modernity within the bloc became particularly significant; and, second, the consumption of material objects to project personal and collective identities, and even to articulate resistance to the state.

Exchanges within the Bloc

At its most simplistic, the totalitarian paradigm reduces the complexities of interactions between Moscow and its satellites to a unidirectional model whereby the former directs and the latter comply. The received view, especially regarding the years before 1956, emphasizes the 'sovietization' and 'stalinization' of the Eastern European satellites through the Soviet Union's coercive imposition of economic, legal, ideological and cultural institutions and norms. Without wishing to deny the coercion exercised by the Soviet Union, especially in the Stalinist period, we suggest that it would be more enlightening to investigate the ways Soviet models, institutions and cultural forms had to be modified or abandoned in the effort to naturalize them into quite dissimilar and sometimes deeply resistant cultures: for what would be the point of rhetoric that found no resonance in the constituency it addressed? Jan Kubik has suggested that while Party ideologues, promoting a new vision of the People's Republic of Poland, presented their programme as revolutionary, in practice they adapted and incorporated long-standing and popular features of the local and national culture in an attempt to secure legitimacy.[12] Similarly, when socialist realism was introduced into East German art it had to be adapted in accordance with German traditions, the existing skills of the artistic body, and the meanings that Germans, as a result of their particular historical experience, attached to such styles as realism or expression-ism.[13] Were the forms given to the material world in Central and Eastern Europe simply imported ready-made from Russia, or were they, rather, the product of dialogue, however unequal? This question has recently been explored in a number of studies of socialist realist architecture published since the mid 1980s.[14] After 1945 leading Soviet architects like Alexei Galaktinov and Lev Rudnev (designer of Moscow University, a landmark building of the post-war period) exported the historicist style characteristic of high Stalinist socialist realism to the People's Republics while at the same time claiming to respond to local traditions in their designs in accordance with official claims that socialist realism was 'national in form, socialist in content'. Was this claim simply empty rhetoric, or might, as Anders Åman has proposed, differing national traditions have been as influential as the direct influence of the Soviet Union?[15] The issue of negotiation and dialogue within the bloc is only directly addressed by a small number of essays in the book, but they point to the need for further investigations.

In considering the cultures of the Soviet empire we surely have much to learn from post-colonial studies concerning both the impact of subaltern cultures on those of imperial regimes such as Britain, and the cross-fertilization of ideas between colonies. In her work on imperialism and travel writing Mary L. Pratt, for example, employs the ethnographic term 'transculturation' to describe 'how subordinated or marginal groups select and invent from materials transmitted to them by a dominant or metropolitan culture. While subjugated peoples cannot readily control what emanates from the dominant culture, they do determine to varying extents what they absorb into their own, and what they use it for.'[16] We might adopt Pratt's 'heretical question': 'how does one speak of transculturation *from the colonies to the metropolis*? While the imperial metropolis tends to understand itself as determining the periphery . . ., it habitually blinds itself to the ways in which the periphery determines the metropolis'.[17] Seeking answers to this question may illuminate cultural relations between the Soviet Union and the subaltern cultures of the People's Republics.

Rather than investigate solely how Moscow imposed its cultural hegemony, then, we should also ask to what extent were developments in Soviet culture and ideology shaped through contact with its satellites? Jacques Rupnik has observed: 'At least until Stalin's death, political innovation was understood very much as a one-way street. Adaptation was essentially an Eastern European problem . . . Soviet adaptation to change initiated in Eastern Europe was not really on the agenda until the Khrushchev era.'[18] Can Rupnik's argument concerning political change be applied equally to economic, technological and artistic innovation? The relative liberalization of cultural strictures and relaxation of Stalinist autarky in the Khrushchev era combined with an urgent, regime-led drive for modernization, 'democratization' and increased attention toward the everyday needs of the ordinary citizen. These circumstances made it possible, and indeed necessary, to learn from the dominion cultures of Eastern Europe. This is one of the factors that makes the period taken by this book a crucial one, not only for the formation of the cultures of the People's Republics but also for that of 'Big Brother'.

Stalin's last years were characterized by isolation and xenophobia. In the field of technology, as in others, for instance, a highly deterministic conception of the 'politics of artifacts' held sway over science. In essence, the argument ran: if the socialist system was the most advanced way of organizing human resources, then it would surely produce the most highly evolved, and thus unique, forms of culture and knowledge.[19] Although they were obliged to remain silent at the time, technical professionals such as architects or engineers in the People's Republics during the Stalin era, and for some years after, saw through the myth of the 'leading' character of Soviet technology as a deceit. Far from leading, the Soviet Union lagged behind its dominions in many fields of industrial development. In the second half of the 1950s Khrushchev, pragmatically recognizing the material and technical advances in the United States and West Europe, encouraged Soviet scientists and technicians to modernize, and at the Twenty-First Congress of the Communist Party of the Soviet Union (CPSU) in 1959 he rashly promised that the Soviet Union would 'catch up' with the United States.[20] International diplomacy and exchange were renewed. Khrushchev travelled avidly and applied the lessons of foreign experience back home. Trade, tourism, scientific and cultural exchange expanded, and cultural agreements were signed not only with socialist countries, but also with capitalist countries such as America (1958).[21] From the growing recognition that superpower status in the post-war world demanded cutting-edge science and technology, it followed that Soviet scientists must be allowed access to the latest foreign research. The principle that socialist countries should pool their scientific and cultural achievements was encoded in the Third Party Programme of 1961. In the strategically crucial areas of science and technology, the Soviet Union systematically exploited the expertise of its more advanced satellites to compensate for its own backwardness. The most obvious example is the process, beginning in 1946, of extracting 'intellectual reparations' from Eastern Germany in the form of deportations of both personnel and equipment to the Soviet Union.[22] The Soviet Union also looked to the 'fraternal countries' for solutions to the new design tasks created by the increased economic and ideological status of consumer goods. The Soviet leadership's ambitious promises to catch up and overtake the West in living standards and industrial production were only realisable by exploiting the more advanced, technically modern satellites such as Czechoslovakia and East Germany. It needed models that could be cheaply produced on a mass scale using the latest synthetic materials and modern production technology. While Soviet defence-related industries and scientific development benefitted from German expertise in organic chemicals, engines and rocket technology, consumer industries also advanced through the importation of synthetics such as the German version of nylon, Perlon. German plastics and synthetic rubber technology, the subject of Raymond Stokes's essay, 'Plastics and the New Society: the German Democratic Republic in the 1950s and 1960s', formed the technical foundation of the Soviet drive to expand the use of plastics in the late 1950s. Both the popular press and specialist design publications hymned 'the polymer epoch' and the brave new plastic world of the future.[23] German technology for television, optics, cameras and film was also exploited.[24] When the USSR Ministry of Culture required high quality photographic images for the catalogue accompanying its display at the Brussels World Fair in 1958, with the aim of promoting a technologically-defined Soviet modernity abroad, it had, ironically, to resort to German film and processing.[25]

In his essay on 'The Aesthetics of Everyday Life in the Khrushchev Thaw in the USSR', design historian Iurii Gerchuk shows how the formation of a modern or 'contemporary style' in Soviet design in the late 1950s was informed by contact with models and publications from Eastern Europe, especially Czechoslovakia or Poland, where the Modern Movement in architecture and design, suppressed in the Soviet Union since the 1930s, had continued to thrive with only a relatively brief interregnum in the late 1940s and early 1950s.[26] The importation of consumer goods, such as mass-produced furniture from Czechoslovakia, and the adoption of Eastern European plans and technology for mass housing construction played a significant role in fulfilling Khrushchev's pledges to raise Soviet living standards. The lively exchange of information and ideas was made possible through exhibitions of furniture, fashion, Czechoslovak glass and Polish industrial design, as well as by publications, conferences and increased opportunities for specialists to travel within the bloc.[27] Thus the texture of daily life in the Soviet Union was modernized and internationalized through the importation of East European models.

Moreover, there is evidence to suggest that the Soviet metropolitan public were ready to accept a degree of modernism in art and design. For example, viewers' responses to a major exhibition of modern furniture design in the 'contemporary style', *Art and Life*, shown in Moscow in 1961, were mainly enthusiastic. A few visitors complained of a loss of national (Russian) characteristics and infiltration of Western modernism into the Soviet way of life, but most objected only that they were unable to purchase the new models because they were not available or were too expensive.[28] This exhibition was the first major public demonstration of Soviet prototypes for mass production. Its title, invoking the constructivist slogan of the 1920s 'Art into Life!' reflected current efforts to promote the 'aesthetics of everyday life' in the context of the emergence of industrial design. These were informed by the rediscovery of the suppressed history of the Soviet avant-garde of the 1920s, including the tentative rehabilitation of the productivist theories of LEF (Left Front of the Arts), and the non-hierarchical conception of material culture or material production.[29]

The permeability of Soviet fine art practice and policy in the Khrushchev Thaw to influence from its politically subordinate neighbours, and the extent to which this contributed to its liberalization, is broached by Susan E. Reid in her essay 'The Exhibition *Art of Socialist Countries*, Moscow 1958–9, and the Contemporary Style of Painting'. To cite Rupnik again, 'The gradual shift from coercion to consent in state–society and centre–periphery relations has raised implicitly the question of the extent to which the search for greater viability and stability of communist regimes in Eastern Europe could provide an incentive, or the impulse, for change in the Soviet Union itself.'[30] To what extent may this observation be applied to transformations in fine art and aesthetics? The art of Central and Eastern Europe, and especially that of Poland, as represented in a major official exhibition *Art of Socialist Countries* which opened in Moscow at the end of 1958, acted, contrary to the intentions of the organizers, as a channel for information about modernist art into the Soviet Union. Its more extreme practices, in the form of Polish abstraction and *art informel*, also served as a foil against which more limited departures from hitherto obligatory standards of verisimilitude, such as expressionist deformation, appeared relatively harmless. The effect of contact with contemporary East European art, Reid argues, was to reinforce and legitimatize the efforts of Soviet cultural reformers to modernize and diversify the domestic practice of socialist realism. At their most extreme, Eastern European developments even called into question the need for socialist art to be realist at all.

It was in Poland that state-condoned divergence from Soviet norms became most pronounced. As Katarzyna Murawska-Muthesius reflects in her contribution to this book, 'Socialist Realism's Self-Reference? Cartoons on Art, c. 1950', socialist realism was never convincingly defined there, but always formulated in reference to the Soviet matrix. In Poland, state influence over cultural forms was not only relaxed in the mid-1950s, but modernism in art and architecture was quickly endorsed, in effect becoming an 'official style'. In this volume, Piotr Piotrowski investigates the ways in which modernism in the fine arts, which he defines by antithesis to the avant-garde commitment to reshape the world, was reconceived after the dismissal of socialist realism. *Tachiste* abstraction and other contemporary hypostases of modernism were not only tolerated by the state but used as evidence of a new liberalism that was central to Poland's self-representation as a modern, tolerant polity, both at home and abroad. The theory and practice of socialist realism was overturned and cast as anachronistic. This dramatic reversal notwithstanding, Piotrowski suggests that there is a correspondence between the official role of art under Stalinism and under destalinization: in eschewing its ideological or propagandistic role after 1956, most artists forfeited art's critical potential. Thus, the revival of modernism in Polish art, which began as a 'revenge' against socialist realism, lent a new legitimacy to the socialist project.

Socialist Consumption

The Thaw period was characterized by fierce competition between the superpowers for possession of the future. In the late 1950s and 1960s, the most potent symbols in this contest were forms of technology such as atomic power, spacecraft and, famously, during the American Exhibition in Moscow in 1959, domestic consumer durables such as washing machines.[31] Increasing emphasis was placed on a technologically driven conception of modernity. As noted, plastics, which were interpreted as an emblem of 'the modern' throughout the world in the 1950s and 1960s, had specific meaning for their advocates in Eastern Europe as the ultimate socialist material. In East Germany, in particular, as Stokes argues, plastics promised a way to channel German expertise in the organic chemicals industry to fashion an image of a progressive, modern and thoroughly socialist economy, enabling a dialectical unity between utility and economy. No longer to be regarded as an inferior ersatz, plastics could both satisfy aesthetic demands and improve the well-being of consumers in the German Democratic Republic. They could thereby bridge the gap between strategic emphasis on producer goods and the need to foster and satisfy consumerism if the regime was to maintain any legitimacy in face of the highly visible example of West Germany's American-injected prosperity.[32] The 'main economic task' was to demonstrate the superiority of the socialist system over the capitalist system. Stokes, taking the Trabant motor car as a telling example, traces the failure of the plastic utopia. The pride of East German industry, symbolizing both its sophisticated technological capability and a commitment to a high standard of living, the Trabant was to be the people's plastic car of the future. The dream foundered, however, on the planned economy's inherent emphasis on quantity rather than quality, and its disincentives against innovation.[33]

In the absence of alternatives, the artifacts produced from German plastics were purchased in spite of the deficiencies of their materials or design and their old-fashioned appearance, but East German citizens could not be quarantined from awareness that better and more modern products were available in West Germany.

Tensions between official ideology and consumption are highlighted in a number of essays in the book. Despite concessions to the consumer, the economies of the bloc were still commanded from above, not driven from below by consumer demand. The satisfaction or, conversely, the control of consumer desires proved to be a thorny problem for communist authorities in Eastern Europe from the outset. The inability of centrally-planned economies based on the national ownership of the means of production and distribution to meet even the basic needs of their populations has been the subject of much comment.[34] Yet for the regimes of Eastern Europe it was an article of faith that central planning would guarantee the best possible conditions of life for the largest part of the population. In an archetypal claim that could have been made at any point in the period under consideration, the Hungarian communist leadership announced in 1960, 'The Hungarian people under a planned socialist economy will be able to rebuild and develop their country to a level of prosperity never experienced before.'[35] Such rhetoric, hyperbolic as it is, warrants study for a number of reasons. It provided a state-sanctioned benchmark against which the actual experience of 'real existing socialism' could be judged and illicit or insubordinate identities could be formed, a point to which we shall return below. Moreover, although such promises about future prosperity were common, political discourse about consumption was far from uniform in the different national contexts of the bloc. It is useful here to separate the experiences of the Eastern European satellites from the Soviet Union.

In the period of stalinization in the People's Republics before 1956, the desire to consume was often represented as a vice that must be kept in check. In Hungary, for example, shopkeepers were discouraged from arranging window displays in ways that might arouse the appetite to consume. The role of display was to be a high-minded, educational one. One Hungarian commentator wrote in 1951: 'There is a need for shop-windows to be arranged tastefully and in an artistic manner, not merely because we intend to display the products of our socialist industry in impressive surroundings; a well-dressed shop can also convey important thoughts and ideas.'[36] Shops were forbidden to compete for the attention and purchasing power of the passer-by, and standardized shop-fascia were introduced to correct the harmful effects of the commercial environment. As retailing was nationalized, advertising in the Western sense was replaced by notices reminding customers of 'correct' attitudes towards consumption. The purpose of advertising in a socialist economy was defined at the Prague conference of Advertising Workers of Socialist Countries in 1957 which set the principles of advertising policy throughout the bloc. These emphasized advertising's threefold purpose: to inform about rational forms of consumption; to raise the culture of trade, that is to improve retail service; and, most importantly, to educate consumers' taste and shape their requirements.[37] The role of domestic advertising in a command economy was not to generate inauthentic and insatiable consumer demand but, rather, to promote 'rational consumption': the all-embracing range of plan culture was to predict and manage popular desires.

During the 1950s and 1960s, however, an ideology of asceticism was increasingly replaced by the promise of consumerism. In his essay here, Stokes notes that in order to maintain any popular legitimacy, the GDR regime found it necessary to bridge the gap between the socialist economy's inherent emphasis on production and the need to provide for consumerism. The increased supply of consumer goods in Eastern Europe has tended to be associated with the period after 1956. But elements of 'consumer socialism' were already evident in the early 1950s, as Mark Pittaway shows in his essay 'Stalinism, Working-Class Housing and Individual Autonomy: the Encouragement of Private House Building in Hungary's Mining Areas, 1950–4'. The process of creating a consumer society went furthest of all in Hungary (Khrushchev famously coined the phrase 'Goulash Socialism' to describe the liberal economic policies of Kádár's regime). In the late 1950s the authorities began to address contradictions between central command and private enterprise, recognizing the 'determining influence' of the consumer. 'At present our economic policy has the important task of complying with the demands of the domestic market and of foreign trade to the greatest possible extent,' wrote a journalist in *Társadalmi Szemle* in 1959, 'production should conform to changing requirements; factories should produce goods that the customer demands, in such a quality and variety as he demands.'[38] The so-called 'guiding directives' issued to the Eighth Congress of the Hungarian Socialist Workers' Party (HSWP) under Kádár in 1962 predicted that one household in three would own a television set by the end of the Five-Year Plan (1960–65), an ambitious increase from the 10,000 sets in the country in 1960.

Even in Kádár's Hungary, however, the legitimacy of consumerism was a matter of contention. Analysing attitudes to consumerism represented in the official press in the period 1960 to 1963, George Gömöri, identified two camps: 'idealists' who lamented the consumer orientation of the Five-Year Plan, and 'realists' who regarded the material improvement of ordinary Hungarians' lives as consonant with the ideals of socialism.[39] For the idealists, Western gadgets spelled the renewal of bourgeois mentality, anti-social individualism and 'technical fetishism', the effect of which was to demoralize 'obsessed' owners. By contrast, the realist position espoused by the HSWP leadership under Kádár represented consumerism as a necessary and logical outcome of a process designed to achieve the material improvement of the lives of the poor and, therefore, hardly antagonistic to the cause of socialism. Far from undermining the system, it believed that the endorsement of domestic consumption would stabilize and preserve communist authority.[40]

If, in the satellites, the rhetoric of austerity associated with Stalinism increasingly gave way to the promise of materialism, in the Soviet Union the Stalinist myth of luxury and abundance was replaced under Khrushchev by what may be characterized by an oxymoron, austere consumerism. The high-rise blocks erected around Moscow between 1947 and 1953 as markers of the Soviet Union's imperial power had typically included luxury shops in the ground floor, complete with chandeliers, mirrors and gilt. But they masked a reality of privation. The appalling living conditions and shortages of consumer goods, resulting from decades of upheaval and from the planned economy's prioritization of capital goods, had been exacerbated by the Second World War: in 1945 consumer goods production, never adequate, had sunk to 59 per cent of its pre-war level.[41] As early as 1952, both contenders for Stalin's throne, Nikita Khrushchev and Georgii Malenkov, recognized that the people could not be persuaded to defer gratification indefinitely.[42] At the height of Khrushchev's reign in 1959, the Party made the attainment of a high living standard for all a precondition for the final, imminent transition to full communism. This standard had, at the very least, to measure up to those of the Central and Eastern European satellites. As contact with the West increased in the mid-1950s the benchmarks included, more ambitiously, West Germany, where the Marshall Plan was taking visible effect, and even the land of conspicuous consumption par excellence, America.[43] Khrushchevist economic policies made a scaled-down dream of domestic comfort and consumption attainable for many, but at the same time concerted efforts were made to hold in check and regulate the forms consumption should take. In setting consumer goods production targets to be achieved by the projected time of transition to full communism around 1980, the Khrushchev regime established 'rational consumption norms' which represented a somewhat austere vision of the promised universal abundance.[44] Promises of consumer goods and better services were tempered by a revival of the ascetic, mobilization spirit of the Cultural Revolution (1928–31) with its rhetoric against petit-bourgeois attachment to possessions. Some of the more radical theoreticians projected that the family and the paraphernalia of domesticity would wither away with the advent of communism: the neo-productivist philosopher Karl Kantor warned that the 'hypertrophy of interest in the individual dwelling is inclined to engender an antisocial, anticommunistic mindset.'[45] And, in the latter years of his administration, Khrushchev pursued a campaign against 'bourgeois acquisitiveness' and private dacha ownership.[46]

The official rhetoric of 'democratism' and mass participation, and the relative openness of public debate in the Thaw, should not mislead us into regarding the period as one of cultural levelling and liberalism; it saw the relegitimation of cultural elitism and the penetration of regimes of taste and behaviour into everyday life.

Figure 1.2 In a Soviet department store. Photo I. Tiufiakov *Ogonek*, no. 11, 1959.

As Iurii Gerchuk notes in this volume, the contemporary style's emphasis on the integrated design of furnishings for the new flats, built to standard plans in the late 1950s and early 1960s, left little room for occupants to customize their home in accordance with their individual sense of taste and comfort. In this regard, Khrushchevism in the Soviet Union was, contrary to its populist rhetoric, thoroughly authoritarian. People's homes and habits of consumption remained within the realm of public discourse, and like other twentieth-century mass housing schemes, the *novostroiki* were also an 'instrument of regimentation of life'.[47] The aesthetics of domestic life became the object of extensive popular advice literature and specialist discourses which aimed to propagate ideals of tasteful 'contemporary' living and to identify this with a stripped-down, modernist aesthetic. 'The interior organizes everyday life', an artists' newspaper proclaimed in 1959,[48] while popular, illustrated magazines such as *Ogonek* and household advice manuals also set out to wean the masses from the heavy, ornate furniture to which they had earlier learned to aspire, and to inculcate a hygienic and rational discipline of living and affordable habits of consumption. Urging that low, light and simple furniture was more appropriate and convenient in the new, small apartment, they encouraged the public to identify good taste with restraint or even austerity, and to see 'laconic', functional forms not as a regrettable necessity, but as contemporary, democratic, and beautiful.[49] The people's taste had to be disciplined both on ideological and aesthetic grounds, as well as to keep aspirations within limits state industrial production might feasibly satisfy. The banishment of superfluous, non-structural ornament from new buildings symbolized the regime's repudiation of the Stalinist proclivity to embellish reality. Khrushchevist truth to function, structural honesty, modernity and good taste were counterposed to Stalinist sham, historicism and vulgar ostentation. In this respect, the discourse surrounding consumption during the Thaw period can be regarded as an important part of efforts to relegitimate and rejuvenate the communist project.[50]

'Making Do'

Whatever norms of rational or cultured consumption and spartan ideals of 'modern' good taste planners and ideologues promoted, official rhetoric can tell us little about how individual subjects made the products of state industry meaningful in the practices of their daily lives. Nevertheless, the traditional emphasis of the socialist economies on production rather than consumption has been reproduced in the Western historiography. As Mary Neuburger notes in her essay for this volume, 'Veils, *Shalvari*, and Matters of Dress: Unraveling the Fabric of Women's Lives in Communist Bulgaria' in this volume, the issues of consumption and material culture to which scholars are increasingly attending with regard to the First and Third Worlds, also demand investigation in the so-called Second World. Since the collapse of the Soviet bloc, consumption in the formerly socialist countries of Eastern Europe has come to be seen as a meaningful, cultural activity, but the focus has been almost exclusively on the period of transition that occurred with the establishment of market economics beginning in 1989.[51] More analysis needs to be made of the communicative and symbolic character of acts of consumption within the socialist, planned economy. As Václav Havel indicated even before the dramatic events of 1989, the emergence of consumer societies in the former Soviet bloc was not simply the result of the collapse of communist authority: rather '*another* form of consumer industrial society' had already begun to appear in Eastern Europe by the late 1950s.

The will to consume represented a potential threat to communist authority. The anthropologist Katherine Verdery has suggested that 'The arousal and frustration of consumer desire, and East Europeans' consequent resistance to their regimes led them to build their social identities specifically *through consuming*. Acquiring consumer goods and objects conferred an identity that set one off from socialism. To acquire objects became a way of constituting your selfhood against a regime you despised.'[52] With the major exceptions of provisioning through the black market and the forms of semi-private enterprise in Poland and Hungary known as the 'second' or 'informal economy', most resources were made available by state command. Theorizing the uses the powerless make of the resources provided by the system to undermine it in the course of everyday life, Michel de Certeau has described popular culture as the 'art of making do with what the system provides'.[53] Although de Certeau was writing in the context of modern capitalist societies, his vivid definition is pertinent to the bloc. Analysis of popular culture, viewed from this perspective, must take into account not only the means provided by the command economy, but also the actions of consumers. Unlike liberal capitalist environments, most resources were 'licensed' and indeed provided by the state in Eastern Europe, even if the meanings attached to them were not. Timothy Ryback, in his study of pop music in Eastern Europe, *Rock Around the Bloc*, presents some of the most curious examples of the unlicensed consumption of legitimate products by the *pásek*, teenage members of Prague's demi-monde in the early 1950s: these fashionable youths pinned precious labels from American cigarette packs discarded by Western visitors onto drab ties which they bought in the city's department stores; they also mimicked the insouciant manner of their beloved American movie stars by chewing paraffin wax as a substitute for gum. In such ways, utilitarian products were stripped of their usefulness and adopted as a badge of conspicuous tastes: they were signs of desires rather than needs.[54] Even material stamped with official opprobrium could be redrafted in consumption: Péter György has described the unanticipated attention attracted by the Hungarian film *Colony Under the Ground* (*Gyarmat a föld alatt*, 1950) as one of the few places where abstract art could be seen, even if it was presented as a measure of the decadence and criminality of the company director who decorated his luxurious home with it.[55]

Differentiated identities could also be enacted (or, in Verdery's terms, 'selfhoods could be constituted') in the ways consumers of 'high culture' such as fine art responded to what they were offered by the state. Reid's study of Soviet viewers' written responses to the exhibition of *Art of Socialist Countries* early in 1959, an official event brought to the people by the USSR Ministry of Culture, shows that while many viewers continued to rehearse clichés provided by the press, others made a serious attempt to engage with unfamiliar expressionist and even abstract work, and to relate it to their own experiences of modern life and the trauma of the war. In spite of the customary efforts to direct public responses, Soviet viewers failed to deliver on the modernist works shown at the exhibition the unanimous condemnation for which a quarter century of socialist realism should have prepared them. Instead, the differentiated response of the Soviet public – officially the final arbiter in matters of art – indicated a readiness among some to accept a diversified and ecumenical conception of realism. This was one aspect of a more general fracturing of the Stalinist facade of a homogeneous and univocal public; it became increasingly necessary to admit that modern Soviet society was a complex organism consisting of multiple constituencies and interest groups. Indeed, from 1959, the

CPSU adopted a 'differentiated approach' to political agitation, acknowledging that the Soviet population was divided along gender, ethnic, generational and other lines with different characteristics, needs and interests.[56]

The most significant loci of consumption where private identities could be articulated against public values were, arguably, the home and the body. Gerchuk's contribution to this volume explores the tension between the collectivist ideals espoused by the Khrushchev regime and the recognition, implicit in its housing policy, of the need for family living units in modern urban industrialized society. Mark Pittaway approaches the issue of self-provision in the relation between public and private by examining the importance of the private housing building pro-gramme in Hungary in the early 1950s. Reflecting the workers' will to autonomy and economic self-sufficiency, private plots cushioned them from the vagaries of state supplies, and private house building allowed workers the possibility of defining their own living environment. Pittaway's research on the mining town of Tatabánya is as sharply-focused on the actual patterns of life of ordinary people as it is on ideology and regulation. It is clear that there is much more work to be done on the ways in which the domestic arrangements of ordinary citizens in the bloc conformed to, or evaded, authority.[57]

Figure 1.3 Fashionable Riga youth dancing a local variant of the Twist on a rooftop in 1968 (Māra Brašmane).

Youth subculture has for some time been an object of investigation by re-
searchers interested in what have been described as forms of ritual dissent in Eastern
Europe and the Soviet Union.[58] Here concepts of style, subcultural identity,
intergenerational confrontation and 'consumption as resistance' have been
particularly important.[59] The word 'style' (*stil'* in Russian) even formed the root
of the name for the most prominent youth counterculture, the *stiliagi*, to which
Mark Svede and Reid refer. 'The word style was key for us. We danced and dressed
"in style",' Artemy Troitsky recalled.[60] The word *stil'*, borrowed from French,
never shook off the suspect connotations of a foreign and somewhat decadent
import (as in the *stil' modern'*). Likewise, the constant charge made against the
stiliagi was that they were anti-social elements: seduced by a mirage of the West
and its consumer goods, they betrayed their Russian, socialist roots. In this volume
Mark Svede looks at the ways in which counter-cultural groups, the beatniks and
hippies in Latvia in the 1960s, articulated alternative identities through dress,
whether through forms of bricolage using items purchased in state stores or on
the black market, or by 'self provision', i.e. by making clothes to compensate for
the limitations of government-issue consumer goods. However, the anti-materialist
and emancipated ethos of these young Latvians entailed rejection both of material
which bore the impress of the state and of the 'crass materialism' associated with
the black market. Observing that the material forms of hippie culture had been
shaped in the West, Svede nevertheless stresses that Latvian hippies were forced
to improvise – or as de Certeau's puts it, to 'make do' – to produce the effects they
desired within the state-planned economy of the Soviet Union. Svede's achievement
here is to draw out, in the Latvian context, the specific register of what might
otherwise be taken as minor semiotic and material differences.

A different tension between socialist authority and censured dress is explored
by Mary Neuburger in her essay. Attracting the attention of modernizing officials
and intellectuals, the 'veil' along with other Turco-Muslim women's garments were
an established symbolic battleground long before the communists took power in
1944. In socialist Bulgaria, however, more effective means of surveillance and
enforcement were available to the Bulgarian Communist Party. Committed to a
course of 'modernization', they promised to liberate women living in Bulgaria, at
the price, Neuburger stresses, of effacing local and ethnic identities. The attempt
to control Muslim women's dress was manifest in the coercive strategies of the
early 1950s and, later, in appeals to consuming desires in the promotion of Western
'European' clothes. In this context, resistance was offered in the course of everyday
life by women who produced and wore veils and *shalvari*. Like Svede, Neuburger's
research counters the myth that the citizens of socialist states were desperate and
undiscriminating consumers, a stereotype widely reproduced in reports of the ubiqui-
tous queue before the collapse of communism and, later, of visits by 'astounded'
citizens of the bloc to Western European shops after 'the fall of the Wall'.

David Crowley and *Susan E. Reid*

The essays commissioned for this book make no claim to constitute the definitive statement about the ways in which the material world was shaped in the Eastern bloc during the consolidation of socialism in the 1950s and 1960s – a task exceeding the ambitions of a single volume or a small group of authors. But they are intended to contribute to a growing body of significant research and to stimulate further enquiry. This era in European history is slowly passing from memory into history. The material environment that it fashioned is slipping away more quickly: a wholesale transformation of Eastern Europe, particularly in urban centres, which seems to have taken place in a remarkably short period, means that the material traces of the communist system are disappearing. The dramatic iconoclasm of pulling down the political memorials of a defunct system – most famously, statues of Lenin, Dzierżyński and Marx – has received a great deal of attention,[61] but one might also reflect on the steady fragmentation of housing estates; the redesignation of public spaces; the dispersal of collections of art and design of this period from museums (sometimes into theme park displays of Stalinism); and even the refurbishment of cafes and private homes. Whether this material deserves preservation in any material form is an argument we must leave for another time and place.[62] But, unquestionably, it demands documentation and analysis, not least because the history of Eastern European cultures in the period of communist authority and perhaps even the fate of this ideology, is inscribed in these objects and in their surrounding discourses.

Notes

1 Iurii Gerchuk, 'Iskusstvo "ottepeli" v poiskakh stilia,' *Tvorchestvo*, no. 6 (1991) p. 28.

2 T. Tikhomirov, 'Zavoiuet li 'russkii stil' Evropu? Sovetskaia kollektsiia mod za 1968 god,' *Moskovskii khudozhnik*, no. 12 (17 March 1967) p. 4. A Christian Dior collection was shown in Moscow in June 1959 and viewed by 130,000 people. T. Trotskaia, 'Parizh pokazyvaet mody', *Ogonek*, no. 26 (21 June 1959).

3 Articles on appropriate, up-to-date dress appeared in *Ogonek*, *Rabotnitsa*, and *Uchitel'skaia gazeta* among others.

4 'O ponimanii mody. Pis'mo s kommentarii,' *Dekorativnoe iskusstvo SSSR* (henceforth *DI SSSR*) no. 1 (1961), pp. 40–2.

5 Writing about 'the search for a socialist technology' in the German Democratic Republic in the 1950s and 1960s, Raymond Stokes has suggested, 'it is worth considering whether or not socialism . . . or any other political system or ideology produced artifacts . . . which uniquely expressed the politics or ideology of their

designers.' Raymond Stokes, 'In Search of the Socialist Artefact: Technology and Ideology in East Germany, 1945–1962', *German History*, vol. 15, no. 2 (1997) pp. 221–2.

6 'O ponimanii mody,' p. 40.

7 L. Efremova, 'Eto seichas modno,' *Ogonek*, no. (1960) inside back cover; N. Khrabrova, 'V poiskakh krasivogo, udobnogo,' *Ogonek*, no. 10 (6 March 1960).

8 'O ponimanii mody,' p. 41.

9 For critiques of the totalitarian model see Ian Kershaw and Moshe Lewin, *Stalinism and Nazism: Dictatorships in Comparison* (Cambridge: Cambridge University Press, 1997); Stephen F. Cohen, *Rethinking the Soviet Experience. Politics and History since 1917* (Oxford: Oxford University Press, 1985).

10 Sheila Fitzpatrick, ed., *Stalinism. New Directions* (London and New York: Routledge, 2000); Sheila Fitzpatrick, *Everday Stalinism. Everyday Life in Extraordinary Times. Soviet Russia in the 1930s* (Oxford: Oxford University Press, 1999); Sheila Fitzpatrick, *The Cultural Front: Power and Culture in Revolutionary Russia* (Ithaca: Cornell University Press, 1992); Sarah Davies, *Popular Opinion in Stalin's Russia. Terror, Propaganda and Dissent, 1934–1941* (Cambridge: Cambridge University Press, 1997); Stephen Kotkin, *Magnetic Mountain. Stalinism as a Civilization* (Chicago: University of Chicago Press, 1995); Jochen Hellbeck, 'Fashioning the Stalinist Soul: The Diary of Stepan Podliubnyi', *Jahrbücher für Geschichte Osteuropas*, vol. 44, no. 3 (1996) pp. 344–73; Vadim Volkov, 'The Concept of Kul'turnost': notes on the Stalinist civilizing process' in Fitzpatrick, *Stalinism. New Directions*, pp. 210–30.

11 The most notable example of this position is I. Golomstock, *Totalitarian Art. Soviet Union, Fascist Italy and the People's Republic of China* (London: Collins Harvill, 1990).

12 Jan Kubik, *The Power of Symbols Against the Symbols of Power* (University Park PA: Penn State Press, 1994) p. 3.

13 See D. Elliott 'Absent Guests,' in I. Rogoff, ed., *The Divided Heritage. Themes and Problems in German Modernism* (Cambridge: Cambridge University Press, 1991); Martin Damus, *Malerei der DDR: Funktionen der bildenden Kunst im Realen Sozialismus* (Hamburg: 1991). For a detailed account of sovietization of German culture that demonstrates the complexities of establishing Soviet hegemony, see Norman M. Naimark, *The Russians in Germany: A History of the Soviet Zone of Occupation, 1945–1949* (Cambridge MA: Harvard University Press, 1995).

14 A. Åman, *Architecture and Ideology in Eastern Europe During the Stalin Era. An Aspect of the Cold War* (Cambridge MA: MIT Press, 1992); W. Włodarczyk, *Socrealizm* (Paris: Libella, 1986); Radomíra Sedláková, ed., *Sorela: Česká*

Architektura Padesátych Let (Prague: Národní Galerie exh. cat., 1994); Országos Müemlékvédelmi Hivatal Magyar Építészeti Múzeum, *Építészet és Tervezés Magyarországon 1945–1959* (Budapest: 1996).

15 Åman, *Architecture and Ideology*.

16 Mary Louise Pratt, *Imperial Eyes: Travel Writing and Transculturation* (London and New York: Routledge, 1992) pp. 6, 229, n. 4. See also Julie F. Codell and Dianne Sachko Macleod, eds, *Orientalism Transposed: The Impact of the Colonies on British Culture* (London: Ashgate, 1998); and Nicolas Thomas, *Possessions. Indigenous Art/Colonial Culture* (London: Thames & Hudson, 1999).

17 Pratt, *Imperial Eyes*, p. 6.

18 Jacques Rupnik, 'Soviet Adaptation to Change in Eastern Europe,' *Journal of Communist Studies*, vol. 2, no 3 (1986) pp. 251–62.

19 The most pronounced examples are the claims made for T. D. Lysenko's 'discoveries' in the field of biology. See David Joravsky, *The Lysenko Affair* (Cambridge, MA: Harvard University Press, 1970); Stephen Fortescue, *The Communist Party and Soviet Science* (Basingstoke and London: Macmillan, 1986).

20 The unrealistic nature of this promise is indicated by Philip Hanson's estimate that in 1964 consumption levels in the Soviet Union were half those even of Britain. Philip Hanson, *The Consumer in the Soviet Economy* (Basingstoke and London: Macmillan, 1968) pp. 48–82.

21 On cultural relations with the US in this period see Walter L. Hixson, *Parting the Curtain: Propaganda, Culture and the Cold War, 1945–1961* (Basingstoke: Macmillan, 1997).

22 Naimark, *Russians in Germany*, pp. 229–32.

23 V. Matveev, 'Plastmassovyi dom budushchego,' *Ogonek*, no. 27 (1958); V. Zvonkov and V. Gartvig, 'Ekspress iz plastmassy,' *Ogonek*, no. 40 (1958); V. Strozhenko, 'Poznakom'tes' so svoistvam plastmass,' *DI SSSR* no. 4 (1960) p. 33.

24 Naimark, *Russians in Germany*, pp. 229–32.

25 Russian State Archive of Literature and Art (henceforth RGALI) f. 2339, op. 4, ed. khr. 880, ll.17, 30.

26 For discussions of post-war design in the satellite states see *50. Léta Užite Um ění a Design* (Prague: Uměleckoprůmyslové Muzeum v Praze, exh. cat., 1988); Gyula Ernyey, *150 Years of Hungarian Design* (Budapest: Rubik Foundation, 1994); David Crowley, 'Building the World Anew: Design in Stalinist and Post-Stalinist Poland', *Journal of Design History*, vol. 7, no. 3 (1994) pp. 187–204; E. Neumann, 'The Planned Economy in Search of the World Standard: reflections on design and advertising in the DDR', *Design Issues*, vol. VIII, no. 2 (1992); and various essays in Piotr Piotrowski, ed., *Odwilź: Sztuka ok. 1956 r.* (Poznań: Muzeum Narodowe, exh. cat., 1995).

27 On the exhibition of Czechoslovak Glass, Moscow, 1959 see RGALI f. 2329, op. 4, ed. khr. 1015.

28 RGALI f. 2329, op. 4, ed. khr. 1391 (visitors' book for exhibition *Art and Life*, April–June 1961).

29 See S. Frederick Starr, 'Writings from the 1960s on the Modern Movement in Russia', *Journal of the Society of Architectural Historians*, vol. 30, no. 2 (1971) pp. 170–8. On the fundamental role played in the revival of productivist ideas by philosopher A.F. Losev, see James P. Scanlan, 'A.F. Losev and Soviet Aesthetics', in J.J. O'Rourke *et al*, eds, *Contemporary Marxism: Essays in Honour of J. M. Bochenski* (Dordrecht: D. Reidel, 1984) pp. 221–35.

30 Rupnik, 'Soviet Adaptation to Change in Eastern Europe', p. 258.

31 See Karal Ann Marling, *As Seen on TV: The Visual Culture of Everyday Life in the 1950s* (Cambridge, MA: Harvard University Press, 1994), chapter 7; and Hixson, *Parting the Curtain*, chaps 6 and 7.

32 See Ina Merkel, 'Consumer Culture in the DDR, or How the Struggle for Antimodernity was Lost on the Battleground of Consumer Culture' in Susan Strasser, Charles McGovern and Matthias Judt, eds, *Getting and Spending. European and American Consumer Societies in the Twentieth Century* (Cambridge: Cambridge University Press, 1998) pp. 281–99.

33 Gert Selle, 'The Lost Innocence of Poverty: On the Disappearance of a Culture Difference,' *Design Issues*, vol. 8, no. 2 (1992) pp. 61–73; Georg C. Bertsch and Ernest Hedler, *SED = Stunning Eastern Design* (Cologne: Taschen, 1994).

34 Useful overviews from the large field of economic history include I. Berend, *Central and Eastern Europe 1944–1993* (Cambridge: Cambridge University Press, 1996); and Michael C. Kaser, ed., *The Economic History of Eastern Europe 1991–1975*, vol. III (Oxford: Oxford University Press, 1987).

35 Tamas Aczel and Tibor Meray, *The Revolt of the Mind: A Case History of Intellectual Resistance behind the Iron Curtain* (New York: Praeger, 1960) p. 153.

36 Erzsébet Markos, 'A kirakatrendezés problémai', *Szabad Müvészet* (June 1961), p. 279, cited by Péter György, 'The Mirror of Everyday Life or the Will to a Period Style' in Péter György and Hedvig Turai, eds, *Art and Society in the Age of Stalin* (Budapest: Corvina, 1992) p. 20.

37 Phillip Hanson, *Advertising and Socialism: the Nature and Extent of Consumer Advertising in the Soviet Union, Poland, Hungary and Yugoslavia* (London and Basingstoke: Macmillan, 1974) p. 29

38 *Társadalmi Szemle* (October 1959) p. 2 cited by G. Gömöri, '"Consumerism" in Hungary', *Problems of Communism*, vol. 12, no. 1 (1963) p. 64.

39 G. Gömöri, '"Consumerism" in Hungary', pp. 64–6.

40 Compare a study of the accommodation between state and the free market in the period of transition at the end of the 1980s by Judit Bodnár, 'Assembling

the Square: Social Transformation in Public Space and the Broken Mirage of the Second Economy in Postsocialist Budapest', *Slavic Review*, no. 3 (1998) pp. 491–515.

41 Julie Hessler, 'A Postwar Perestroika? Towards a History of Private Enterprise in the USSR", *Slavic Review*, no. 3 (1998) p. 527; Eugène Zaleski, *Stalinist Planning for Economic Growth, 1933–1952*, trans. M. C. MacAndrew and J. H. Moore (Chapel Hill, 1980) pp. 579, 603.

42 See for example 'Arkhitektura – na uroven' novykh zadach', *Sovetskoe iskusstvo* (10 January 1953).

43 The East-West comparison was much more pronounced in the case of Berlin before the erection of the Wall in 1961. Before then, as Steiner notes, consumers could compare the merits of the two economic systems by taking a short journey across the city. See André Steiner, 'Dissolution of the "Dictatorship of Needs"? Consumer Behavior and Economic reform in East Germany in the 1960s' in Strasser, McGovern and Judt, eds, *Getting and Spending,* pp. 170–1. See also R.A. Medvedev and Z.A. Medvedev, *Khrushchev: The Years in Power* (New York: Columbia University Press, 1978) p. 39.

44 Hanson, *Advertising and Socialism*, p. 7.

45 Cited by Iurii Gerchuk, 'Stochki zreniia shestidesiatnika', *DI SSSR*, no. 7 (1991) p. 9.

46 Alec Nove, *An Economic History of the USSR* (Harmondsworth: Penguin, rev. ed., 1982) p. 364.

47 V. E. Khazanova, 'Arkhitektura v poru "Ottepeli" in V.E. Lebedeva, ed., *Ot shestidesiatykh k vos'midesiatym. Vosprosy sovremennoi kul'tury* (Moscow: VNIII, mimeograph 1991), p. 77

48 Anon., 'Iskusstvo inter'era', *Muskovskii khudozhnik*, no. 10–11 (June 1959), p. 1.

49 N. Svetlova, 'Tvoi dom', *Ogonek*, no. 3 (11 January 1959) pp. 14–16; O.G. Baiar & P. N. Blashkevich, *Kvartira i ee ubranstvo* (Moscow: 1962).

50 Susan E. Reid, 'Destalinization and Taste, 1953–1963', *Journal of Design History*, vol. 10, no. 2 (1997) pp. 177–201; and Victor Buchli, 'Khrushchev, Modernism, and the Fight Against Petit-bourgeois Consciousness', *Journal of Design History*, vol. 10, no. 2 (1997) pp. 161–76.

51 For example, C. Humphrey, 'Creating a culture of disillusionment: consumption in Moscow, a chronicle of changing times' in Daniel Miller, ed., *Worlds Apart. Modernity Through the Prism of the Local* (London and New York: Routledge, 1995): Catriona Kelly 'Creating a Consumer. Advertising and Commercialization', C. Kelly and D. Shepherd, eds, *Russian Cultural Studies* (Oxford: Oxford University Press, 1998); and Milena Veenis, 'Consumption in East Germany. The Seduction and Betrayal of Things', *Journal of Material Culture*, vol. 4, no. 1 (1999) pp. 79–112.

52 K. Verdery cited by Humphrey, 'Creating a culture of disillusionment' in Miller, *World's Apart*, p. 56.

53 Michel de Certeau, *The Practice of Everyday Life* (Berkeley: University of California Press, 1984).

54 Timothy Ryback, *Rock Around the Bloc: A History of Rock Music in Eastern Europe and the Soviet Union* (New York and Oxford: Oxford University Press, 1990) p. 10.

55 György, 'The Mirror of Everyday Life', p. 21.

56 See Mary Buckley, *Women and Ideology in the Soviet Union* (New York and London: Harvester, Wheatsheaf, 1989) p. 144.

57 Victor Buchli, in a recent study, has brought a fruitful approach to a building designed by the celebrated modernist architect, Moisei Ginzburg, in 1928–30, the Narkomfin Communal House in Moscow. This single building is considered as a site of repression, conciliation and resistance at different points in its history from the first Five-Year Plan (1928–32) to the collapse of the Soviet Union in the early 1990s. Buchli sets out to explore how 'individuals coped with rapidly changing social contingencies by examining their negotiations with domestic architectural space', a concrete space designed to stimulate the social trans-formations which the Bolsheviks had believed would hasten communism. See Victor Buchli, *An Archaeology of Socialism* (Oxford: Berg, 1999).

58 See Uta G. Poiger, 'Rock 'n' Roll, Female Sexuality, and the Cold War Battle over German Identities', *The Journal of Modern History*, 68, (1996) pp. 577-616; John Bushnell, 'Soviet Hippies', *Harriman Institute Forum*; Hilary Pilkington, *Russia's Youth and its Culture: A Nation's Constructors and Constructed* (London and New York: Routledge, 1994); Rodger Potocki, 'The Life and Times of Poland's "Bikini Boys"', *The Polish Review*, no. 3 (1994) pp. 259–90; Jim Riordan, *Soviet Youth Culture* (London and Basingstoke: Macmillan, 1989); Sabrina Petra Ramet, *Social Currents in Eastern Europe. The Sources and Consequences of the Great Transformation* (Durham: Duke University Press, 1995) pp. 234–61; Sabrina Petra Ramet, ed., *Rocking the State: Rock Music and Politics in Eastern Europe* (Boulder, Colorado: Westview Press, 1994); Paul Neuburg, *The Hero's Children: the Postwar Generation in Eastern Europe* (London: Constable, 1972).

59 See, for example, Stuart Hall and Tony Jefferson, eds., *Resistance Through Rituals: Youth Subcultures in Post-war Britain* (London and New York: Routledge, 1998, first published in 1976); Tracey Skelton and Gill Valentine, eds, *Cool Places: Geographies of Youth Cultures* (London and New York: Routledge, 1998); Dick Hebdige, *Subculture: The Meaning of Style* (London and New York: Routledge, 1988).

60 Artemy Troitsky, *Back in the USSR* (London: Faber & Faber, 1987); and see Pilkington, *Russia's Youth and its Culture*, pp. 277–8.

61 S. Michalski, *Public Monuments: Art in Political Bondage, 1870–1997* (London: Reaktion, 1998); N. Leach, ed., *Architecture and Revolution: Contemporary Perspectives on Central and Eastern Europe* (London and New York: Routledge, 1999).

62 Efforts to preserve the material culture of socialism include the work of the Dokumentationszentrum Alltagskultur der DDR in Eisenhüttenstadt. See A. Ludwig and M. Stumpfe, *Alltagskultur der DDR: Begleitbuch zur Austellung Tempolinsen und P2* (Berlin: be.bra Verlag, 1995).

–2–

Warsaw's Shops, Stalinism and the Thaw
David Crowley

In 1978 Václav Havel described the political and economic system which prevailed in Moscow's satellites:

> Our system is most frequently characterized as a dictatorship or, more precisely, the dictatorship of a bureaucracy over a society. I am afraid that the term 'dictatorship' . . . tends to obscure rather than clarify the real nature of power in this system . . . What we have here is simply another form of consumer and industrial society . . . [T]he post-totalitarian system has been built on foundations laid by the historical encounter between dictatorship and the consumer society.[1]

Havel suggests that consumer societies in Eastern Europe were congruous with communist rule. This view is at odds with what was perhaps the most widely reported impression of 'Eastern Bloc' societies during the Cold War; that is, of shortage, typically represented by the long, trailing queue outside state shops. The notion of a 'consumer society' suggests not only that a large part of the population possess the means to consume goods above the level at which ordinary needs are satisfied, but that a choice to consume one commodity over another performing a similar function can be made.[2] Moreover, commodities with minor distinctions in terms of use have different associations or meanings attached to them by both producers and consumers. As such, the circulation of goods is determined by the distribution of particular kinds of knowledge within a society. Moreover, the commodity is part of a system of representation in that it is not only the thing itself that is required by the consumer society but also its image. In other words, commodities can carry meanings even for those who do not have the means or the desire to materially consume them. One might therefore not only ask if and when Poles living in the People's Republic had the means to consume, but where did their understanding of the things that they acquired and used come from? In a social and economic system that laid great store by the equality of its citizens, how could the consumer articulate social differences through the consumption of things (in other words what is sometimes called 'positional consumption')? And how could subjective concepts like fashion or taste be accommodated by a centrally-planned system of production that claimed to be oriented to comprehensively meeting needs?

This paper investigates one particularly charged and public aspect of the changing discourse of consumption in Poland from the consolidation of power by the Stalinists in the late 1940s to the period of destalinization in the mid 1950s, that of the 'official' view of the shop as well as alternative, illicit ways of provisioning. The state shop was the point at which production and consumption met. Not simply a place where consumption was subordinated to the plan, the shop was also a critical opportunity to propagate views about exemplary consumptive practices. This was not just a matter of rhetoric in the periphrasis of the plan or directive; the design and arrangement of shops themselves was shaped by the discourse of consumption. However, before examining the shop and, to some extent, the practice of shopping, it is important to explore the official view of consumption during Bolesław Bierut's regime (as First Secretary of the Party between 1948 and 1956). The effective depression of consumption at the beginning of communist rule marked the level against which subsequent administrations measured their own accomplishments.

Plan Culture under Bierut

Pronouncements about domestic consumption after the formation of a one-party state in Poland in 1949 were usually bland and often disingenuous. The Polish communists did not subscribe to a coherent or comprehensive theory of consumption.[3] Although Marx offered a critique of the alienating effects of commodification in his theory of commodity fetishism, production has tended to dominate over distribution and consumption in classical Marxist thinking, a preoccupation shared by Soviet practice in all its manifestations. Actual policy was often *ad hoc* and opportunistic, patterned by Soviet precedent. The communist system was built on unambiguous promises of material progress. The Poles were constantly reminded of their good fate to be living in a socialist country allied to the Soviet Union, despite the privations that they faced in everyday life. They were perpetually on the threshold of the promised land. Socialism, therefore, aroused the desire to consume by its promises of material improvement.

Frank acknowledgment of the actual economic system that had been imposed on Poland only came after the political 'Thaw' of the mid 1950s. Oskar Lange, the leading reform economist of the period, described it as a 'war economy' based on the depression of consumption. Stalinist economics were based on massive investment in heavy industry; full nationalization entailing the closure of many small enterprises so that resources could be channelled into larger, 'more efficient' industrial concerns; the imposition of a new financial system controlled by a central bank, thereby keeping all investment in state hands; and, most importantly, the establishment of central-planning mechanisms that would manage demand according to a Soviet-style 'Five Year Plan'.[4] Like the Soviet Union in the 1930s, great emphasis was placed on rapid industrial growth in the iron and steel industries as well as in engineering. State ideology claimed that only intervention into the organization of resources could raise standards of living for all. By the early 1950s central control over the industrial economy was almost complete. Enacting policies adumbrated by the Party, the *Centralny Urząd Planowania* (Central Planning Bureau) drew up detailed plans for each manufacturing concern. Copious calculations determined investment levels, the supply of raw materials and other resources, as well as the range of different products to be manufactured. This was understood as a politically determined system. Competition, profit and market prices were eliminated. The price paid by consumers, whether for basic foodstuffs or for scarce consumer durables, did not result from an assessment of real relative costs but from a judgement about the 'correct' relationship between the value of things and the role that they played in the lives of ordinary Poles. High demand and low levels of production, as well as an artificial pricing regime meant that this was a 'producer's market' in which the consumer had relatively little sway over the things which reached the shops. In fact, the volume of production and the quality of goods were not determined by demand but by state command. As plan culture was built on quantitative markers rather than measures of quality, there was little incentive to introduce flexibility or new technology into industrial production. (This was reinforced by Poland's rejection of the Marshall Plan in 1948 and forced entry into COMECON, which resulted in exchanges of materials and technologies with the Soviet Union). Consequently, whilst, for example, millions of shoes or spoons may have been made to order, the plan had little to say about the quality or design of those products.[5]

Consumption under Attack

Future bounty was promised in return for suppression of the appetite to consume in the present. The supply of commonplace products was a low political priority during the late 1940s and early 1950s as the state established the means to regulate and shape consumption. This took the form of control over retailing by eliminating private shops as well as prohibition of certain goods. This was initially known as the '*bitwa o handel*' (battle over trade) which was waged from the Spring of 1947, even before the communists assumed power.[6] Although denunciations of 'profiteers, speculators and dishonest merchants' were largely expressed with the aim of controlling prices of essential commodities, like food for a hungry population, some particularly 'nietowarzystki' (anti-social) commodities such as Western music or motorcars were singled out. However, in Poland, provision of basic consumer goods was a matter of urgency. Levels of destruction in cities like Warsaw were extremely high and, consequently, the need for everyday goods like furniture and utensils was very strong. Not surprisingly, luxury was ruled unacceptable by the sober mood that accompanied the period of reconstruction as well as the Party's inflated attack on the excesses and luxuries of bourgeois life. The moral economy which operated during the period of reconstruction meant that popular opinion disapproved of conspicuous consumption without necessarily affirming the Party's vilification of the private shopkeeper and other visible members of the 'bourgeoisie'.

Restraint was more than just a matter of hard-nosed austerity measures (after all, rationing was a feature of the mixed economies of Western Europe at this time as well). Consumption, in the context of the Cold War, became a symbolic field of conflict on which allies and enemies could be plotted. For instance, a campaign was mounted against the *Bikiniarze* (Bikini Boys) – young people, largely from Warsaw, who affected, as devotees of American popular culture, '*nietowarzystki*' and distinctly '*niepartyjny*' ('unpartylike') styles of dress and mannerisms.[7] The *Bikiniarze* engaged in a form of highly conspicuous consumption, dressing and living out what they imagined to be the style of fashionable American youth: their preferred music was jazz; their cigarettes were Camels; they adopted English nicknames from American movies and popular songs. During the height of Stalinism in Poland, the state stigmatized the *Bikiniarze* by characterizing them as *chuligani* (hooligans) engaged in anti-social, promiscuous and immoral behaviour. Like many contemporary reports of spectacular youth cultures in the West, this characterization placed stress on an 'unprincipled' desire to consume. Moreover, it tended to focus on the *Bikiniarze*'s obsessive interest in the details of a disparaged material culture, that of the US. In October 1947, following Zhadanov's lead in the Soviet Union, the Central Committee launched a campaign in the press and schools against the 'American way of life' and its influence in Poland. The 'American way of life' – a caricature – was associated with the impoverishment and commercialization of culture. Adam Ważyk in his poem, *Piosenka o Coca-cola*, described the drink as 'the official symbol of the horrors of American civilization'. Similarly, 'Americanization' was introduced into the Polish vocabulary with negative associations, particularly when describing the effects of the Marshall Aid programme in Western Europe. Rodger Potocki describes how an exhibition entitled *Oto Ameryka* (*This is America*) that circulated through the people's republics in early 1952 sought to ridicule 'capitalist culture' by exhibiting kitsch.[8] The US could be understood by the banal things which Americans reputedly consumed. Despite the best efforts of the authorities, this exhibition proved to be extremely popular not least, one might reasonably assume, with the *Bikiniarze*.

Party attitudes to consumption in the home were far from encouraging. Although President Bierut promised to spread the 'ideas of everyday beauty into every home in Poland' in 1952,[9] attacks on the notion of private life made too much attention to one's home seem an anti-social trait. In discussion of the new society, the image of the home was sketched in little more than broad outline. Nevertheless, certain traits emerge strongly. In the early years of the 1950s it was represented in the press by new residences from the Warsaw reconstruction program (see the discussion of MDM below). Older housing stock – whether the large middle class apartment or cramped workers' quarters – was represented negatively as an index of the inequity of pre-war capitalism. The ideal home was rarely conceived as much more than a place where practical needs could be met. Although modernism as an architectural aesthetic was denounced by Party ideologues,[10] a utilitarian attitude to the home was encouraged. The value of a 'functional kitchen' or multi-purpose furniture was emphasized to resonate with the mood of vigilant asceticism that the Party sought to promote in the country. One commentator in March 1953 wrote, somewhat zealously, of the new dwellings being built under the aegis of the Six-Year Plan:

> The new, bright and comfortable flats are not only a place of rest for the working man. They are also a place where one can work on self-improvement, a place where one may work out many of the ideas about efficiency which present themselves in the course of professional work.[11]

New homes were places for the reproduction of the new socialist citizen. They were rarely discussed, even in genuinely popular magazines, as a site of memory, decoration or leisure. Such conceptions were not given currency until the political Thaw of the mid 1950s.

The attendant concept of 'private life' was a condition also viewed with suspicion. In 1950, for example, a 'discussion' held in the pages of *Sztandar Młodych* (Banner of Youth), the organ of the *Związek Młodzieży Polskiej* (ZMP/ Union of Polish Youth), rehearsed the most fervent position of those who supported the right of the Party organization to shape all aspects of life. This was prompted by a non-conformist letter from Comrade Jankowska which claimed that besides 'work in school or factory . . . discussions on the subject of Marx and the People's Republic of China and studying Stalin' even the most ardent activist should be able to enjoy 'non-controlled' pleasures such as using make-up or be able 'to dance with a comrade in suede boots . . .'. According to the results of a questionnaire conducted by the paper's editors, it was widely and enthusiastically agreed that the private lives of communist youth should be 'completely subordinated to the interests of class warfare' and that to demand 'non-controlled' pleasures was to display signs of 'bourgeois individualism'.[12] The essentially public and ascetic culture promoted by the most zealous strains of Polish Stalinism viewed the feminine and private values which might be expressed in the consumption of commonplace things – even domesticity itself – with suspicion. As Berend has noted 'Forced collectivism . . . embodied peevish intolerance against otherness'.[13]

In a polarization characteristic of Soviet ideology since the 1920s, 'profligate' consumption was contrasted against worthy production. In fact, a hierarchy of virtue credited those fields of production most distant from domestic consumption with greatest social worth: engineering, mining and steel production were adopted as symbols of the vigour of communist industry. In the Soviet manner, these sectors were personified in the celebrity accorded to labour heroes such as Wincenty Pstrowski, a miner credited with great feats of productivity.[14] Reports of their achievements often contained altruistic expressions of the satisfaction to be found in deferring consumption: 'After all, we do not work with the immediate aim of consuming. Today we lay the greatest stress on the manufacture of those products which will further our industry.'[15] In 1950 Wojciech Fangor painted *Postaci* (Figures), an archetypal expression of the Stalinist exaltation of production over consumption (Figure 2.1). Three figures are shown standing in front of the kind of a socialist realist building being planned for Warsaw at that time. Two are dressed in the stereotypical uniform of the worker, their productivity symbolized in the firm grasp of a pick-axe or shovel: the third figure, heavily made up and clothed

Figure 2.1 Wojciech Fangor, *Postaci* (Figures), 1950, oil painting, Muzeum Sztuki in Łódż.

in a fashionably-cut dress printed with the words 'Coca-cola' and 'Wall Street', clutches onto her purse, a sign of selfish desires. The steady gaze of labour casts an accusation at this extravagant figure who hides behind dark sunglasses. Fangor's painting reproduced a cluster of binary oppositions which were conjoined in communist ideology in the early 1950s: production/consumption; work/leisure; masculine/feminine and Soviet/West.

Exceptions to the negative characterization of consumption did exist. The worker employed in nationalized factories and reconstruction schemes was encouraged to beat production targets with material rewards. From 1948 mass labour competitions were initiated with bonuses or prizes (usually radios and sewing machines) being awarded to the winners. The relatively luxurious and scarce goods offered as reward for hard-work in 'the path of building socialism' escaped the bad odour of commodification because they were awarded by the state to the worker. They were a public demonstration of the productivity of the socialist economy. There was, in fact, a growing recognition that the distribution and availability of almost all products was, in some sense, in the gift of the state. Consumption was clearly determined by politics, sometimes in quite literal ways. In 1954 the journalist Leopold Tyrmand kept a diary of his life in Warsaw. An eclectic set of reflections on popular culture as well as literature, and sardonic comments about the communist regime, *Dziennik 1954*, contained some thoughtful reflections on the 'communist style of life'. Tyrmand, for example, recorded on 5 March that:

> In Warsaw you can feel the heated preparations for the second PZPR (Polish United Workers Party) congress. It will be weighty political event in Polish life. At once goods appear in great profusion, as if thrown into the shops. It is always this way. Great assemblies, congresses, national and international conferences result in shop displays garnished with expensive commodities. You can now acquire without difficulty sausage, sprats and better material for trousers . . . I overheard a lovely conversation on the bus today. An old, fat woman – the kind who is mistress of the house – said, 'You know, beef sirloin can be had at our co-operative shop . . .'. The old thin woman – the kind who is a professional clerk – replied 'Of course, it's the congress . . .'.[16]

If sporadic abundance in the shops could be understood as being politically managed, so, of course, could routine shortage.

Shopping with Stalin

In the first years after the war as the communists sought to consolidate their authority over Poland, a mixed economy first came under the discipline of the Three-Year Plan (1947–9), and was then brought under total control by a programme of nationalization guided by the Six-Year Plan passed by Parliament in

July 1950. Consequently, between 1947 and 1955 the number of private retailers in Poland dropped dramatically from 131,218 to 7,567 businesses (to 5.76 per cent of the 1947 figure).[17] In tandem with campaigns against the black market and speculation, the range and disposition of shops throughout the country came under centralized control.[18] Planners established norms so that each locality would be served by a predetermined number of shops selling a specified range of products. '*Społem*', a co-operative business established in 1908 and effectively nationalized in 1948, for example, sold basic foodstuffs in the towns, whilst '*Delikatesy*', a new feature in the urban landscape from 1952, sold more luxurious items such as imported goods like coffee, confectionery, and Russian Champagne. Clothes and consumer durables, when available, were sold in central department stores known as a 'Pedet' (*Powszechny Dom Towarowy*) in many towns and cities. By establishing a certain hierarchy of functions and, more generally, by keeping consumption under tight rein, competition between shops was largely extinguished.

The nationalization of retailing in the early 1950s had effects in other aspects of Polish life. Advertisements – unnecessary in a command economy and, by this time, taken as a symptom of the malaise of capitalism – rapidly disappeared from the pages of Polish magazines and from city streets. In fact, Polish commentators such as Ignacy Witz, writing in *Życie Warszawy* in 1953, drew a comparison between the political and cultural posters celebrating May Day or announcing the latest film in Polish cinemas and commercial advertising in the West:

> Capitalist advertising posters do not convince, do not speak, do not teach: they simply scream. Our poster is a professional friend of the masses . . . The difference between posters of capitalist societies and those in progressive countries is like that between a lying, noisy trader and a cultured, whole-hearted advocate of the rights of society.[19]

For Witz the clamorousness of the street in the West was measure of the 'decadence' of the system which shaped it.

The widely used propaganda technique of binary opposition – in Witz's case between West and East – was also employed to draw comparison between present conditions and life before the Second World War. *Stolica*, a weekly magazine dedicated to the reconstruction of Warsaw, often reproduced contrasting pictures of Warsaw past and present: for instance, the Bentkowski House (1819–22) on Nowy Świat, once a major commercial street in the capital, was revealed in a 1939 image as once having been disfigured with 'tempting' signs and the advertisements of the 'business interests' that occupied its ground floors: in contrast, its unpolluted state and new role as a scientific institute in 1953 was presented as a measure of the new value system prevailing in Poland.[20] Whilst the revolution of 1917 had been the harbinger of modernity in Russia, the decisive political transformation of the late 1940s in Poland was from one order of modernity to another. Between the world wars, a large part of urban Polish society had experienced modern forms of mass consumption.[21] This had important consequences in that the capitalist 'other' denounced by Stalinist ideology in Poland could not simply be a burlesque representation. It necessarily had to encompass the Polish past; a past which was within recent, living memory.

Culture Versus Commerce

The Stalinist assault on commerce drew upon a deeply embedded vein in national mythology, that of the preeminence of culture.[22] To be *kulturalny* (cultured) has been a confidently asserted state of being since the early nineteenth century. This, of course, has been a general European phenomenon but the particular circumstances of Polish history gave added emphasis to the 'value' of culture. Hampered by strictures placed on public life during the period of partitions (1795–1918) as well as by the underdevelopment of a commercial, bourgeois class, some Poles postulated an ideal Polishness based on high levels of education and a traditional notion of social and moral conduct. These two qualities were connected in that one should be knowledgeable about culture and to draw from it lessons for the conduct of life, of whatever station. In the 1950s the communists, despite their pretensions to be the vanguard of the working class, sustained this idealistic though inherently elitist view of culture as an edifying force (conveniently echoing Lenin who had argued after 1917 that it was necessary to hold onto the finest aspects of Russian culture to build a more cultured society).[23] *Kulturalny* attitudes and patterns of consumption were heavily promoted in state propaganda: ordinary Poles were invited – particularly during the *Dni oświaty książki i prasy* (Days of education, literature and the press), a campaign mounted each May – to purchase 'improving' cultural products such as cheap editions of nineteenth-century novels and Russian language publications. By the same measure, failure to maintain 'kulturalny' patterns of behaviour was cast as anti-social. Poles were reminded, for example, that 'a cultured person does not get drunk' in campaigns against alcoholism by the social affairs section of WAG, a state publishing house.

Culture and commerce were generally polarized in the discourse over consumption. An echo of the disdain in which commerce was held can be found in 1954 when *Świat*, a photojournal based on *Life* magazine, reproduced a touched-up photograph of an Italian highway marred by a rash of advertisements for petrol.[24] In the accompanying article entitled, '*Zamerykanizowany krajobraz*' ('Americanized landscape'), the author elaborated a comparison between the beautiful landscape (nature improved by culture) and the trickery of advertising (culture spoiled by greed). Advertising was an index of the corruption of culture. However, the benefits of culture could be brought to salvage the defects of commerce. One of the functions of a shop in People's Poland was to be that of improvement: a well designed shop 'represented the high culture of service and aesthetics of socialist trade'.[25] Shopping was to be an elevating and cultured experience. Inside state shops, established forms of advertising such as the trade-card disappeared. In its place, state offices reminded customers of the 'correct' attitudes to consumption. A small poster displaying the image of a crane swinging the number six into place (symbolizing the Six-Year Plan) captioned with the slogan, 'Collective trade ('*handel uspołeczniony*') is the path to socialism', regularly adorned the walls of '*Delikatesy*' shops in the 1950s. At the same time, a publicity campaign cautioned against the illicit consumption of goods on the black market, a theme to which I will return. The political transformation from private ownership to public control was also evident in the packaging of common products. The popular confectioner, Wedel, which had been in business in Warsaw since 1851, was renamed *Zakłady przemysłu cukierniczego im. '22 Lipca'* (The '22nd of July' Confectionery Manufacturer), the date of the announcement of the People's Republic in 1944 by the Soviet backed Polski Komitet Wyzwolenia Narodowego (Polish Committee of National Liberation). This date was adopted as a national holiday; a day invariably occupied with grand, honorific events designed to show off the achievements of the socialist state. Chocolate boxes now bore this political hallmark too. Ordinary products were branded with names and images that carried strong associations with the new regime. In the 1950s, for example, Polish smokers could buy 'MDM' cigarettes bearing the widely reproduced image of the monumental socialist realist lamps illuminating Plac Konstitucji (Constitution Square) in the capital. In such mundane ways, ideology was domesticated, and ordinary things linked to the grand cause of building socialism. In fact, MDM (*Marszałkowska Dzielnica Mieszkaniowa*/Marszałkowska Residential District) warrants particular investigation because it was presented as a paradigm for the modern, socialist townscape.

Warsaw's Shops

The reconstruction of Warsaw from devastation in 1944 was keenly embraced by the communists as a cause through which they could secure popular support and demonstrate the superiority of state management of the economy and national resources.[26] Following the announcement of a Six-Year Plan for the reconstruction of the capital[27] and the introduction of an official architectural style, socialist realism, at a meeting of Krajowej Partyjnej Naradzie Architektów (National Party Council of Architects) in the Party headquarters in Warsaw in June 1949, the principal building schemes in the capital took on an unmistakably political character. MDM, a scheme that combined residential buildings, an impressive square, and social agencies and services as well as shops, was particularly significant (although the full extent of the 1950–1 plan for this part of the city was

Figure 2.2 General view of *Plac Konstutucji* (Constitution Square), Warsaw designed by Stanisław Jankowski, Jan Knothe, Józef Sigalin and Zygmunt Stępiński in 1949 and opened in 1952.

never completed).[28] As an integrated district in the heart of the city, it was presented as a model (albeit a short-lived one), in terms of architectural language as well as the 'socialist' distribution of space, for other urban schemes in the country. Its location, just south of the historical core of the city, and its provision of high-density accommodation as well as shops and offices had symbolic and practical purpose: in contrast to the suburbanization of cities in Western Europe after 1945, the working classes were returned to the heart of the city – not to live in slums but in a planned and purpose-built district. MDM was planned to house 42,000 inhabitants and to operate as Poland's first 'city centre of socialist business' providing 'shops and facilities necessary for the collective life of the masses' (Figure 2.2). MDM was planned as the image of a fully integrated city without the functional divisions between work and leisure or culture and politics, characteristic of the West. In realizing the new socialist city, the planners intended to realize the whole socialist citizen.

Plac Konstitucji, the core of MDM completed in July 1952, is a large square flanked by monumental buildings based on the proportions and stylistic language of small corpus of neo-classical buildings constructed in the city before the First World War. The ground floor of each building was occupied by shops and cafes, with apartments on the floors above. In the handsome book published to chronicle MDM's apotheosis, a telling photographic comparison was made between the private shops found in the city immediately after the war and those located around Plac Konstitucji.[29] A terrace of single-story shacks extended by stalls that spilled out into the street was counterposed with a view of the elegant, deep arcade that left the shop fascia behind in deep shadow, obscuring the window displays. The reader, just like the passer-by, was encouraged to admire the overall and harmonious effect of monumental classical forms rather than the goods for sale. In marked contrast to the view of street as marketplace with the disorder and hubbub that this experience entailed, Warsaw's new architecture vigilantly framed and contained the activities that it housed. In fact, when socialist realist schemes came under attack from modernist architects after 1955, they singled out the lifelessness of MDM in particular as a failing of this phase in urban planning.[30] In this criticism of Stalinist aesthetics, the typical aspects of the commercial city could now be invoked as enlivening, positive features of the cityscape. Jerzy Wierzbicki wrote:

> Note the absence of advertising, lighting and neon: the elements which in the evening hours give the city streets the greatest liveliness and diversity. The city centre must be a concentration of hotels, restaurants, cafes, travel offices, attractive shop premises. The life of a great city presses for them . . .[31]

Moreover, far from being a site of consumer spectacle (associated in Wierzbicki's mind with Paris in particular), MDM maintained the Stalinist fetish for production. The buildings flanking the north side of the square were given sculptural reliefs above tall ground floor windows. In a narrative sequence, they told a story of the origins and construction of the MDM scheme itself like the stations of the cross. And massive figures representing generic 'positive types' associated with a productive economy such as the miner (sculpted by Józef Gazy) and the mother (by Karol Tchorek) were set into niches along a section of the main thoroughfare running through MDM. One of the primary functions of the square as a site of consumption was subordinated to the communist mania for production.

Inside MDM's shops, the quality of design and, in particular, the fittings was patently higher than that which had been available to most private retailers in the immediate post-war period. Expensive materials such as marble used to clad walls as well as opulent fittings such as hand-woven carpets and candelabra lent an air of gentle luxury to the shops selling jewellery and domestic furnishings. As a mode of shopping, these retailers drew upon the model of the department store: the customer, so it appear from press reports, would be brought goods for inspection by one of the many shop assistants whilst waiting comfortably on one of the many elegant chairs. The shop's stock was not accessible: a small range of examples was placed in cabinets like museum cases for leisurely and disinterested inspection. If the department store had been a 'palace' for the middle classes in the nineteenth century affecting an image of what Rachel Bowlby has called 'opulent leisure',[32] MDM's pretentious shops gave the impression of democratizing consumption even further across the social scale. Even in shops selling more commonplace commodities such as food an emphatically *kulturalny* approach to layout and retailing was envisaged. The interior of a branch of *Delikatesy*, frequently reproduced in propaganda in the early 1950s, was furnished with lofty classical figures flourishing symbols of bounty. At the same time, its restrained and tasteful displays of bottles of wine and other products corresponded with the vein of controlled asceticism which the state encouraged as part of its strategy of containing consumption.

Warsaw's Markets

The state, despite its policies of nationalization, did not have a monopoly over the exchange of commodities in Poland. The wartime black market continued to thrive in the 1950s fueled by the goods – particularly clothes, linen and cosmetics – sent to Poland by relief schemes organized by Polonia (émigré Poles and their families abroad) and the United Nations Relief and Rehabilitation Administration, as well as by smuggling conducted by those fortunate to have opportunities to travel abroad. Major conduits for this illicit trade were Warsaw's street markets, particularly the Rożycki Bazaar and '*Ciuchy*' (slang for clothes) on Plac Szembeka at the periphery of the city (Figure 2.3). Whilst the former included some fixed stalls, '*Ciuchy*' was a more informal system with sellers staking a claim on a patch of ground on which to spread their wares. Tyrmand, the diarist, was a habitué of Warsaw's markets. After visiting the Rożycki Bazaar in March 1954, he described it as 'the last true, red-blooded reserve of commercial life in Warsaw, a reserve of Warsaw humour and petty villainy.'[33] Although selling and buying on the black market were prohibited, such street markets were tolerated because, like a safety valve, they satisfied demands that Polish industry could not. (And, in fact, a network of shops known as '*Komisy*' was established to combat black-market trade. Poles could legitimately sell clothes and other valuable goods, usually received from relatives abroad, through these state shops.)

Before 1956 Warsaw's street markets were usually the subject of negative comment in the press: one typical report mocked 'the offal of a transatlantic culture' on sale.[34] The failure of the state to meet the needs of consumers became a legitimate subject of public debate – a discussion licensed by destalinization – and a spate of articles appeared reporting in the spirit of social investigation the popularity of the 'department store under open skies'.[35] In December 1956 a particularly uninhibited article on '*Ciuchy*' appeared in *Przekrój* (*Profile*), an

David Crowley

Figure 2.3 Cover of *Przejkrój* magazine, December 1956. The caption to the covershot reads 'Men and women's, old and new, fashionable and unfashionable shoes on one of the shoddy Warsaw stalls'.

illustrated weekly reporting culture and fashion.[36] Its author, after acknowledging the twin embarrassment that not only were the goods on sale originally sent as aid, but that Polish manufacturers could not produce such things, offered a thoughtful analysis of the motivations of shoppers. Shopping was a qualitatively different experience at *Ciuchy* compared to that promoted by the state shop because it was based on different values. Not only did the street market offer the opportunity to engage the senses in direct and prohibited ways – fingers to touch, eyes to range over and compare all the goods on display – but it was also an 'adventure' made up of chance encounters with things. Chance, it seemed, had been extinguished by the meticulous, if flawed, scope of the Plan. The fact that many of these things came from 'beyond the iron curtain' added to their appeal as 'forbidden fruit': 'Obviously, a Czechoslovak or Bulgarian thing cannot be "*ciuchy*". They may be good products but they are bought with reason and not from love.' The archetypal example of '*ciuchy*', for this author, were military fatigues on which American soldiers had painted cryptic military letters and numbers. Such commodities carried a mysterious and illicit charge. For these reasons, he claimed that the official network of '*Komisy*' 'could never replace the street-market even if they were improved by people attentive to the "*kulturalny*" . . . appearance of the city and if leading heroes of the class war replaced the grannies selling nylon knickers . . .'.

For Tyrmand writing in 1954 before critical social comment could be freely vented, the goods available at '*Ciuchy*' were a distinct and unmistakable feature of Warsaw life:

> It is paradoxical that Prague and Budapest, two intact cities with an excellent supply of clothing factories, appear less elegant than Warsaw. Of course, it is clear that the general state of dress of the crowds on the streets is incomparably higher but in Warsaw you can see a few people, chiefly young university students, dressed in a specific 'ciuchy' style thereby giving Warsaw's streets the colour of European chic. The young, without regard for 'the march of society', are the most fervent carriers of 'ciuchy' elegance. Amongst the young, socks with coloured stripes are a uniform and, at the same time, a manifesto. With these socks the young engage in a heroic battle with communist schools, with communist youth organizations, with the whole communist system. These socks stand in recent years as the sign of a holy war over the right to have your own taste . . .[37]

Striped socks had a synechdochical relationship to an entire taste culture that Tyrmand later described as 'applied fantastic'.[38] This strange compound inferred both commitment, in the effort required to produce the intended effect, and escape, in the pursuit of exotic style. Fantasy was measured by the cultural and material austerity of post-war life, as well as the political charge attached to consumption. The diverse range of clothes and other goods at '*Ciuchy*' constituted, for Tyrmand, a *style*, not in terms of design or manufacture but in the manner of their consumption. Moreover, consumption was interpreted as resistance. It would seem that Tyrmand's interpretation concurs with numerous studies of spectacular sub-cultures in the affluent West from the 1950s onwards. The idea that commodities have been deployed in a conflict over meaning in consumer cultures is a familiar theme developed by numerous authors.[39] The Lévi-Straussian idea of 'bricolage' and the Situationist practice of 'détournement' – processes by which the marg-inalized and opponents of consumerism have tried to reclaim the steady stream of commodities produced by modern societies – have often been invoked in explorations of the idea of consumption as resistance. However, 'insubordinate consumption' in capitalist countries has usually met with little opposition: after all, capitalism encourages little interest among manufacturers in the life of their products after they are sold. In contrast, in Bierut's Poland '*ciuchy*' was not only condemned but, as we have seen, consumption itself was critically circumscribed by what Tyrmand called a 'spartan ideology'. The early example of '*Ciuchy*' would seem to illustrate Katherine Verdery's observation that 'The arousal and frustration of consumer desire and East Europeans' consequent resistance to their regimes led them to build their social identities specifically *through consuming*. Acquiring consumer goods and objects conferred an identity that set one off from socialism. To acquire objects became a way of constituting your selfhood against a regime you despised.'[40] When Poland was cast in opposition to the consumer society, '*Ciuchy*' provided the means for this kind of resistance. However, during the Thaw official attitudes to consumption became both more encouraging and more ambiguous at the same time.

The Thaw

The waves of destalinization that swelled from 1954 touched many aspects of Polish life. Although the Thaw has tended to be measured by the freedoms extended to the esoteric realms of high culture such as abstract art[41] or in terms of the reform of political life, its impact on ordinary Poles was largely felt in the ways that consumption was conceived anew. In fact, one might even say that the changing appearance of the street was a more certain demonstration of the effects of the Thaw, than any 'internal' changes in personnel in Party headquarters. For a short period (which had ended at the time of the Third Party Congress in March 1959) communist authority was moderated by a degree of tolerance (extended only in part by design).

The Thaw in Poland was precipitated by events in Moscow and accelerated by popular pressure from within. In the climactic events of 1956 Poles in Poznań and elsewhere protested their discontent with shortage by taking to the streets. After October the Party, under the new leadership of Władysław Gomułka, embarked on a course of reform that aimed to sustain and revive a set of basic dogmas, not least the commanding role of the Party in Polish life. One of the promises made by Gomułka's colleagues was the improvement of standards of living. This concept was defined materially rather than in terms of education, political consciousness or, as the Stalinists had viewed it, culture. Under the influence of economists like Lange, a partial market economy was introduced in 1957 with the intention of increasing the production of consumer goods. The strategy of introducing greater flexibility and decentralization in industrial production had the effect of encouraging Polish manufacturers to compete with one other. Reform economists even argued for profit – once a wretched offence against the working class – as the measure by which productivity should be gauged. Although the intention was to improve the range of consumer goods available, Lange and others were careful to argue against their distribution as a political salve. Although the state continued to subscribe to central planning as well as national ownership of the means of production, an element of pluralism entered into Polish economic life in 1957–8 not least in the form of private businesses such as taxi services, restaurants and tailors. One estimate suggested that more than 10,000 new private shops and kiosks opened in 1957 alone.[42]

At the same time, the state reduced its interest in many spheres of culture and science in an attempt to lower the ideological temperature. The Polish post-Stalinists declared a technocratic view of progress – one that did not measure human works by ideology alone. They sustained their claim on the leadership of Polish society by vaunting their hold on modernity. In this context, the discourse of consumption thickened and took on a multifaceted and sometimes contradictory disposition. Although the availability of consumer goods only increased at a slow rate during the second half of the 1950s, *images* of consumption expanded exponentially, not least because magazine and newspaper editors were no longer under pressure to represent the world outside exclusively in terms of Cold-War polarities. Events and patterns of life – whether fashion from France or American jazz – could now be reported in the spirit of social documentary. A pre-war magazine, *Dookoła Świata* (Around the World), was revived by the ZMP in January 1954 with this intention; Tyrmand called it a 'concession' made by the regime (a type of commodity almost exclusive to the Eastern bloc).[43] Until October 1959 when the Central Committee castigated such popular magazines for exhibiting uncritical enthusiasm for 'Western culture',[44] they were important catalysts of change. From 1956 American and Western European films were widely distributed by the *Centralna Wynajmu Film* attracting much higher audiences than East European imports.[45] Against a flood of images of life in the West, a number of Stalinist shibboleths were depoliticized: shopping and consumption in general were increasingly associated with pleasure and, by the same process, leisure was released from the improving sphere of *kulturalny* activity. Consequently, articles appeared in the press on shopping as an enjoyable and leisurely occupation;[46] advertising returned to the pages of popular magazines; and the home was increasingly represented as a site of individualism and self-expression. A new magazine, *Ty i Ja*, first published in 1960, ran a regular feature, '*Moje hobby to mieszkanie*' ('My hobby is my flat') which took its readers to the homes of well-known artists and actors, high profile members of an emerging *klasy średniej socjalizmu* (socialist middle class). On its pages the home was presented as an expression of taste and identity: old furniture, 'exotic' souvenirs and *staroci* (bibelots) could be used to tell personal histories that did not necessarily conform to an 'approved' reading of history. Consumption, at least vicariously on the pages of magazines, was increasingly associated with the exercise of individual taste rather than the 'rational' and collective judgement of utility.

New Shops

Against the background of an efflorescence of images of consumption, the shop was reassessed by architects and urban planners. Again, Warsaw, as the most prestigious site of state activity, offers the most exaggerated examples. The new economic model encouraged an explosion of new private shops and kiosks. State-owned retailers also expanded during the late 1950s to sell the new consumer goods manufactured by state enterprises as well as imports.[47] According to Hansjakob Stehle, writing in 1965, the proliferation of new retailers brought about the demise of the street market.[48] One could argue that, in fact, Warsaw's new shops incorporated modes of selling that were far closer to *Ciuchy* than MDM. One of the earliest examples of these new structures was the temporary building designed in 1957 by Tadeusz Tomicki and Ryszard Trzaska for the *Stołeczny Zarząd Handlu* on Marszałkowska Street, close to MDM. This steel-framed and glass-walled 'pavilion' called '*Śródmieście*' (City Centre) accommodated 42 private stalls selling clothes and household goods. A modernist box deposited on the paving stones, *Śródmieście* was fronted with glass giving the impression of projecting the goods for sale into the street. At night this glass box was illuminated from within so that the skeletal structure almost disappeared and the merchandise appeared to be suspended in the light. Such shops were increasingly conceived as part of an urban spectacle offering diversity and surprise.[49] Architects and planners conceiving new schemes in Warsaw imagined lively streets filled with bright shops and flanked with billboards. A popular theme was the city at night illuminated with neon advertisements. The (usually unacknowledged) source for this conception of the urban environment was the capitalist city.

Another novelty imported from the West on Warsaw's streets was the super-market, the most conspicuous example being 'Supersam' at the start of Puławska Street, designed in 1959 by Jerzy Hryniewiecki, Maciek Krasiński and Ewa Krasińska (Figure 2.4). This landmark building was a dramatic statement of faith

Figure 2.4 'Supersam' supermarket, Warsaw designed in 1959 by Jerzy Hryniewiecki, Maciek Krasiński and Ewa Krasińska.

on the part of the architects and the authorities, in a technologically determined conception of modernity: in the use of 'industrial' materials such as reinforced concrete and in ostentatious structural forms such as the cantilevered concrete canopy over the door and dramatically cambered beams which spanned the brightly lit shopping hall. The shift towards self-service associated with the 'open shop' was understood as empowering consumers in that they were now able to judge goods in hitherto prohibited ways. (This idea caused some controversy: some state retailers, fearful of theft and breakage, called for programmes to educate consumers in this new 'culture' of shopping.)[50] Shelves were to be stacked high with products giving the unmistakable impression of profusion. The supermarket, as a style of retailing, was evidently not modelled on Soviet precedents but on American ones. In the period of destalinization in the Soviet Union, America was characterized by official ideology in new ways. Although the Gomułka administration was not the mirror of Khrushchev's regime, the image of America in official rhetoric became more ambiguous in Poland as well. For example, architects writing in a Polish magazine on the problems of kitchen design turned to America because, they claimed with a little ideological sleight of hand, the greatest problem that both countries shared was that of mass housing.[51] The fact that the ideological and economic outlook of the two countries was polarized was less important than the usefulness of the technical knowledge which the American building industry could supply. In a similar fashion, the supermarket was presented (not least by architects, a technocratic lobby) as a quintessentially modern development and, as such, one that the communists were compelled to introduce to Poland. Warsaw, it seemed in the late 1950s, was being remade in the image of the consumer society. In this aspect of life (and I would suggest others), the communists modulated their claim about the unique and superior nature of the socialist system.

Conclusion

The Thaw released a range of new and rehabilitated images of consumption, not least in the appearance of Warsaw's shops. At this time Poland appears to have become a mass consumer society, albeit in a peculiar fashion. The Poles were not transformed into aspiring consumers by the possibility of acquiring a new wave of goods. In fact, estimates about the increased availability of consumer goods in Poland during the late 1950s and early 1960s suggest that only a small part of demand was met.[52] Moreover, many complaints were raised about the poor quality of these products. (At this time a new word entered Polish speech, *brakorobstwo*, to describe the faulty products of Polish industry). The consumer 'revolution' in Poland at this time was almost exclusively an eidetic one: the 'liberation' promised by consumption existed rather more in the realm of images than in the potential of material things. Socialist Poland, after all, remained a country where the unavailability of bread triggered riots. The Thaw, in this respect, conforms to the cycle of arousal and frustration which characterized the unhappy history of the People's Republic.

Notes

1 Václav Havel, *The Power of the Powerless* (1978) (London: Faber & Faber, 1987) pp. 37–40.
2 The literature on the history and nature of the consumer society is very large. A useful survey of this literature is Daniel Miller, ed., *Acknowledging Consumption* (London: Routledge, 1995).
3 The Communist Party was known from 1948 as the *Polska Zjednoczona Partia Robotnycza* (Polish United Workers' Party). Before this date, post-war political

life was dominated by members of the *Polska Partia Robotnicza* (PPR/Polish Workers' Party). Leading members of the PPR held the most important portfolios in the Provisional Government of National Unity (1945–7) and in the first elected government after the January election of 1947. There is much continuity between the two parties, not least in their subordination to Moscow, and for the sake of clarity I have chosen simply to describe them as the Communists.

4 My description of this process is necessarily a brief summary. See Ivan T. Berend, *Central and Eastern Europe 1944–1993* (Cambridge: Cambridge University Press, 1996) pp. 3–94; and Michael C. Kaser, ed., *The Economic History of Eastern Europe 1991–1975*, vol. III (Oxford: Oxford University Press, 1987).

5 Lange, who was associated with the steps towards greater flexibility in state planning in the late 1950s, was fond of noting that at one time there had been no hairpins in Poland because they had been overlooked in the plan. See Hansjakob Stehle, *The Independent Satellite* (London: Pall Mall Press, 1965) p. 152.

6 Padraic Kenney, *Rebuilding Poland, Workers and Communists 1945–1950* (Ithaca: Cornell University Press, 1997) p. 192–8.

7 This discussion of the bikiniarze draws on Rodger P. Potocki's excellent essay, 'The Life and Times of Poland's "Bikini Boys"', *The Polish Review*, no. 3 (1994) pp. 259–90.

8 Ibid., p. 278.

9 Bolesław Bierut cited by Maria Starzewska, *Polska ceramika artystyczna pierwszej połowy xx wieku* (Wrocław: 1952) p. 47.

10 See Anders Åman, *Architecture and Ideology in Eastern Europe during the Stalin Era* (Cambridge, Mass. and London: MIT Press, 1992).

11 St. Komornicki, 'Jak urządzić nowe mieszkanie' in *Stolica* (1 March 1953) p. 11.

12 *Sztandar Młodych* (10 September 1950).

13 Berend, *Central and Eastern Europe, 1944–1993*, p. 84.

14 See 'Początek wspózawodnctwa pracy' in Anon., *Kalendarz Robotniczy na 1949 rok* (Łódź: Książka Wiedza, 1948) pp. 216–24.

15 Anon. 'Polsce, prezydentowi, sobie . . .', *Przekrój* (23 March 1952) p. 3.

16 Leopold Tyrmand, *Dziennik 1954*, entry for 5 March 1954 (Warsaw: Tenten, 1995) p. 240.

17 See Zbigniew Landau and Jerzy Tomaszewski, *The Polish Economy in the Twentieth Century* (Beckenham: Croom Helm, 1985) p. 206.

18 It should be noted that until 1956 the state operated *konsumy specjalne* (speciality stores) where members of the nomenklatura could purchase foreign goods. Somewhat of a special case, they are beyond the terms of this paper.

19 I. Witz, 'Nasz Plakat' (originally published in *Życie Warszawy* in 1953) in *Przechadzki po warszawskich wystawach 1945–1968* (Warsaw: PIW, 1972) p. 53.

20 Stanisław Herbst, 'Nowa Historia Warszawy', *Stolica* (1 February 1953) p.13.

21 Wiktor Herer and Władysław Sadowski, 'The incompatability of system and culture and the Polish crisis' in Stanisław Gomułka and Antony Polonsky, eds, *Polish Paradoxes* (London: Routledge, 1990) p. 129–33.

22 The preeminence given to culture was also a feature of Soviet communism. See Svetlana Boym, *Common Places. Mythologies of Everyday Life in Russia* (Cambridge MA: Harvard University Press, 1994) pp. 102–9.

23 See Anne White, *Destalinisation and the House of Culture* (London: Routledge, 1990) p. 19 and passim.

24 Anon, 'Zamerykanizowany krajobraz' in *Świat* (24 October 1954) p. 21.

25 Catalogue to the *Pierwsza Powszechna Wystawa Architektury Polskiej Ludowej*, (Warsaw: 1953) p. 59.

26 See my 'People's Warsaw/Popular Warsaw', *Journal of Design History*, vol. 10, no. 2 (1997) pp. 203–24.

27 See Bolesław Bierut, *Sześcioletni plan odbudowy Warszawy* (Warsaw: Książka i Wiedza, 1951).

28 Complete data is provided in Stanisław Jankowski et al, 'Marszałkowska Dzielnica Mieszkaniowa', *Architektura*, nr. 7 (1951) pp. 223–32.

29 Stanisław Jankowski, ed., *MDM. Marszałkowska 1730–1954* (Warsaw: 1955).

30 See, for example, Jerzy Wierzbicki, 'Parter ulicy w Warszawie', *Architektura*, no. 7 (July 1955) pp. 196–200.

31 Ibid, p. 198.

32 Rachel Bowlby, 'Supermarket futures' in Pasi Falk and Colin Campbell, eds, *The Shopping Experience* (London: Sage, 1997) p. 97.

33 Tyrmand, *Dziennik*, pp. 254–5.

34 Unacknowledged newspaper report quoted by Stewart Steven, *The Poles* (London: Collins Harvill, 1978) p. 338.

35 Anon. '"Pedet" pod niebem', *Świat* (2 September 1956) p. 21.

36 Bracia Rojek, 'Ciuchy', *Przekrój* (9 December 1956) p. 8–9.

37 Tyrmand, *Dziennik*, p. 143.

38 When Tyrmand revised his diary for publication he introduced this term into a passage about the dress of the young in Warsaw. It has appeared in most editions of the book. See, for example, *Dziennik 1954* (London: Puls, 1993) p. 45. This term was adopted by Wojciech Lipowicz in a discussion of the applied arts in the catalogue for the '*Użytkowa fantastyka lat pięćdziesiątych*' exhibition held at the Muzeum Rzemiosł Artystycznych, a branch of the Muzeum Narodowe in Poznań, in 1991.

39 Examples include Michel de Certeau, *The Practice of Everyday Life* (Berkeley: University of California Press, 1984); Nigel Whiteley and Nicholas Abercrombie, eds, *The Authority of the Consumer* (London: Routledge, 1992).

40 K. Verdery cited by C. Humphrey, 'Creating a culture of disillusionment: consumption in Moscow, a chronicle of changing times' in Daniel Miller, ed., *Worlds Apart. Modernity Through the Prism of the Local* (London: Routledge, 1995) p. 56.

41 A good recent example is the *Odwilż* exhibition and catalogue edited by Piotr Piotrowski (Poznań: Muzeum Narodowe, 1996).

42 Stehle, *Independent Satellite*, p. 171.

43 Tyrmand, *Dziennik*, p. 182.

44 Tomasz Goban-Klas, *The Orchestration of the Media* (Boulder: Westview Press, 1994) p. 119.

45 Stehle, *Independent Satellite*, pp. 209–10

46 See, for example, Anna Bankowska, 'Wiosna i kobieta', *Stolica* (17 April 1960) pp. 2–3.

47 An interview with the director of the main department store in Warsaw describing how decentralization would improve the supply of goods for sale was published in *Stolica*. See Barbara Ubysz, 'Handel zwycięza dystribucję', *Stolica*, 48, XI (25 November 1956) pp. 2–3.

48 Stehle, *Independent Satellite*, p. 172.

49 See, for example, Stefan Koziński, 'O projektowaniu obiektów dla handlu', *Architektura*, no. 9 (1960) pp. 360–2.

50 Józef Łowiński, 'Sklepy warszawskie', *Architektura*, 1 (1959) p. 48.

51 Jan Maass and Maria Referowska, 'Kuchnia', *Architektura*, 2 (1959) pp. 28–9.

52 Frank Gibney, *The Frozen Revolution: Poland, a Study in Communist Decay* (New York: Farrar, Straus and Cudahy, 1959) p. 248.

–3–

Stalinism, Working-Class Housing and Individual Autonomy: The Encouragement of Private House Building in Hungary's Mining Areas, 1950–4
Mark Pittaway

Introduction

Between 1952 and 1954 waste ground and agricultural land on the fringes of the western Hungarian mining town of Tatabánya was transformed into a 'garden suburb' with 240 private homes. Each home was set in its own plot with a small garden at the front for the cultivation of 'rosebushes, fruit trees and flowers'.[1] Behind the houses, concealed from the view of passers-by, was the part of the plot where vegetables were grown, chickens, and in some cases a pig were kept. The houses themselves were made of red brick.[2] They were also large by the standards of much miners' housing in the town. Each had an entrance hall, while some had one and others had two large rooms for use as bedrooms or living rooms and a separate kitchen.[3] The houses were to be connected to the electrical power supply, though would not themselves have running water. All the local authority had undertaken to do was to provide wells within easy reach of the new private homes.[4]

The Party in the town and the local authorities promoted the development of a 'garden suburb' for miners as an achievement of the socialist state. The local newspaper quoted the wife of one of the new owner-occupiers stating that 'we have been married eighteen years, but before the liberation we simply couldn't think that we would ever own our house. Before, a radio, or new kitchen furniture was simply an unachievable goal for us. And now, I own my own house'.[5] The new residents in the Tatabánya suburb were the beneficiaries of a state-organized programme to help solve the chronic housing shortage in mining areas through granting aid to miners and their families to build their own homes. On 2 July 1952 the Ministry of Mining and Energy initiated a campaign to supply private house builders with materials and practical assistance. It envisaged that 500 private houses would be constructed nationally by the end of 1952, and a total of 1500 would be built by August 1953. Credit up to 70% of the cost of building the house was

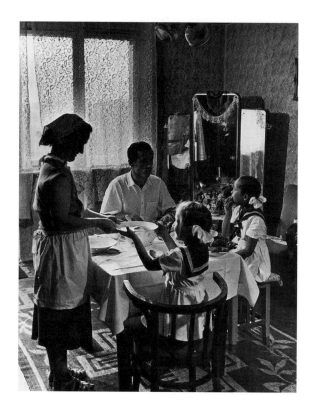

Figure 3.1 Mineworkers' homes and stalinist domesticity. In new housing on the Petöfi Mining Colony in 1954 stakhanorite coal hewer István Mészáros enjoys Sunday lunch with his family. Photograph courtesy of the Hungarian National Museum, Budapest.

offered: 23,000 Forints for a one room house, and 30,000 Forints for a two-room dwelling. The remaining 30% was met by the miner-builder personally and would amount to around 6–7,000 Forints (about eight times the average monthly wage).[6]

The promotion of private house building and 'petty-bourgeois' attitudes by a Stalinist regime seems a little strange. During the Stalinist years, officially permitted discourse amongst architects and town planners revolved around the best means to plan new environments in ways in which the use of collective services would be promoted, co-operative forms of living would be encouraged and the development of privatized mentalities would be prevented. When the notion of building family houses was publicly discussed at the end of the 1950s and in the early 1960s it aroused bitter controversy among the planners. Given widely held assumptions about the extreme collectivism of the Stalinist regime the widespread encouragement of private house building in Hungary from the 1960s onwards has been seen as a natural consequence of the reformism of the post-Stalinist state.[7]

Figure 3.2 The image of pre-socialist miners' housing, Sálgótárján, 1950. Photograph courtesy of the Hungarian National Museum.

Furthermore the homes of the 'garden suburb' – single storey private houses, set in individual plots – contrasted strongly with much of the new building of the Stalinist years, in both Tatabánya and the country as a whole. Tatabánya was one focus of Stalinist urban policy. An amalgam of four villages, it had become a significant mining and industrial centre by the time it was formally given town status in 1947. Tatabánya did not have the infrastructure of a town and therefore in 1950 a plan was adopted to create it. In addition to the construction of new roads and public buildings the plan contained a major flat building programme to re-house miners living in run-down company accommodation built at the turn of the century.[8] Tatabánya's new town suburb, which was beginning to take shape by the mid-1950s, provided the showcase for this re-housing programme. Buildings containing fifty-six small family flats were erected for miners' families, close to schools, shops and other facilities that would – at least in theory – allow miners to use collective facilities for eating, shopping, childcare, and certain chores like washing that had previously been done within the household. The flats were conceived only as places of rest for the miners and their families.[9]

Why then did the regime encourage private housebuilding by miners, and why did its propaganda organs at local level support owner occupancy? Official histories of the town written in the socialist era explained this in two ways. The first was to explain it through housing shortage – for many miners to build a private house was the only way to secure reasonable family accommodation. The second was to argue that the miners who built houses were predominantly 'new' workers recruited from agriculture who wished to retain something of their old way of life.[10] The account presented here substantially differs from these versions of events.

The state had a more ambiguous attitude to the private sphere than attention either to the debates of Budapest-based architects or to the ideas that informed the construction of Tatabánya's new town might suggest. Much propaganda argued that the male worker required a stable home environment in order to work productively, based on the nuclear family and a modified version of traditional gender roles. In her analysis of pamphlets produced by the official womens' organization Joanna Goven has shown how the expansion of female employment was accompanied by the publication of manuals that showed new 'working women' how to combine work in the socialist labour force with household 'duties'.[11] Such assumptions permeated the way in which officials analysed the causes of worker 'indiscipline'. Officials connected the poor work discipline of 'new' young workers living in workers' hostels to the fact that these workers were living collectively, rather than in what they regarded as a stable domestic environment. In such circumstances the assumptions generated by this ideology of Stalinist domesticity interacted with more 'petty-bourgeois' social attitudes and pragmatic considerations to create official enthusiasm for the promotion of home ownership. During the mid-1950s the private house building schemes directed at Tatabánya miners were expanded to cover the workers in the power plants of the town. Both the management of the plants and local Party officials welcomed these plans arguing that encouraging private house building had two advantages over state construction. The first was that 'the workers would better care for their own house' than they would for state property and that 'maintenance would therefore require less use of state property and the financial burden would be born by the worker'. The second was that 'labour discipline would be favourably affected if the loan for building the house was linked to their workplace. The building of private houses therefore helps the creation of a stable workforce'.[12]

I argue that state encouragement of private house building drew on the notions of domesticity described above. This combined with the problems of housing shortage in Hungary's mining areas, and those of labour management and discipline pushed the state down this road. Private house building was enthusiastically supported by the relatively small number of miners who could afford to participate because it offered them the possibility of attaining a sphere of relative autonomy from the failures of the shortage economy and the socialist state around them. To both state officials and miners the private house symbolized a secure private sphere. The policy makers assumed that it offered miners a degree of security and as such would improve their work performance, whereas miners saw it as a means of securing a degree of household self-sufficiency in the face of a chaotic economy.

In order to develop this argument the chapter focuses on private house building in the town of Tatabánya during the early 1950s, firstly considering the interaction between housing conditions, labour policy and the workforce, and thus setting the context for a discussion of the attraction of private house building to miners themselves. The chapter then concludes by evaluating the effectiveness of the campaign and assesses what private house building reveals about social relations in industrial Hungary during the early 1950s.

The Politics of Labour and the Politics of Housing

The link between housing shortage and the problems of creating a stable workforce had been foremost in the minds of many officials when they designed the programme to encourage private house building in the early part of the decade.[13] In Tatabánya, as in most of the mining communities across the country, patterns of settlement inherited from the pre-socialist period interacted with poor housing conditions and increased employment opportunities created by socialist industrialization to drive both the politics of labour and the politics of housing in the town.

During the inter-war years the workforce of the Tatabánya mines was stratified by settlement in a way typical of mining in provincial Hungary, in particular by the process known as 'colonization' (*kolónizálás*). In part this term was used by social observers beginning with Zoltán Szabó in the 1930s to describe the way in which employers in heavy industry across provincial Hungary sought to integrate a workforce drawn from the peasantry, from different ethnicities and nationalities, and with diverse experiences of work, into the rhythms and practices of industrial labour. The colony (*kolónia*) was the company housing and the facilities built around it for the benefit of the workers. Often benefiting the best-paid workers within the core of the workforce, this policy had a disciplinary objective. In the late 1930s one social observer reported that mineworkers who lived on the *kolónia* in Tatabánya complained that mine management sought to dictate the newspaper they should read and indeed to determine 'which restaurants they were allowed to go in'.[14]

Patterns of settlement were to interact with the social organization of mine work to stratify the workforce during the inter-war period. In 1939 the total number of mineworkers stood at 5,129, of which 3,367 worked underground and a further 1,762 worked above ground. While the division of skill within the labour process and the differentiation between overground and underground workers stratified workers within mining, division due to settlement had a much greater role. Those who lived on the *kolóniák* were made up of either those miners who had been brought from parts of the monarchy other than Hungary prior to 1914, their descendants, or those who had been recruited from among the rural poor. Of the underground mineworkers who lived in the *kolóniák* in 1939, 28.6 per cent had begun work in mining, 37.8 per cent were former agricultural day labourers and 17.1 per cent had been smallholders whose land had been too small to guarantee an income. On entering the mining *kolónia* they effectively left the land behind.[15]

The second important group in the workforce was the worker-peasant one. Many worker-peasants had small land holdings of under 1.5 hectares, and could not make a living from them. They or family members went to work in the mines to guarantee the family an income, or where they could cover the basic needs of the household from the land, generate a surplus from which more land could be bought and their dreams of securing an existence as an independent smallholder be realized. Some of these workers were seasonally employed and took jobs in the mine during the winter, leaving in summer for the harvest. Others were more permanent and sought to accumulate wealth to buy either land or build a house. From a total of 11,763 employees in the Tatabánya mines in 1947 some 3,832 fell into the category of commuting village dwellers.[16]

Socialist industrialization was to re-stratify the workforce and create problems of labour discipline and labour shortage. These problems were driven by the interaction of the dissatisfaction of young workers with working and living conditions, particularly housing, and the expansion of the workforce demanded by socialist industrialization. In 1950 the increasing intensity of work, the poor safety record in the mines, a wage system that tended to depress wages exacerbated by a norm revision and the poor provision of food in the shops led to increased discontent. Many miners felt that the communist regime was not delivering to its key constituents in the mining towns.[17]

Poor housing conditions were one major cause of this discontent, particularly among miners who lived in the nationalized *kolóniák*. In 1950 a report on housing conditions in the *kolóniák* in Tatabánya concluded that 5,860 mineworkers lived with their families in 4,987 flats with 5,905 rooms in total. This meant considerable overcrowding; it was stated that there was an average of 3.2 people living in a room in company housing, but there were rooms which had to be shared by as many as twelve people. The majority of the flats had been built at the turn of the century. They were contained in 'six doored' (*hat ajtósok*) houses, so-called because each one contained six small family flats. Attached to each house was a collective toilet and small yard. A minority, built in the inter-war years, consisted of four-flat houses. In addition to the overcrowded conditions inside, many of the houses were regarded as appalling. A journalist visiting with a group of doctors in 1948 remarked that 'most miners' families live together in one room, even though on average they have 3 or 4 kids and often young married couples have to live with their parents'. According to the local newspaper in 1947 'ten live together in a one room flat . . . There is only one bed. The road is at the height of the roof and because of it dust comes down into the flat as a result of the road traffic'.[18]

Increasingly young miners anxious to set up families sought employment outside mining in order to guarantee better housing conditions. In 1950 with the beginning of socialist industrialization an increasing number of miners requested that management agree to their departure on the grounds that 'in Tatabánya they could not start a family': 1,672 underground workers had already left during 1949 and 1,264 left during the first half of 1950 alone. At the same time as the mines struggled to retain labour, they were compelled to prepare to shoulder their part of the burden of increasing national coal production in order to provide fuel for Hungary's rapidly expanding heavy industrial sector. Despite this, no spectacular expansion of the labour force in the mines occurred between 1950 and 1955. In 1950 9,343 manual workers were employed by the Tatabánya coal mines, a figure that rose to 10,244 in 1955. Furthermore between 1950 and 1951 despite huge increases in plan targets the number of manual workers in the mines actually fell.[19]

The labour shortage these processes generated was not merely a matter of a lack of unskilled workers that could be solved through organized labour recruitment. Skilled young coal hewers left Tatabánya in droves. As a result, alongside campaigns to recruit unskilled labour for coal transportation in the mines, the state began to introduce crash courses to train coal hewers. Traditionally such workers had undergone an apprenticeship alongside a more experienced hewer for six to eight years. Under the terms of new crash training courses 'new' workers were able to work as hewers at the coal face after only a year's training.[20]

These processes drove a huge re-composition of the workforce in the Tatabánya mines. In 1957 when the coal hewers were surveyed only 35 per cent had been working in the mines for ten years or over – in other words just over a third of skilled workers in the coal mines had worked in the pits prior to the beginning of socialist industrialization: 39.2 per cent had begun work in the mines between 1947 and 1954 as plan targets demanded constantly increased coal production. Workers in the mines remembered the changes to the town as the children of older miners left during these years and they were replaced by new residents. These new residents were the children of the agricultural poor from the rural Great Plain regions in the east of the country. There was little improvement in housing conditions, the flats on the *kolóniák* remained overcrowded. There was little investment in state housing in the town during the early 1950s, and the plans for new housing investment in the town were never realized. 'New' workers from agriculture who wished to settle permanently in the town had nowhere to go but the workers' hostels. As a result of the influx of 'new' workers in a climate of housing shortage the percentage of the workforce resident in the hostels grew rapidly: in 1950 the State Supervision Agency calculated that 5.1 per cent of the workforce in the mines lived in them. By 1953 this proportion had risen to 30 per cent.[21]

The result was the creation in the hostels of a specific culture among the largely young male workers who were resident in them that was regarded by the state as a cause for some concern. For workers living in the Tatabánya hostels conditions were poor; in September 1951 it was reported that one of the hostels was constantly 'dirty, the reason being that there is often no water; as a result the workers cannot bathe and go to sleep dirty . . . there is no water, cold or hot. There are no furnishings in the rooms, nowhere to put either food or clothes.' Doctors came to believe that the conditions of the workers' hostels were responsible for a significant amount of illness among the mineworkers. Many of the hostels were originally intended to be temporary. They were originally buildings with other uses and had been quickly converted for the purpose of accommodating 'new' workers. As a result of the lack of investment in housing in the town such 'temporary' accommodation had become semi-permanent. They were reported to be 'messy, they are cleaned rarely, the beds are changed only every 6 to 8 weeks'. In addition theft was reported to be a major problem.[22]

The life of residents of the workers' hostels was one of relative isolation from the world around them, punctuated only by weekend visits to their families and mitigated by the temporary community of the hostel: 'after a hard day's work people didn't really go out' reported one resident. Another described his leisure activities as walking 'to the cinema. If I had enough money I went into the cinema, but most of the time I didn't have enough for a ticket' or reading 'forbidden paperback westerns' published in the 1930s. At the same time a solidarity built up between most of the hostel residents, 'the residents would not have betrayed their neighbours' remembered one. Often they spent their spare time listening to Western radio stations 'if they could find the station'. Listening to Western radio often formed a kind of initiation into the culture of the hostel; 'the guys watched each other to see how they all reacted to the things they heard, how they behaved. We warned those who had just arrived that if they told anybody there would be problems made for them'.[23]

This culture of alienated, young, 'working class' males forced out of agriculture by an oppressive state bred political dissent – a fact that was recognized by the state. Young workers from Tatabánya who escaped to the West in 1953 recounted how under cover of darkness they would go from the workers' hostel into the town to tear down posters inviting them to produce 'More coal for the homeland', or exhorted them to 'Sign up for peace loans, build a future for your family and your children', and replaced them with their own home-made posters with slogans like 'Long live the Americans!' or 'Don't work for such low wages!'[24] More importantly the state was confronted with a major problem of absenteeism and other forms of 'indiscipline' in the mines. This they linked to the culture of the workers' hostels. In response, the state sought to enact punitive legislation to control the behaviour of the young male workers within them while it sought in the long term to domesticate hostel residents. In its propaganda it held up examples of 'disciplined' workers leaving the hostels, taking state aid to build houses and settling down with their families, as an ideal to be followed.[25]

Miners and Private House Building

For the authorities private house building offered the potential of both alleviating housing shortage and easing the problems inherent in the management of labour. By offering those workers who could afford to do so the chance of aid to build and own their home they aimed to tie them to the mine. By allowing workers the chance of creating their own private space and granting them the promise of autonomy from the privations of Stalinist Hungary they sought to create more disciplined, contented workers. The miners who participated in the private house building schemes bought in to the promise of autonomy and privatization that their own home offered, even if their precise motives were often not appreciated by the representatives of either the local authorities or the national state.

A private family house as opposed to a state flat, or, worse, renting a bed or living in a workers' hostel, offered private house builders the opportunity to become more self-sufficient especially in food. In summer 1953 the local newspaper in Tatabánya reported on the case of one 'new' worker and his family. The family was characterized by a clear gender division of labour: while the husband worked in the mine the wife took responsibility for managing the household. She pointed to the importance of the garden of the house which made such management easier, stating that 'my father didn't like houses but his daughter is growing cucumbers in her own garden to eat during the winter'. The garden contained more than cucumbers as the wife aimed to meet a substantial proportion of household needs through growing tomatoes. In addition she was growing corn and potatoes for the winter and kept chickens.[26]

State propaganda at the time, and official explanations during the socialist period, sought to portray state encouragement of private house building as part of a bargain between the authorities and 'new' miners who had recently left agriculture. Of the articles written on families moving into their new homes published in the town's local newspaper in 1953 and 1954 most dealt with 'new' workers and their families. In each case the 'new' miner had come from an agrarian household and had been recruited into the workforce during the 1950s. After an initial, unhappy period living in a workers' hostel while his wife and children lived on their smallholding at the other side of the country, the worker's enterprise offered him a loan to build a private house. Acceptance resulted in the miner and his family moving together to an adequate family home in Tatabánya.[27] This narrative is backed by an official history that argues private house building was designed to accommodate those miners who 'would readily live in a family house with a garden in accordance with their previous way of life'.[28]

Although we lack precise information on the social composition of those who took out state loans, there is considerable evidence that they did not constitute a majority of private house-builders. Archival evidence suggests that miners whose families had lived on the *kolóniák* constituted a majority of those who took up the state's offer. It points to the attraction of programme for large numbers of miners seeking to escape inadequate accommodation.[29] This is backed to some extent by evidence from the town's local newspaper – among the families they wrote about were several who left the *kolóniák* to find better housing.[30]

Why might a miner and his family who had lived in the *kolóniák*, whose grandparents had left the land for good and adopted an urban miner's lifestyle, wish to build a private house? Part of the answer lay in the access a private house gave to a garden in which vegetables could be grown, or chickens bred. The period immediately following the Second World War was one of tremendous inflation in post-war Hungary. Money, and with it wages, became valueless during the first post-war years. In Tatabánya this had led to the spread of the practice of cultivating allotments in the town. In households where the men were still prisoners of war the women cultivated the allotment.[31] As wages rose and many men returned home from the prisoner-of-war camps in the late 1940s, the importance of growing food lessened, yet the desire for a garden close to the place of residence remained strong. Sz.J., a worker in the machine repair plant attached to the mines, remembered being allocated a flat in four-flat house built at the end of the 1940s. For him a key advantage of this accommodation over flats was the small garden, which he could use to keep chickens, and grow vegetables.[32]

The onset of socialist industrialization was to strengthen the importance of the role that a garden might play in satisfying household needs as real wages declined and shortages increased. Goods and food shortages caused considerable discontent among Tatabánya mineworkers from 1950 onwards. Official organs received complaints in 1950 from consumers who had had to queue for sugar, especially from members of households where all members worked and as a result were unable to queue and were forced to go without for weeks on end.[33] As far as workers in the VI pit of the mines were concerned, 'that workers had to run around after them [groceries]' was a sign that the regime 'continually talks about rising living standards yet gives us nothing'. Another stated that living standards were declining because 'on the market there aren't any goods'. The shortages meant that the workers 'only earn salt and paprika now'.[34]

These shortages and the general inadequacy of public services led to the rise of an ideal of privatized autonomy from the ideologized, shortage-ridden, insecure public realm directed by the Stalinist state. This fed a desire for household self-sufficiency that was not attainable, but was nevertheless craved. A private house functioned as a means of giving concrete expression to the desire to become more self-sufficient. One miner who had become a new home owner expressed his desire to apply for a fishing licence in order that he could therefore help to feed his family.[35]

The development of such privatized ideals pushed 'new' and 'old' miners and their families together at least in terms of their attitudes within the community. The circumstances of socialist industrialization increased the importance of wage labour to the rural poor. The maintenance of a garden along with an industrial job was one of the ways in which industrial and agricultural activity were combined in socialist Hungary. Miners whose families had been employed in industry over several generations bought into an ideal of self-sufficiency, and many began to look toward combining work in a garden with a wage as a hedge against the shortages experienced in the world outside.[36] In the attitudes which made the construction of private houses in Tatabánya's garden suburb attractive to miners, traces of longer-term social change can be seen. The sharp differentiation between the urbanized worker and the member of a rural smallholder household who, perhaps occasionally, took work in industry that characterized the world of the poor in inter-war Hungary was breaking down. A unified culture embracing all of 'the working people' was beginning to emerge whose members would be differentiated only by their access to different sources of income.[37]

The attraction of the private house was driven by the same attitudes that were beginning to re-shape 'working class' culture by the mid-1950s. They were in large part a reaction to the failure of the state to satisfy the needs of its 'working class' constituency. This can be illustrated by returning to the emerging 'garden suburb' and to the 'new town suburb' while paying particular attention to the experiences of the new residents of both as they took up residence during mid-1953. Both suburbs were plagued by the failure of the local authority to provide adequate public transport, electricity, or shopping facilities. In the new town suburb housewifes had to queue daily for vegetables. Consequently, reported the local newspaper, lunch in the new flats was not prepared until late afternoon.[38] In the garden suburb one housewife, however, was able to cook what she had cultivated in the garden of her house ready for lunchtime[39] – thus underlining the difference a house with a garden could make in the shortage economy of 1950s Hungary.

Conclusion

The growth of an ideal of household self-sufficiency throughout Hungary during the 1950s affected miners as much as it did other groups of workers and clearly fuelled their desire to build their own home. The actual ability of miners to build their own homes was restricted. Between the launch of the campaign in 1952 and

1954 only 240 family houses were built in the garden suburb in Tatabánya. In a climate of endemic poverty the amount of money miners had to find from their own resources represented a serious constraint unless the miner concerned had either savings or his employer was able to secure a larger loan for the miner. Furthermore in order to build a private house the miner had to negotiate the bottlenecks and shortages of the socialist economy in order to secure the necessary cement and other construction materials that were required.[40]

Nevertheless the examination of the motives of both the state and of working-class housebuilders at a local level is important in that it opens to examination many commonly held assumptions about Stalinism and its nature. It has been assumed that Stalinism was highly collectivist and that the state aimed to destroy or at least undermine traditional institutions. In this context it seems surprising that the state supported private housebuilding at all, or that a propaganda organ, even at the local level, could celebrate the promotion of owner occupancy or household-based food production as an achievement of the regime. Those who have studied the gender politics of the regime in Stalinist Hungary would perhaps find this less surprising. While the early socialist state nationalized enterprises and politicized production it seems to have been much more conservative where the sphere of reproduction was concerned.

When therefore the state was faced with the shortage of labour and its perceived indiscipline and sought solutions in the sphere of housing, it tended to be more conservative in its solutions than the discussions of avant-garde architects and planners suggests. Furthermore, the acceptance by miners of an ideal of household self-sufficiency openly contradicts the notion of early socialist Hungary as a collectivist society. As this author has argued in much greater depth elsewhere,[41] the need to survive the shortage economy and the despotism of the Stalinist state forced industrial workers to resort to strategies that were often individualistic or based on the membership of particular groups or the adoption of particular social identities. Such identities and patterns of behaviour were highly corrosive of broader social identities and solidarities.

Although the initiative described in this chapter lay at the margins of Hungarian social policy in the early socialist period it is important because it enables us to illustrate themes that must be central to any consideration of the nature of state socialism or its social impact. Firstly the case of private house-building draws our attention to the fact that the assumptions many of its policy makers made about the private sphere were often quite conservative. Secondly, it illustrates the degree to which society responded to shortage within the economy and the radicalism of the state by adopting strategies which promoted social privatization. This led – to borrow a phrase from one anthropologist who studied Romania in the 1980s – socialist societies to be characterised by 'solitude within an intense social field'.[42]

Notes

1 *Harc a Szénért*, 6 May 1954.
2 *Harc a Szénért*, 26 June 1953.
3 *Harc a Szénért*, 13 February 1953.
4 *Harc a Szénért*, 13 November 1953.
5 *Harc a Szénért*, 26 June 1953.
6 Szakszervezetek Közpönti Levéltár (Central Archive of the Trade Unions, hereafter SZKL) Szakszervezetek Országos Tanácsa (National Council of Trade Unions, hereafter SZOT) Szociálpolitika/16d./1952; *Feljegyzés Bányász lakásakció helyzetéről*, pp. 1–2.
7 For a sample of the kinds of debates that were conducted by architects in particular during the period see the contributions reprinted in Máté Major and Judit Osskó, eds. *Új építészet, új társadalom 1945–1978. Válogátás az elmúlt évtizedek építészeti vitáiból, dokumentumaiból* (Budapest: Corvina Kiadó, 1981) especially pp. 97–144; for a sample of the existing literature which associates private house building with economic reform and the development of a 'second economy' see István Kemény 'The Unregistered Economy in Hungary', *Soviet Studies*, vol. XXXIV, no. 3 (July 1982), pp. 349–66; Endre Sik 'Reciprocal Exchange of Labour in Hungary' in R.E. Pahl, ed. *On Work: Historical, Comparative and Theoretical Approaches,* (Oxford: Basil Blackwell, 1988).
8 Géza Horváth 'A Városépítés Története' in Gábor Gombkötö (ed.) et al. (eds) *Tatabánya Története. Helytörténeti Tanulmányok I. Kötet*, pp. 193–6 (Tatabánya: A Tatabányai Városi Tanács Végrehajtó Bizottsága, 1972).
9 *Harc a Szénért*, 18 November 1953.
10 Horváth, 'A Városépítés Története', pp.198–9.
11 Joanna Goven *The Gendered Foundations of Hungarian Socialism: State, Society and the Anti-Politics of Anti-Feminism, 1948–1990*, pp. 30–108, PhD. dissertation, (Berkeley: University of California, 1993).
12 See Komárom-Esztergom Megyei Levéltár (Komárom-Esztergom County Archive, hereafter KEML), Magyar Szocialista Munkáspárt Komárom Megyei Bizottság Archivium iratai (Papers of the Hungarian Socialist Workers' Party, Komárom County Committee Archive, hereafter MSZMP KMBA ir.) 32f.4/ 12ö.e., p. 33.
13 SZKL SZOT Szociálpolitika/16d./1952; *Feljegyzés Bányász lakásakció helyzetéről*, pp. 1–2.
14 For initial discussion of the concept of 'colonization' based on observation of mining districts in north-east Hungary see Zoltán Szabó *Cifra Nyomorúság: A Cserhát, Mátra, Bükk Földje és Népe*, (Budapest: Cserépfálvi Könyvkiadó, 1938) pp. 127–67; Ferenc Szvircsek 'Kolonizálás, mint a Salgótarjáni Kőszénbánya

Rt. munkáspolitikájának része' in Anikó Fûrészné Molnár, ed. *Tatabánya 45 Éve Város*, pp. 99–105 (Tatabánya: Tatabánya Museum, 1992); for Tatabánya itself see Molnár Anikó Fürészné 'Lakáshelyzet, otthonkultúra az ipartelepeken' in Fûrészné Molnár, ed. *Tatabánya 45 Éve Város*, pp. 87–98; Zoltán Magyary and István Kiss *A közigazgatás és az emberek. Ténymegállapító tanulmány a tatai járás közigazgatásáról*, (Budapest: Pécsi Egyetemi Könyvkiadó és Nyomda Rt., 1939) p. 99.

15 Ferenc Szántó 'A szénbányászat és a gyáripar fejlõdése a két világháború között' in Gombkötö et al. eds. *Tatabánya Története*, especially p. 162; Magyary and Kiss *A közigazgatás és az emberek*, p. 101; Imre Bán 'Szénbányászok' in Gyula Rézler, ed. *Magyar Gyári Munkásság: Szociális Helyzetkép*, (Budapest: Magyar Közgazdasági, 1940) pp. 222–5.

16 See Bán 'Szénbányászok', pp. 222–5; András Tóth *From Agriculture to Industry*, unpublished manuscript, Budapest, 1992; Private papers of Samuel Droppa; *Munkavállalók Létszáma, Létszámváltozásai, Évi Munkanapok, Mûszakok és Tejlesitmények*; Private papers of Samuel Droppa; *Létszámkimutatás a közeli falvakban lakó munkavállalókról 1947, 1948, 1949.*

17 KEML MSZMP KMBA ir. 32f.4/17ö.e., p. 211; KEML MSZMP KMBA ir. 32f.4/17ö.e., pp. 217–9; SZKL Komárom SZMT (Komárom County Union Organisation) /42d./1950; *Titkári Jelentés 1950 év szeptember hóról*, pp. 3–5; SZKL Komárom SZMT/42d./1950; *Titkári jelentés 1950 év november hóról*, p. 1.

18 KEML MSZMP KMBA ir.32f.4/17ö.e., p. 213; Pál Germuska *A fürdõszobát meg hírbõl sem ismerik. A tatabányai bányászok lakáskörülmények az 1948 és 1959 közötti idõszakban*, (unpublished mss. Tatabányai: Tatabányai Múzeum Adattára, 1992) pp. 2–3; Molnár Fûrészné 'Lakáshelyzet, otthonkultúra az ipartelepeken'; *Forum*, vol. 2, no. 5, (May 1948) pp. 383; *Komárom-Esztergom Vármegyei Dolgozók Lapja*, (22 July 1947).

19 KEML MSZMP KMBA ir.32f.4/17ö.e., p. 214; Sándor Rozsnyói 'A város nagyüzemei' in Gábor Gombkötö et al. eds. *Tatabánya Története. Helytörténeti Tanulmányok II. Kötet*, p. 87, (Tatabánya: A Tatabányai Városi Tanács Végrehajtó Bizottsága, 1972); Private papers of Samuel Droppa; *Munkavállalók Létszáma, Létszámváltozásai, Évi Munkanapok, Mûszakok és Tejlesitmények.*

20 KEML MSZMP KMBA ir.32f.4/15ö.e., p. 66; Magyar Országos Levéltár (Hungarian National Archive, hereafter MOL) XXIX-F-107-m/51d.; *Tb. Alsó Szénbányák Dolgozó Létszámkimutatása 1951 év dec. hó*; MOL XXIX-F-107-m/51d.; *Törzskönyvi (Állományi) Létszámkimutatása Tb. Szénbányák, 1951. június hó*; MOL XXIX-F-107-m/51d.; *Törzskönyvi (Állományi) Létszámkimutatása Tb. Szénbányák, 1951. április hó*; MOL XXIX-F-107-m/51d.; *Törzskönyvi (Állományi) Létszámkimutatása Tb. Szénbányák, 1951. február hó*; MOL XXIX-F-107-m/52d.; *Törzskönyvi (Állományi) Létszámkimutatása*

Tb. Felsõ Szénbányák, 1951. október hó; MOL XXIX-F-107-m/52d; *Törzskönyvi (Állományi) Létszámkimutatása Tb. Felsõ Szénbányák, 1951. augusztus hó*; KEML MSZMP KMBA ir.32f.4/15ö.e., p. 26.

21 MOL XXIX-F-107-m/54d.; *Kimutatás az 1957. október 1-i állapotnak megfelelõ adatokról*; Personal interview with T.J., Tatabányai Múzeum, 10 August 1995; SZKL SZOT Szociálpolitika/16d./1952; *Feljegyzés a Komárom megyei lakásépitkezésekrõl, Tatabánya-újváros, Oroszlány, és Eterniti épitkezések ellenõrzése alapján*, p. 1; *Harc a Szénért*, 17 July 1953; for overcrowded housing in the town in 1954 see *Komárom Megye Fontosabb Statisztikai Adatok 1952–1955*, pp. 120–46, KSH Komárommegyei Igazgatósága, Tatabánya, 1956; KEML MSZMP KMBA ir. 32f.1/17ö.e., p. 213; MOL MDP- MSZMP Közpönti Szervek iratai (Papers' of the Central Organs of the Hungarian Workers' Party – Hungarian Socialist Workers' Party, hereafter M-KS-)276f.88/249ö.e., p. 13.

22 SZKL Bányász Szakszervezet (Mineworkers' Union, hereafter Bányász)/460d./1951; *Jelentés Tatabánya nõi- és legényszálló: Budapest, 1951. szeptember 18.*; SZKL Bányász/542d./1952; *Jelentés a tatabányai ankétról és a tatabányai Bányagépgyártó Vállalat Szakszervezeti munkájáról*, p. 1; *Harc a Szénért*, 22 November 1951; SZKL Bányász/460d./1951; *Jelentés, 1951 julius 11*, p. 2.

23 Open Society Archives (OSA) Radio Free Europe, Hungarian Research Materials (RFE Magyar Gy.6)/ Item No. 06852/53, p.13; OSA RFE Magyar Gy.6/ Item No. 06687/53, pp. 3–6.

24 OSA RFE Magyar Gy.6/ Item No. 06687/53, p. 5.

25 *Harc a Szénért*, 28 August 1953.

25 *Harc a Szénért*, 13 May 1954.

26 *Harc a Szénért*, 26 August 1953.

27 *Harc a Szénért*, 13 May 1954; *Harc a Szénért*, 28 August 1953; *Harc a Szénért*, 13 February 1953.

28 Horváth, 'A Városépités Története', p. 199.

29 SZKL SZOT Szociálpolitika/16d./1952; *Feljegyzés a bányász sajátlakás épitésakció helyzetérõl*, p. 1.

30 *Harc a Szénért*, 13 February 1953.

31 MOL Magyar Általános Kõszénbánya Személyzeti Osztály iratai (Papers of the Personnel Department of the Hungarian General Coal-Mining Company) Z254/10cs/38t., p. 493.

32 Personal interview with Sz.J., Tatabánya Múzeum, 15 August 1995.

33 SZKL Komárom SZMT/42d./1950; *Titkári jelentés 1950 év november hóról (Secretarial report about November 1950)*, p. 1.

34 SZKL Komárom SZMT/43d./1950; *Szakszervezetek Országos Tanácsa Esztergom-Komárom Megye Bizottság 393./1950 sz. Hangulat jelentés (National Council of Trade Unions. Komárom-Esztergom County Committee.*

Report on the climate of opinion 1950/303), pp. 1–2; SZKL Komárom SZMT/ 43d./1950; *Szakszervezetek Országos Tanácsa Esztergom-Komárom Megye Bizottság 419./1950 sz. Hangulat jelentés (National Council of Trade Unions. Komárom-Esztergom County Committee. Report on the climate of opinion 1950/ 419)*, p. 2.

35 *Harc a Szénért*, 28 August 1953.

36 Mark Pittaway *Retreat from Collective Protest: Household, Gender, Work and Popular Opposition in Stalinist Hungary*, Paper presented at the workshop 'From household strategies to collective action', Internationaal Insituut voor Sociale Geschiedens, Amsterdam, 28–29 May 1999.

37 ibid.

38 *Harc a Szénért*, 10 June 1953.

39 *Harc a Szénért*, 26 June 1953.

40 For the figures on the number of houses built see *Harc a Szénért*, 6 May 1954; on the financial problems of workers in joining the programme see SZKL SZOT Szociálpolitika/16d./1952; *Feljegyzés Bányász lakásakció helyzetérõl*, pp. 1–2; for one case where management assisted one worker see *Harc a Szénért*, 28 August 1953; for the problems with the supply of construction materials see SZKL SZOT Szociálpolitika/16d./1952; *Feljegyzés a bányász sajátlakás épitésakció helyzetérõl*, p. 1.

41 Mark Pittaway *Industrial Workers, Socialist Industrialisation and the State in Hungary, 1948–1958*, PhD. thesis, Department of Economic & Social History, University of Liverpool, 1998.

42 David A. Kideckel *The Solitude of Collectivism: Romanian Villagers to the Revolution and Beyond* (Ithaca and London: Cornell University Press, 1993).

−4−

Plastics and the New Society: The German Democratic Republic in the 1950s and 1960s[1]
Raymond G. Stokes

Introduction

Dustin Hoffmann's character Benjamin in the 1967 film, *The Graduate*, was accosted at one point by his prospective father-in-law, who told the younger man (whose mind was on other things) that the future lay in plastics. The older man's character was in many ways quintessentially American. But in his enthusiasm for plastics, he could have been a chemist, chemical engineer, designer, or bureaucratic visionary from Walter Ulbricht's East Germany. Indeed, his vision of virtually unlimited potential for growth in the plastics industry would have been shared by elites in most of the industrialized world in the 1950s and 1960s.

For a vast number of people around the world in those decades, plastics represented the modern. For some in Eastern Europe, they represented the ultimate socialist material. For most East German politicians, managers and engineers, such views represented very good news indeed: they might well be able to parlay traditional German strength in the organic chemical industry into a reputation for being progressive, modern and thoroughly socialist. Not at all incidentally, plastics – the product of that industry – might help square the circle of East Germany's main economic dilemma: how to maintain a modern industrial economy despite having few resources besides coal, a shrinking labour force and ever more limited outlets for export. In all, plastics appeared to be excellent politics, malleable and serving several purposes at once.

Plastics became, at one point in East German history, a panacea, just as other technologies had been or would become.[2] Production capability, aesthetic impulse and the desires of consumers might be melded through the new materials into a beautiful unity. In the event, all were disappointed. The purpose of this article is to explore the disjunction between vision and reality by concentrating not just on the production of plastics, but also on their ideological functions and on their consumption. For just as East German planners and managers focused overly much on production at the expense of consumption, so have historians of the country.

The links between the producer and the consumer are generally neglected, which is unfortunate since examining them can shed light on real life under 'real existing socialism', the reasons the system lasted as long as it did and its ultimate failure.

I start with a brief overview of the traditional role of the chemical industry in German politics and society, before turning to its ever more central role in the initial years of the German Democratic Republic (GDR), culminating in the so-called 'chemicalization' (*Chemisierung*) programme, which began in 1958. The next section explores the implementation of this programme and its reception by East German designers and consumers, and the last section explores the ramifications of this study for the history of the GDR and of Eastern Europe more generally.

The Chemical Industry in German Politics and Society through 1945

Although Germany was not the first country to exploit the potential of the new organic chemicals industry in the late nineteenth century, it was the most successful. During the decade before the unification of the country under Prussian leadership in 1871, a number of firms were founded to produce lucrative and scientifically challenging dyestuffs on the basis of by-products of the processing of German coal. This small number of firms included BASF, Bayer and Hoechst, and they and a handful of others pioneered in the application of science to this new technology through the founding of dedicated industrial laboratories; pushed into new areas such as pharmaceuticals and high-pressure chemistry; and, by the beginning of the twentieth century, came to dominate world export markets in chemical products. In fact, they controlled an estimated ninety per cent of world trade in chemicals by 1913, and they contributed mightily to Germany's economic and political power on the eve of the First World War.[3]

From the beginning, the German organic chemical industry seemed especially suited to the country's geopolitical and international economic situation. Not only was the industry a substantial contributor to keeping Germany's balance of trade in good order, something especially important for a country so reliant on foreign trade because of its relatively poor endowment with natural resources. Just as importantly, it did not itself draw in any major way upon foreign sources of raw materials, relying instead primarily on German coal, water, air and ingenuity. The industry could, even more crucially, provide substitutes for imported raw materials and finished goods, something absolutely essential in case of economic or political conflict with other nations, and especially Great Britain, which could control the seas. Indeed the German word *ersatz* (or substitute material) entered the English language around the time of the First World War precisely because of the German success in manufacturing substitutes for previously imported materials. Two German chemists, one an employee of BASF and the other an academic closely associated with the company, were to win a Nobel prize for their success in developing synthetic nitrogen, the key ingredient in vital fertilizer and ammunition. The most significant facility for manufacturing synthetic nitrogen was BASF's Leuna Works in what later became the GDR.

The industry's ability and willingness to provide substitutes for imported material grew to even more impressive proportions in the years following 1918, and especially under the aegis of its new company, IG Farben. Formed in 1925, the IG was a trust established by BASF, Bayer, Hoechst and other important German chemical firms and brought the substantial financial, managerial and technological capabilities of those companies under one roof. It was the largest industrial corporation in Germany and one of the largest in the world. By the end of the 1920s, the IG was producing petrol, rubber and a variety of other products on the basis of German coal. Naturally, this ability attracted the National Socialists, who came to power in 1933, and led eventually to disastrous and destructive collusion between the Nazi regime and the IG.[4]

It is worth noting that by the 1920s and 1930s at the latest, the IG and the rest of the German chemical industry were moving well beyond development and production of materials which were merely substitutes and into the realm of new materials. Indeed the word 'substitute' itself began to lose some of its connotations of being acceptable only in a pinch. After all, petrol produced at the Leuna Works performed virtually identically to that produced at traditional refineries in Hamburg-Harburg. And some characteristics of synthetic rubbers were actually superior to those of the natural product. From other materials which emerged from German laboratories and factories through 1945, such as various plastics and synthetic fibres, new and different products could be produced. Or they could be deployed to design machines with characteristics (such as portability and/or lightweight construction) that traditional materials would not permit.

Not all of the German experience during the Nazi period with the *ersatz* and new materials was positive, of course. And many plastics and artificial fibres gained a reputation for shoddiness, poor quality and, frequently, ugliness that was difficult to shake in the post-war period. But post-war trends in production and consumption of plastics in both German successor states appear to indicate that the wartime experience had nothing to curb the Germans' voracious appetite for plastic products. As Table 4.1 indicates, West Germany ranked high in per capita consumption of plastics throughout most of the post-war period and led all industrialized countries, including the US, during the decade of the 1960s. By 1969, West Germans consumed on average nearly 50 kilos of plastic each, which was almost half again the rate consumed by the average American and nearly twice that of West Germany's nearest European rival, France.[5]

East German figures, presented in Table 4.2, are more difficult to assess on a comparative basis since they are based on different definitions of plastics. They

Table 4.1: Per Capita Consumption of Plastics in Western Industrial Nations (kg per Capita)

	1950	*1955*	*1960*	*1961*	*1962*	*1963*	*1964*	*1965*	*1966*	*1967*	*1968*	*1969*
USA	6.4	8.0	10.7	17.0	18.1	19.1	20.8	24.6	28.5	28.7	32.5	34.7
UK	2.5	5.2	9.1	9.5	10.4	11.5	13.9	15.1	15.5	17.3	20.4	21.7
FRG	1.9	5.8	15.0	15.5	21.4	19.5	24.5	26.7	28.5	31.6	40.4	49.9
Fra.	0.9	2.8	7.5	8.3	9.5	10.8	12.5	14.1	17.2	18.9	21.6	26.8
It.	0.6	1.7	5.0	6.7	8.6	10.2	11.0	11.8	14.7	17.7	19.3	23.5
Neth.	1.2	3.5	9.1	9.8	10.5	10.6	14.7	16.6	16.5	18.5	18.8	23.6
Japan	0.2	1.4	3.8	8.4	10.6	10.8	13.6	14.2	17.0	23.4	29.0	32.8

(Includes all plastics, whether cellulosic or synthetic, but excludes elastomers and fibres.)

Source: B.G. Reuben and M.L. Burstall, *The Chemical Economy: A Guide to the Technology and Economics of the Chemical Industry* (London: Longman, 1973), p. 35.

are also based on production rather than consumption, which is perhaps unsurprising given the productivist orientation of the communist country. But they can nonetheless serve as an indicator of general orders of magnitude for consumption of synthetic materials when set against the figures for the Western industrialized nations. In 1955, the GDR produced four kilos of plastics and synthetic resins per inhabitant, which seems to indicate a rank of fourth in the industrialized world behind the US, Britain and West Germany. By the 1960s, the Americans and West Germans were far outstripping the East Germans in their consumption of plastics, but the GDR figures indicate a level of production – and probably also consumption – of plastic products not far behind that of France, the UK, Italy and the Netherlands.[6]

Table 4.2: Per Capita Production of Plastics and Synthetic Resins in the GDR (kg per Capita)

	1955	*1960*	*1964*	*1965*	*1966*	*1967*	*1968*	*1969*	*1970*	*1971*
GDR	4.0	6.7	12.0	12.9	14.6	16.3	17.9	19.2	21.7	24.6

Source: *Statistisches Jahrburch der Deutschen Demokratischen Republik,* 1966, p. 169; 1967, p. 167; 1970, p. 114; 1972, p. 128; 1975, p. 1.

In 1945 in the immediate aftermath of the war, however, these triumphs for the chemical industry lay in the distant future and would have appeared an especially unlikely outcome of the post-war situation. IG Farben was the target not just of Allied trust-busting attempts, but also of Allied scientific and technical investigators and reparations and removals teams. For the mightiest factories of the IG Farben concern, which lay in the Soviet zone of occupation, the later GDR, the impact of

Allied policy was especially devastating. They were cut off from the main research and development facilities, which were in the West. Removals to the Soviet Union eliminated about 50 per cent of capacity at the Leuna Works. Combined with war losses of one-fourth at the factory, this left only about one-fourth of its substance intact. Similar war damage, reparations and removals severely curtailed production capacity in many other factories. Patents were seized and made available to companies around the world free of charge. Key scientists and engineers from the chemical plants were transported to the Soviet Union to work on projects there for up to ten years beginning in 1946. And even after the removals stopped, the largest factories were seized by the Soviets, made into Soviet corporations (*Sowjetische Aktiengesellschaften,* or SAGs) and forced to produce for the Soviet economy through 1953.[7]

It was for all of these reasons that the GDR chemical industry was slow to resume its previous prominence in the economy and culture. By 1951, however, research was already underway at Leuna to develop polyethylene production capability as well as that for modern plastics and synthetic fibres. The companies engaged in the arduous process of reconstruction and technical renewal with redoubled efforts after they were turned over to the East German state in 1954 and became 'Factories owned by the people' (*Volkseigene Betriebe,* or VEBs). It was the late 1950s, however, before GDR committed itself to an ambitious programme to expand the economic and cultural role of its chemical industry, with important effects on production, design and consumption.

The Chemicalization Programme

In 1957, in the context of growing Cold-War tension and systematic competition between capitalism and socialism, the GDR Party apparatus joined the rest of the Eastern bloc in ideological and programmatic discussions on the role of science and technology in communist society. Through those debates, science became, like other fundamental economic forces, a 'force of production', a term popularized by Gerhard Kosel's 1957 book, *Produktivkraft Wissenschaft.* Official communist dogma finally ratified this generally accepted position at the Twenty-Second Congress of the CPSU in 1961.[8] In the meantime, in 1958 the V. *Parteitag* of the ruling Socialist Unity Party in East Germany agreed that the 'main economic task' for the GDR was to demonstrate within just a few years the superiority of the socialist system over the capitalist one (and specifically of the GDR over the FRG) in terms of per capita consumption, not just of plastics, but of all commodities produced in all industrial sectors, This, of course, would only be attained through an increase in productivity on the basis of science and technology. Later that same year, the chemical industry was singled out for a major programme to accomplish this ambitious aim.

Walter Ulbricht himself used the occasion of a special conference in Leuna in November 1958 of the Party's Central Committee and the State Planning Commission to sketch out the GDR's chemical programme under the slogan *Chemie gibt Brot – Wohlstand – Schönheit* ('Chemistry gives bread, prosperity and beauty!'). Although his speech was an especially lengthy performance, essentially he made three main points. First, he announced a greater commitment to research and development in the chemical industry. Second, he announced the transition of much of the GDR chemical industry to petrochemical feedstocks (on the basis of petroleum supplied by the Soviet Union), and, simultaneously, the expansion of existing coal-based chemical capacity. Third, he singled out plastics and synthetic fibres as products for the GDR to concentrate upon in order to improve the well-being of GDR consumers and to be able to reach lucrative export markets.[9]

The 'chemicalization' of the GDR economy, which the chemicals programme was to accomplish, was an odd mixture of the traditional and the new. It marked a renewed commitment to coal-based chemistry (which the rest of the industrialized world was in the process of abandoning), especially at the Buna Works in Schkopau (see Figure 4.4). This was, to some extent, a frank acceptance that the GDR would continue to rely on domestic coal, water and ingenuity to produce its rubber, plastics and elastics. But it was also a concession to the desire of prominent and powerful engineers in the GDR, such as Buna's Johannes Nelles, who wished to pursue Germany's coal-based traditions to greater glory. In any case, heightened resolve to produce using coal-based chemistry was accompanied by a firm embrace of new petrochemicals technology. The petroleum itself would be supplied by the GDR's socialist big brother, the Soviet Union, and refined at a new, purpose-built facility at Schwedt near the Polish border. From there, it would be sent by the 'Friendship' pipeline to the traditional factories of the 'chemical triangle' as feedstocks to produce plastics and other materials. The chemicalization programme thus reinforced commitment to autarkic practices while at the same time announcing greater dependence on imports for raw materials and on exports of finished products.

Its contradictions and inconsistencies were, however, symptomatic of the hopes and fears of the GDR's leadership at the beginning of the Second Berlin Crisis. Loss of population to the West, especially pronounced among scientific and technical personnel, and ever-increasing disparities between economic performance and technological level between East and West Germany engendered a feeling that bordered on despair. The chemicals programme, however, like the launch of the new Trabant automobile and a host of other displays of technological competence in the late 1950s, were meant to demonstrate that the GDR's commitment to achieving the 'main economic task' was more than just whistling in the dark. Virtually all of these programmes and displays were meant to bridge the gap between productivism, which had been emphasized by the GDR leadership from

Figure 4.1 The millionth Trabant, November 1973. Named after the first Sputnik, the Trabant's futuristic all plastic body was admired in the West as well (reproduced from *DDR Werden und Wachsen*, Dietz Verlag Berlin 1975).

the beginning and consumerism, which it would be necessary to foster and satisfy if the regime were to survive. Plastics, it was hoped, would play a vital role in the bridging process, and the designer would be the link between the two.

Chemicalization in Action: The Impact on Design and Consumption

Even before Ulbricht inaugurated the chemicals programme in autumn 1958, the first Trabant automobiles were rolling off the assembly line (see Figure 4.1). They were the pride of East German industry, indicating sophisticated technological capability, a commitment to mobility and the determination to forge a high standard of living for the country's population. The name of the new vehicle (*Trabant* is the German word for satellite) demonstrated admiration for the Soviet Union's recent and spectacular technological accomplishment of launching the world's first artificial satellite, Sputnik. The East German government was even willing to lay out some of its limited foreign exchange to acquire the rights to use the name

Figure 4.2 Camping dishes made from Meladur. Design by Hanz Merz, 1957/58.

  These two sets of camping dishes in plastic were designed in the late 1950s and were inspired by the GDR's chemicalization programme. They used contrasting materials: the lighter and more modern version (Figure 4.3) employed polyethylene, while the more traditional version (Figure 4.2) employed a coal-based plastic called Meladur. Since polyethylene production capability largely eluded the GDR chemical industry until the mid-1960s, the more modern version of the dishes could not be mass-produced. Technological limitations had an impact on design capability for the consumer market. Reproduced by kind permission of: Sammlung Industrielle Formgestaltung, Berling.

from a Swiss firm.[10] In projecting its potent message encompassing competence, confidence, pride and progressivism, the Trabant relied primarily on its design, and most importantly, its futuristic, all-plastic body.

  In the post-Cold War era, when the Trabant became a symbol of the GDR's economic and technological failure, it is important to remember the initial enthusiasm the car's introduction engendered. At the same time, it is just as important to push the analysis a bit further. For the Trabant, like the Soviet Sputnik, could not live up to its initial promises: on closer inspection, both demonstrated the technological weaknesses of the Eastern bloc even more than its strengths.

Figure 4.3 Camping dishes made from polyethylene. Design by Giese, 1959/60.

Take, for example, the Trabant's plastic body. The car's exterior was 'presented to the public [rather successfully at first, both at home and abroad] as a statement of modern design.' At the same time, it must be mentioned that the *Rennpappe*, or 'cardboard racing car', as the Trabi came affectionately to be known, was a 'creative response to a shortage of sheet metal'.[11] It was intended to cover up, and initially succeeded in covering up, a major systemic failure by drawing upon the chemical industry's traditional ability to supply *ersatz*. But the cover-up was more far-reaching than that: the plastic used to produce a statement of the modern was itself out of date. German Democratic Republic designers deployed a material called Duroplast for the Trabi, which was composed of 47 per cent Soviet cotton and 53 per cent East German phenolic resins. Essentially, then, the car's body was made out of a variation on Bakelite, a plastic of the 1920s and 1930s more than the 1960s. The material was brittle, cumbersome and did not take colour well, while 'modern' plastics proved undesirable for car bodies, being (like later composite materials) better suited for interior and hidden applications. It may be partly for this reason that other manufacturers around the world, who had toyed with the idea of plastic cars in the 1940s and 1950s,[12] ultimately discarded the idea. This may also be part of the reason that, despite alterations and interesting designs in the 1960s and beyond, there was a 'near neglect of the car's design and engineering' as it was actually produced through 1990.[13]

Duroplast was but one instance of a more general characteristic of the GDR's plastics production palette. For, although the country was in general keeping up with the rest of the industrialized world in *per capita* plastics manufacture, its production was composed to a much higher degree of older types of plastics. Until the mid 1960s, the bulk of GDR plastics production was polyvinyl chloride (PVC), a plastic which come of age before the Second World War. Other industrialized nations continued to produce PVC as well, because it has a wide variety of applications. Consumers, however, had unpleasant memories of the plastic during the war and its immediate aftermath, when it was used to manufacture all sorts of products, regardless of suitability. They therefore were reluctant to accept it when a wider variety of choices became available in the 1950s.[14] Manufacturers and their customers therefore turned to other plastics of more recent vintage, including polyethylene, polypropylene and others. By 1966, world production of polyethylene had already overtaken output of PVC in terms of volume. Well out of step with this development, the GDR continued to produce PVC on a large scale, amounting to fully 48 per cent of total plastics output in the mid 1960s. Meanwhile, polyethylene production, dogged by numerous difficulties, amounted to just two per cent of all plastics produced.[15]

But why is the production palette for thermoplastics in the GDR important? I would argue that the main significance of this failure in production – which itself indicated a severe and startling break with the German tradition of chemical innovation at IG Farben and its predecessors – lies in the effects on design and consumption, which were considerable. Let us examine each in turn.

Designers responded with alacrity to Ulbricht's announcement of the chemicals programme in late 1958.[16] Earlier that year, Berlin's Institute for Applied Art published an illustrated book on industrial design that featured just two items made from plastic, a set of camping dishes (see Figure 4.3) and a door knob. By 1959, however, the Institute published Horst Redeker's *Chemistry gives Beauty*, which accorded to plastics the central position in design that Ulbricht had intended.[17]

Redeker used his book in part to enthuse about the chemicals programme not just as a production programme, but also as 'a potent cultural programme' in which the designer had a role to play. Design, he continued, was 'a part of the process of industrial refinement', adding value to goods through making them more useful and attractive; but it is also allowed the expression of cultural values. Redeker contended that the chemistry of plastics and synthetic fibres, along with automation, mechanization and peaceful use of nuclear power, "represent a revolution in technology that contradicts in every way the conservative capitalistic relations of production'. Plastics lent themselves especially well to socialist societies since they enabled 'a dialectical unity between utility and economy'.[18]

In practical terms, the socialist designer could help demonstrate the superiority of the socialist over the capitalist system (the 'main economic task') through design of plastic artefacts. Redeker contrasted practice in the US with that in East Germany in this regard:

> in the USA, it is true, large amounts of plastics are produced. But they are made in the main into worthless, cheap and shockingly kitschy mass wares, into Woolworth products. Owing to their mania for ornamentation, these in turn tend to be rendered quickly obsolete by something new and more fashionable. Through this, at the very least, they work against the natural [sic] durability of the material in the interest of ever new markets and new profits. For us, it is a matter of viewing the new materials 'in spite of' their relative cheap price (which, from our perspective, is not a defect providing high quality is preserved, but rather an advantage) not as artificial materials in the sense of ersatz materials, but rather in the sense of materials which are worthy of complete commercial-artistic design. These goods should not be seen as less excellent than natural ones, but rather as materials whose excellence lies in their being simultaneously useful and profitable.[19]

Redeker was most interested in the possibilities for designers of new synthetic materials, which he emphasized, 'allow . . . to a degree previously unknown the union of manifold and varied characteristics in the same material, the fusion of qualities which had previously been mutually exclusive.' He mentioned in particular the possibilities presented by polyethylene and polystyrene and quoted Ulbricht's comments at the chemistry conference in Leuna in 1958 at length about the possibilities for packaging and building materials which these plastics presented.[20] And here we come to the dilemma which designers in the GDR faced: how to design new products using new plastics given the limited production of those very new materials?

The illustrations in Redeker's book demonstrate this dilemma especially clearly. True, he does not have to resort to a picture of the door knob used in the Institute for Applied Art's 1958 publication, but he does present, as did the Institute, the set of camping dishes made of Meladur, a phenolic resin, which are admittedly quite attractive (see Figure 4.2). There are also three light fixtures made of Meladur or similar material and five examples of furniture designs which employ thin plastic sheets of various colours for upholstery. It is a startlingly small number of examples. Not a single design is based on the new plastics Redeker extols in his book, mainly because those plastics were not available to the GDR designer and would not become generally available until well into the 1960s.[21]

It is not that designers in the GDR were incapable of alternative, more modern designs. In fact, an alternative design for camping dishes was produced in 1959/

60, these made from polyethylene rather than Meladur (see Figure 4.3). The former are clearly 'modern' looking, but they were impossible to produce in any quantity owing to the fact that the GDR's capability for manufacturing the required raw polyethylene was negligible until the second half of the 1960s. Practically speaking, then, the designer in the GDR in the late 1950s and early 1960s was limited in materials to just a handful of older plastics. What is more, once consumer goods of plastic or other materials were produced, designers could not present them in 'modern' containers and packaging, a particularly suitable application for the new plastics such as polyethylene and polypropylene. An additional problem was that the number of designers was clearly too small for the burgeoning plastics finishing industry; despite the industry having a motto in the early 1960s of 'Every week a new household article from plastic,'[22] this rate of design output paled in comparison to the thousands of designs pouring out of the capitalist West during these years.

The constraints on design posed by the plastics palette in the GDR and the limited manpower allocated to the design process through the mid 1960s naturally had an impact on consumption as well. Consumers in the GDR were in a sense a captive audience, because there were few consumer manufactures available from abroad. The artefacts produced using the output of the GDR chemical industry tended to be purchased, regardless of the deficiencies in their design or materials. But many GDR consumers of the 1950s had lived through the war and, like their West German counterparts, viewed PVC with some suspicion and reluctance. As has already been mentioned, however, PVC was, along with older plastics still, the material from which most East German plastic wares of necessity were made. To make matters worse, East German consumers were well aware that other materials and designs based on them were available, not least because the West Germans were among the most successful countries in the world in switching to new plastics in the second half of the 1950s. This was part of the reason why the East German consumer, despite having an abundance of goods available by the late 1950s, was 'perennially dissatisfied, always searching for something special, with an unsatisfied desire for something else'.[23]

Concluding Remarks

Examining the production and consumption of plastics in the GDR through the mid 1960s allows some insights into the reasons for the ultimate collapse of the GDR and, at the same time, its ability to survive for as long as it did. Clearly, on the plus side, the country's chemical industry showed formidable capability, producing similar amounts *per capita* of plastics during the 1950s and 1960s to other key industrialized countries, even in the capitalist world. The output allowed the GDR to supply its own and export markets with a large variety and quantity of goods made from plastics and synthetic fibres, facilitating the construction of a

Figure 4.4 Neon sign advertising 'Plastics and elastics from the Buna Works in Schkopau'. Virtually all of the Buna Works' products were manufactured using traditional coal-based feedstocks, something which was intensified by the 'chemicalization' programme of the late 1950s. This occurred at the same time that other industrialized countries were moving away from coal-based, and into petroleum-based chemistry. Reproduced with kind permission of: BSL GmbH, Schkopau.

socialist consumer society by the 1960s. But at the same time, there was a downside, which played its part in pushing the GDR towards ultimate collapse. The industry's shortcomings in bringing new sorts of plastics into production meant that goods were often of poor quality, old-fashioned in appearance and/or not varied enough in design – or at least they seemed that way compared to those produced in the West. Such perceptions, in turn, had an impact on production, because apparently inferior consumer goods could not motivate workers, who continued to manufacture both inferior consumer and producer goods. Inferior producer goods ensured that the vicious cycle would continue.[24]

Plastics had appeared to be excellent politics for the GDR in the late 1950s: ideologically sound, malleable and solving a host of economic and political problems all at once. By the mid 1960s, as some of the new synthetic materials finally came on line in the GDR, plastics were causing at least as many problems as they solved.

Notes

1 I would like to thank David Crowley, Susan Reid and an anonymous referee for helpful comments and suggestions. Research for this article was generously supported by the German Marshall Fund of the United States, the Deutscher Akademischer Austauschdienst (DAAD) and the University of Glasgow.

2 This was a characteristic of all Eastern-bloc countries. See, for instance, Raymond Hutchings, *Soviet Science, Technology, Design: Interaction and Convergence* (London/New York: Oxford University Press, 1976) p. 118.

3 L.F. Haber, *The Chemical Industry in the Nineteenth Century* (Oxford: Clarendon Press, 1958); John Beer, *The Emergence of the German Dye Industry* (Urbana: University of Illinois Press, 1959); Ernst Homburg, 'The Emergence of Research Laboratories in the Dyestuffs Industry, 1870–1900', *British Journal of the History of Science,* 25 (1992) pp. 91–112; Ulrich Marsch, 'Strategies for Success: Research Organization in German Chemical Companies and IG Farben until 1936', *History and Technology* 12 (1994) pp. 23–77.

4 Peter Hayes, *Industry and Ideology: IG Farben in the Nazi Era* (Cambridge: Cambridge University Press, 1987, Peter Morris, 'The Development of Acetylene Chemistry and Synthetic Rubber by IG Farbenindustrie Aktiengesellschaft, 1926–1945', PhD Thesis, Oxford University, 1982.

5 Figures from B.G. Reuben and M.L. Burstall, *The Chemical Economy: A Guide to the Technology and Economics of the Chemical Industry* (London: Longman, 1973), p. 35.

6 Figures are calculated on the basis of those presented in *Statistisches Jahrbuch der DDR,* 1966, p. 169; 1967, p. 167; 1970. p. 114; 1972, p. 128; 1975, p. 1.

7 Rainer Karlsch, 'Capacity Losses, Reconstruction and Unfinished Modernization: The Chemical Industry in the Soviet Zone of Occupation/GDR, 1945–1965', in Gerald Feldman and John Lesch, eds, *The German Chemical Industry in the Twentieth Century* (Amsterdam: Kluwer Academic Publishers, forthcoming); more generally, Rainer Karlsch, *Allein bexahlt: Die Reparationsleistungen der SBZ/DDR 1945–1953* (Berlin: Ch. Links, 1993). See also Ulrich Albrecht, Andreas Heinemann-Grüder and Arend Wellmann, *Die Spezialisten: Deutsche Naturwissenschaftler und Techniker in der Sowjetunion nach 1945* (Berlin: Dietz, 1992).

8 Gerhard Kosel, *Produktivkraft Wissenschaft* (Berlin: Verlag Die Wirtschaft, 1957); *Jahrbuch der Deutschen Demokratischen Republik 1958* (Berlin: Verlag Die Wirtschaft, 1958), p. 187; Martin McCauley, *The German Democratic Republic since 1945* (New York: St. Martin's Press, 1983) p. 125.

9 Ulbricht's speech and the main proceedings of the conference are printed in *Chemie gibt Brot – Wohlstand – Schönheit. Chemiekonferenz des Zentralkomitees der SED und der Staatlichen Plankomission in Leuna am 3. und 4. November 1958* (Berlin, 1958).

10 Abt. Inv., Forschung und Technik, Sektor Forschung und Technik (Dr. Schwarz), 'Betr. Valutaplan für Lizenzhanmen der Abteilungen der SPK', 14 September 1959. P. 4, Bundesarchiv Berlin (formerly Potsdam) [BAP] DE1/14195.

11 See Jonathan R. Zaitlin, 'The Vehicle of Desire: The Trabant, the Wartburg and the End of the GDR', *German History* 15 (1997) p. 359.

12 For Ford's experiment in this regard in the early 1940s, see Jeffrey L. Meikle, 'Plastics in the American Machine Age, 1920–1950', p. 50, in Penny Spake, ed., *The Plastics Age: From Modernity to Post-Modernity* (London: Victoria and Albert Museum, 1990).

13 Zaitlin, 'The Vehicle of Desire', p. 367. The designers Clauss Dietel and Lutz Rudolph produced a number of alternative designs for the Trabant and for the more expensive Wartburg in the 1960s which were never implemented.

14 Morris Kaufman, *The History of PVC: The Chemistry and Industrial Production of Polyvinyl Chloride* (London: Maclaren & Sons, 1969), pp. 166–7; Robert V. Milby, *Plastics Technology* (New York: McGraw Hill, 1973), pp. 263–71.

15 Forschungsrat der DDR. Ministerium fur Wissenschaft und Technik, 'Prognose. Organische hochpolymere Werkstoffe und ihr effektiver Einsatz in der Volkswirtschaft', December 1967, pp. 8–9, Bundesarchiv Hoppegarten [BAH] DF4/19860. The story of polyethylene development in the GDR is in Raymond Stokes, 'Chemie und chemische Industrie im Sozialismus', pp. 288–91, in Dieter Hoffmann and Kristie Macrakis, eds, *Naturwissenschaft und Technik in der DDR* (Berlin: Akademie-verlag, 1997). An English version is in

Hoffmann and Macrakis, eds., *Science Under Socialism* (Cambridge, MA: Harvard University Press, 1999).

16 Heinz Hirdina, 'Gegenstand und Utopie', pp. 48–61 in Neue Gesellschaft fur Bildende Kunst, ed., *Wunderwirtschaft DDR – Konsumkultur in den 60er Jahren* (Weimar: Böhlau, 1996); Heinz Hirdina, *Gestalten für die Serie: Design in der DDR 1949–1985* (Dresden: VEB Verlag der Kunst, 1988).

17 *Gute Formgebung, schöne Industriewaren* (Berlin: Institut für angewandte Kunst, 1958); Horst Redeker, *Chemie gibt Schönheit* (Berlin: Institut für angewandte Kunst, 1959).

18 Redeker, *Chemie gibt Schönheit,* quotations from pp. 6, 12, 17.

19 Ibid, pp. 30–1.

20 Ibid, pp. 37–8, quotation p. 40, emphasis in original.

21 Ibid. A similar discrepancy between text and illustrations crops up in E. Blank, 'Die Anwendung von Plasten im Maschinenbau', *Maschinenbautechnik* 9 (1960) pp. 175–8.

22 Protokoll, 'Rundtischgespräch "Neue Wege in der industriellen Formgebung"', 9 March 1961, p. 5, BAP DE1/29195.

23 Ina Merkel, 'Der aufhaltsame Aufbruch in die Konsumgesellschaft', p. 20, in Neue Gesellschaft für Bildende Kunst, ed., *Wunderwirtschaft DDR.*

24 I make a similar point in 'In Search of the Socialist Artefact', *German History* 15 (1997) pp. 238–9, while treating the subject of technology in the GDR in greater breadth and detail in *Constructing Socialism: Technology and Change in East Germany* (Baltimore, MD: Johns Hopkins University Press, 2000).

−5−

The Aesthetics of Everyday Life in the
Khrushchev Thaw in the USSR (1954–64)
Iurii Gerchuk

The 'Thaw', as the decade of relative liberalization of Soviet social and political life after the death of Stalin is known, was a time of numerous but unsystematic individual reforms; of risky and inconsistent attempts by the regime to establish contact with the vital forces of society, which, although demoralized by Stalinist terror, was beginning to 'thaw out'; and of liberal gestures combined with dictatorial barking. As First Secretary of the Party, Nikita Khrushchev tried in vain to combine the essential and inevitable liberalization with the preservation of ideological dictatorship. The unsettled political weather of the Thaw was connected as much with the volatile, contradictory and capricious character of the leader, the combination of his practical ability with an incredible lack of culture, of his energy for action with the burden of indestructible ideological clichés of Stalinist times, as with more fundamental causes. No consistent liberal reforms in either practical or purely intellectual spheres could be compatible with the sacrosanct, ossified ideological dogmas of official 'Marxism' and the authoritarianism associated with the personal power attached to the leadership, even that of a reform-oriented leader.

All the same, the demand for change in both the highest levels of total control of culture and of the organization and design of everyday life of citizens of this impoverished country was extraordinarily high. Society came back to life, and a fundamental transformation took place in the visual appearance of cities, homes, and everyday things.

The speed at which these changes took place in various spheres of material culture made it necessary to draw on the example of various foreign models. This was encouraged by the perception that the country had at last caught up with world artistic development after many years of enforced stagnation. In the more liberal climate of the Thaw, contacts with foreign culture, harshly restricted in the previous period, were somewhat eased, although they remained, nonetheless, under vigilant ideological control. The nearest and relatively uncensored (and sometimes even encouraged) sources of cultural influence were the socialist countries of Eastern Europe, which were ideologically close to and politically dependent upon the Soviet

Union – primarily Czechoslovakia, Poland and East Germany. Exhibitions were quite regularly brought from these countries, including those of applied arts and design, posters and book design. Soviet artists were now able to subscribe to general and specialist art journals from these countries, and to buy books in special shops (West European and American publications only rarely fell into our hands). A broad stream of everyday goods also flowed from these countries: fabric and clothing, shoes, tableware, lamps, furniture, and various items of decorative art. There was a demand for these things among the Soviet public who preferred them to domestic products which seemed, in contrast, to be largely clumsy and old fashioned.

Yet another source of influence was the 'inner abroad', the Baltic Republics, which actively contributed to the transformation of the aesthetic milieu of Soviet everyday life and to the formation of a new style. Annexed to the Soviet Union only on the eve of the Second World War, they had had little time to submit to official culture's levelling down and, during the Thaw, recovered more quickly than those regions that had been Soviet from the start. For us, the products of the Baltic bore the unmistakable stamp of the European culture we so desired.

The Revolution from Above in Soviet Architecture

Architecture was the first of the arts to throw off the corset of Stalinist eclectic, pompous pseudoclassicism. Not that architects were braver than the rest. Rather, the need for change in this area was realized by the Party leader, Khrushchev. At the All-Union Conference of Constructors in November 1954 he launched a sharp attack on extravagance and backward construction technology, on unforgivable 'excesses' in the decoration of facades, and on the unjustified use of one-off projects for standard building types. The ostentatious edifices which had only recently been awarded Stalin prizes were denounced for 'embellishment'. This was a 'revolution from above' in which aesthetic considerations played only a minor role. Ideological and economic considerations were paramount: 'Architects must learn to count public money'.[1]

Blame for past extravagance was pinned on the architects themselves. According to Khrushchev, it appeared as if they had indulged in luxury on their own initiative: 'They amused themselves by building spires and so these buildings come to look like churches. You like the silhouette of churches? I don't want to argue about taste, but we don't need buildings that look like this for housing. A contemporary apartment block must not start to look like a church or museum. That does not provide any services to the residents and only complicates maintenance of the building and raises its costs.'[2] Prominent Moscow architect G. Zakharov was singled out for *ad hominem* criticism. 'He needs beautiful silhouettes, but the people need apartments.'[3] 'On the example of master architects many young architects who are barely out of college and haven't yet found their feet, want to design only one-off buildings and hurry to build monuments to themselves.'[4] There is, however, no question that it was the Stalin regime that ordered architectural embellishment and that it engaged in its own self-aggrandizement. I remember the story of one of the architects of the time who was told by his regional Party secretary that 'if we spend money on construction then it must convince the man in the street of the rightness of Soviet power.' During the Thaw the situation changed. Khrushchev recognized that 'the people' must be given tangible benefits and not superficial appearances. But the time for criticism, even partial, of the real culprits had not yet arrived.

The indignation with which Khrushchev fulminated against the architecture of the high Stalin period with all his down-to-earth practicality was, of course, sincere. However the timely idea could have been suggested to him by others, along with many of its justifications and concrete proposals originating from professionals who understood these matters. The direction taken by the discussion resulted from a backstage struggle, of which Khrushchev himself gave a glimpse in his speech. During preparations for the conference the architect G. Gradov, who worked at the Academy of Architecture, approached the Central Committee. He harshly criticized its leadership, above all the President of the Academy Arkadii Mordvinov who had declared architecture to be an art and who, for art's sake, encouraged extravagance. Mordvinov, as Khrushchev said, tried to prevent Gradov from addressing the meeting. But, with the Central Committee's support, Gradov spoke, egged on by sympathetic interjections from Khrushchev.

In Gradov's words, the Union of Architects and the Academy 'directed our architects to deal primarily with artistic and decorative tasks'. ('Tell us about this in more detail, reveal your secrets to us', said Khrushchev.) Settling accounts with his colleagues, Gradov saw them as the culprits of unnecessary 'copying of the classics', while 'our state leadership repeatedly warned architects that our architecture must be functional.' His own position can be summarized as 'the foundation of architecture should not be pure aesthetics but, above all, a concern for material-technical content.' It was necessary to 'overcome formalist distortions and stagnation in architecture, to subordinate architecture entirely to the essential needs of our society and bring it closer to contemporary technology.' He proposed organizing a single 'USSR Academy of Architectural Construction'.[5] The idea soon became a reality: in 1955–6 an Academy of Construction and Architecture was established, with a clear emphasis on technical rather than artistic problems.

That architectural reform was initiated from 'above' had both positive and negative implications. Architecture freed itself surprisingly quickly of outdated forms and was enabled to make accelerated stylistic development at a time when, in fine art, such reform processes were impeded in every way. It became possible to rework and make selective use of the legacy of Russian Constructivism of the

1920s and early 1930s, hitherto condemned out of hand. From the mid-1930s the architectural experiments of the avant-garde had been declared ugly, gloomy and, above all, 'formalist' (the stock charge against artistic tendencies repudiated by Soviet ideology). At the same time it turned out to be vitally necessary to draw on the experience of foreign architecture, recently regarded as 'bourgeois', 'formalist' and 'anti-human'. Although architects were still warned against making 'uncritical' use of foreign example, according to ancient ideological tradition, (and special meetings were even organized on the subject), it was no longer possible to cut ourselves off from world architectural development. Books appeared about modern Western architecture: first of all translated texts, soon followed by original ones. One of the first came out in 1956, Italian engineer Pier Luigi Nervi's *Costruire Corretamente* (Milan 1955, translated into English as *Structures,* New York, 1956 and into Russian as *Stroit' pravil'no* – Transl.), which visually demonstrated the tectonic elegance and plastic expression of exposed and unembellished monolithic ferroconcrete constructions. The respect due to the great names of Le Corbusier, Frank Lloyd Wright, Walter Gropius and Ludwig Mies van der Rohe – denigrated in the years of embellishment and struggle against 'cosmopolitanism' – was now restored. We also found out about contemporary architects such as Oscar Niemeyer, the subject of a monograph published in 1963.

As international contacts began to expand, models of foreign architecture could occasionally be experienced at first hand. In the summer of 1959 workers wearing strange helmets of coloured plastic appeared in Sokol'niki Park, Moscow, and began to erect an openwork, tubular, spherical construction, which they filled with a six-sided honeycomb with gauffred metal panels: it was the 'geodesic dome', the central pavilion of the forthcoming American National Exhibition. This was an extraordinary event for the time and it attracted universal attention. For the first time the US, about which we had been told nothing but bad things, was permitted to show its achievements in Moscow. The architecture of the pavilion was equally extraordinary. The lightness and openness of its construction, its demonstrative simplicity and strange, purely technological elegance, quite incompatible with any kind of applied ornament, was received as a visual lesson in genuinely contemporary architecture. And next to the cupola sprung up a grove of plastic columns that spread out overhead like fans, also with a multi-faceted, semi-transparent covering. A typical American home was also displayed at the exhibition: a small house for which there was always a long queue of visitors.

Our new architecture, in turn, took its first steps on foreign soil: the glass, gauffred prism of the Soviet pavilion at the 1958 Brussels World Fair (architects A. B. Boretskii, Iu. I. Abramov, V. A. Dubov and Anatolii Polianskii) (Figure 5.1) demonstrated the decisive break with the tradition of 'embellishment'. It is telling that when Sokol'niki Park was prepared for the American National Exhibition new, transparent cafes were built there from glass held in light tubular constructions

Figure 5.1 Soviet Pavilion, 1958 World Fair, Brussels. Architects A. B. Boretski, Iu. I. Abramov, V. A. Dubov and A. T. Polianskii, and engineers Iu. V. Ratskevich and K.N. Vasil'eva.

(architect Igor Vinogradskii), which at the time had a thoroughly 'foreign' look.

Reform did not by any means liberate Soviet architecture, but set new and very strict directives. However, the new principles corresponded, to some degree, to the spiritual and intellectual needs of the time and the inner potential of architecture, which had been stuck in the dead end of showy stylization. The possibility of new, dynamic and complex spatial resolutions opened up, as did the freedom to find new means and devices for decoration. The democratic urge and rationalism of the art of the Thaw gained their first foothold precisely in the new architecture.

On the other hand the 'new tendency' in architecture was narrowly conceived and energetically implemented. Architecture's development as an art was ruthlessly subordinated to state regulation. It could exist only within the framework of state planning organizations under the control of tight budgets, corsetted by rigorously observed 'Construction Norms and Regulations'. The tendency to subordinate architectural considerations to elementary technical-economic functions reinforced utilitarian tendencies both in practice (especially in mass construction) and even in architectural theory which was now reborn from a *tabula rasa*. 'Apartment blocks designed by engineer Vitalii Lagutenko' – such was the name of one of the first series of cut-price, standard-plan buildings. It seemed possible, at this stage, to resolve the eternal dualism of architecture very simply: aesthetic and utilitarian principles were sharply differentiated and priority was given to the latter. Economics, technology and organization of construction ousted artistic tasks and quality, which were reduced to external decorativeness alone. This elementarism left a clear imprint on all architectural practice of the Thaw and above all on mass housing construction.

The appearance and character of all new construction were radically transformed. After a short stage of purifying familiar projects of superfluous tower superstructures and facade mouldings, there followed a total re-examination of the goals and methods of architectural design. A programme of mass housing construction was proposed, based on maximally economical, standardized projects utilizing prefabricated elements and industrial construction technology.

Such a programme was, without doubt, long overdue, and its social significance was enormous. This, of all the Khrushchev reforms, had the most radical impact on the living conditions of significant strata of society. Stalinist housing construction, externally very dignified and impressive, lagged far behind the country's requirements. The majority of urban families occupied one or two rooms of a communal apartment with shared entrance, kitchen and bathroom. The transition to contemporary mass production of cheap housing had become an urgent necessity.

After housing, various types of public building were standardized – schools and hospitals, cinemas and clubs. Prefabricated ferro-concrete was declared, in the spirit of the times, a technological and economic panacea. Its widest possible application in construction was strictly monitored, sweeping away other proposals even where they were technically feasible. A slogan was coined, 'Architects into the factories!' Industrial production of housing was to determine the creative tasks of the new architecture. Its theoreticians dismissed brick as a material that was too traditional, insufficiently economic, and which hindered industrialization. All the same, as late as 1963, three quarters of all housing was built of brick, but it was held that 'the general path of development of the new style lies not here but in the broad application of new, progressive construction materials and above all of prefabricated, reinforced concrete.'[6] Style was to be shaped directly by technology and become a function of technological progress.

The second determinant of the new style lay in finding solutions to architecture's social tasks. The purely artistic concept of an 'architectural ensemble' gave way to 'micro-regions' designed according to the functional principle. Freer and more complex spatial deployment of buildings as a system took the place of formal, symmetrical plans. Apartment blocks were set perpendicular to the street or at an angle to it, in ladder formation, and enclosed perimetral building in residential areas gave way to new, larger quarters interspersed with open space. The concept of the yard disappeared and the living environment was united and socialized, its firm inner boundaries and divisions removed. The yard dissolved into a residential quarter which, open on all sides, flowed into the general space of the urban region. This solution was seen as bringing, alongside aesthetic and functional advantages, a certain social purpose: life in the new quarters would be less hermetic and 'private', and consequently the collective, communist principle would be strengthened. To this end, even in the old areas of Moscow the fences separating yards were broken down on an order from above. Only later did the real and not always desired social consequences of this socialization of yard space become manifest.

These principles were tried out in the design and construction of Moscow's then-famous experimental Ninth Quarter: Novye Cheremushki (1956–57, architects Natan Osterman *et al.*) (Figure 5.2), one of the first experiments in economical, standardized mass housing design, became a household name, but with time, as the shortcomings of simplified system building became clear, it took on derisory associations.

Figure 5.2 Standardized housing blocks in Novye Cheremushki region, Moscow, late 1950s.

To spare the need for lifts, the majority of housing in towns was five storeys high. This was a false economy, however, since the new housing schemes took up vast territory, thus attenuating urban communications. The appearance of this kind of system-built, five-storey housing was simplified to the point of complete facelessness. To simplify construction, the plan was reduced to a simple rectangle and the elevation to a monotonous grid of identical windows. The dull elementarism of the architectural design was exacerbated in mass production-line construction by the extremely low quality of building and finishing work and even of the prefabricated details.

'Comfort' was also conceived in very frugal terms. Design norms were revised in the direction of extreme economy. In the standardized housing designs accepted and applied at the turn of the 1950s–60s, ceiling heights were reduced to 2.5 m. In the tiny, cramped flats the space for auxiliary rooms was cut to the bare minimum. The size of the kitchen was reduced from 7 to 4.5 sq m and it opened directly off the living room. The toilet was combined with the bathroom. Convenience was sacrificed not only to save space but to simplify the construction process.

All the same, Khrushchev's slogan, 'each family will have its own flat', found a place in the hearts of millions of people, languishing amidst the squabbles of the old, cramped communal apartments. In 1961 the pledge was inscribed in the new programme of the CPSU: 'Each family, including newly-weds, will have a well-appointed flat in accordance with the requirements of hygiene and cultured living.'[7] However, this was to be achieved, according to state projections, in twenty years, along with the advent of communism.

Khrushchev's slogan projecting into the communist future (whose visual realization, Novye Cheremushki, was being constructed at that time) signalled a certain crisis of Party ideology, albeit unclear at the time, concerning the subordination of the individual to the collective. Private life, enclosed in the family circle by the walls of the individual dwelling, was acknowledged to be a social value and one of the goals of social development. This contradicted the collectivist ideals that, far from having been officially repudiated, were, in fact, being reinvigorated in the utopias of the Thaw period, including specifically architectural ones. A number of architects tried to overcome this contradiction by connecting separate apartments with a developed system of public services, largely located within a single building or group of buildings joined by covered passages. Here were envisaged attractive rooms for collective leisure, communal dining, amateur workshops and so forth (a project by the architects Natan Osterman, K. Ivanov *et al.*). Such a complex might include a kindergarten and crèche where the majority of children would stay day and night. This made it possible to save space in the flats, which in such cases were not intended to accommodate children (a project by Gradov). Economy also dictated that proper kitchens be replaced by 'compact kitchen aggregates' for warming up food brought from the canteen complex.

However, economic considerations were not the most important factor here; the dominant motives were ideological. 'Clearly the main thing in the search for a new type of housing is the social problem of the communist restructuring of everyday life, the development of public services and of such forms of daily life in which the spirit of collectivism and genuine comradeship will take the place of individual isolation', declared the author of an article dedicated to these designs.[8] In his opinion, the developed communal rooms in the new living complexes 'must be more attractive than the individual quarters, because it is in these rooms that people must have the opportunity to spend most of their leisure time in mutual contact.' Furthermore, 'in the aesthetics of the new dwelling the stress on intimacy and privacy [*kamernost'*], which many consider inseparable from the individual flat of today, will no longer play the main role. The development of the social principle will bring to the fore the synthesis of architecture with monumental-decorative art, bringing grand social ideas into everyday life.'[9]

Nobody asked the future residents of these 'complexes' whether they longed to exchange the intimate isolation of the flats promised to them for the opportunities of collective leisure among stained glass and frescoes in the company of their former neighbours from the hated communal apartment; whether they were ready to sacrifice the dimensions of their flat for the wealth and spaciousness of these 'common' (or rather nobody's) rooms; or, finally, whether they were interested in the 24-hour childcare facilities, which would practically remove children from parental influence, excluding the family from the process of their upbringing.

The 'Contemporary Style' and Taste

One of the most characteristic features of the artistic culture of the Thaw was the direct, active intervention of art in the daily life of millions of people. It seemed necessary to reorganize this life in a new, rational way that would correspond to the norms of contemporary taste. In this way it would be rendered both 'correct' and beautiful. This concern raised the social status of all the arts connected with forming the human spatial environment and everyday surroundings. The decorative and applied arts, which in the Stalin decades were considered to lag behind the most directly ideologized and programmatic – and hence dominant – arts of painting and sculpture, suddenly took the lead, along with city planning and architecture. They were ahead in their capacity to develop rapidly and break old canons, both because limitations imposed from above were not so strict here, and because they attracted, as never before, many creatively energetic young talents. They were also more advanced in regard to art criticism and theory.

The important social mission of these arts, as it was now conceived, was to ennoble everyday life, to introduce into it rational order, beauty and healthy, contemporary taste. This vision was opposed to the *meshchanstvo*, or 'philistinism' that embodied the spiritual atrophy of the old social order that was passing away. The *meshchanin* – the petit-bourgeois or philistine – as the collective image of opposition to the Thaw ideals and changes, was one of the key tropes of journalism and art criticism of those years. Although this concept carried social resonance, the criteria of *meshchanstvo* were largely aesthetic, in that people of bad, retrograde, 'philistine' tastes were understood to be artistically uneducated and unable to distinguish crude sham and stage-prop luxury from genuine art, with its intelligent simplicity and inner, unostentatious dignity.

'Petit-bourgeois taste', as the embodiment of unculturedness, stagnant conformism and coarse self-interest, became enemy number one of the new style. The battle against 'tastelessness' was waged by journals and newspapers, and by public lectures organized by the Society for the Dissemination of Knowledge. For the new ideals to become reality it was necessary to overcome everything that made people 'philistines'. Philistinism was caused, in part, by tasteless, commercial trash, such as paper flowers, amateur postcards from resorts, or boxes decorated with shells, but also by expensive objects that demonstrated the self-satisfied wellbeing of their owners: heavy crystal cut with diamond facets, services with little flowers, cumbersome, polished and carved furniture.

For the first time the artistic organization of everyday life became the subject of broad public attention. Denouncing 'tastelessness', journals explained how the apartment should be furnished 'in the contemporary manner'. Special manuals were published for those moving into new flats. Exhibitions demonstrated whole rooms furnished with models of the new furniture, papered with new wallpapers, and decorated with new lamps and curtains. The ensemble also included the latest tableware, a ceramic vase and a print in a light frame, all typical of the 'contemporary style'. Architects and artists used their prerogative as specialists to introduce the contemporary style as the general norm, varying only within narrow parameters. Materialized in industrial manufacture, it was to become universal. To this end, a major programmatic exhibition of applied art entitled 'Art and Life' was held in Moscow in 1961.

In practice and in theory, a concerted effort was made to define the artistic language of contemporaneity that would be the antithesis of heavy, Stalinist pomposity and traditionalism. The term 'contemporary' became the fundamental criterion of artistic quality. The new applied arts proposed 'democratic' criteria of beauty: laconic forms, freed from fragmented detailing (just as buildings were freed from mouldings); economy and clear functionality; and the culture of simple materials whose natural qualities must be visibly manifested in the manufacturing process. Beauty was to be inseparable from utility, and must be rational and universally accessible.

Recent, large-scale construction of housing made the problem of the renovation of living conditions a topical issue for hundreds of thousand of consumers. Their massive old furniture, rickety and shabby, did not look right in the low-ceilinged little rooms of thin-walled, panel houses, being out of proportion with them. The active promotion of the contemporary style also had some effect on ordinary people. Around the rubbish skips in the yards of older parts of town a connoisseur could put together whole collections of antique furniture, in need of restoration but often of museum quality.

Meanwhile, Soviet-made items in the new style were more often to be seen at exhibition than on sale in the shops. Sluggish Soviet industry reconstructed itself only slowly, so that the demand for the new style had to be satisfied mainly by imports. These came primarily from Eastern Europe. The coloured silk lampshades popular before the war became one of the symbols of 'philistine taste'. They were forced into extinction by multi-armed light fittings and double glass shades consisting of a matt inner layer encased in a sparsely ornamented outer shell, which were imported mainly from East Germany. Thence, too, came furniture that was sound but rather heavy. Lighter models, of more modern construction, were offered by Czechoslovakia. You could do more than just admire them at industrial exhibitions such as *Czechoslovakia 1960,* which took place in Sokol'niki Park, or at specialized exhibitions such as that of furniture, lighting, glass and musical instruments held at the same venue in May–June 1964; you could buy them in the shops at quite affordable prices. Finally, ultra-contemporary designs of metal and plastic furniture imported from Finland filled public interiors, especially cafés for young people, which were energetically modernized at this time.

However, the demand created by the beginning of mass housing construction required the decisive modernization and mechanization of Soviet furniture production, too, that is, its transformation from a still semi-artisanal activity to industrial production. And this dictated changes in its form towards simpler and lighter construction. The general tendency of stylistic change and avid assim-ilation of the most recent foreign developments pointed in the same direction, towards laconic form, lightness and rationalism. Different materials were now used: natural wood was displaced by plywood. Beaded panels gave way to very simple, smooth surfaces. Embellishment of any sort, carving, convex or concave details disappeared. Here the demands of economy and technology were corrob-orated by the evolution of public taste. Strict rationalism, constructive clarity, laconicism of form – all these characteristics of the new architecture also spread to furniture.

The system-built dwelling also influenced the appearance of furniture more directly: its dimensions accommodated themselves to the lower ceilings and niggardly proportions of living and auxiliary rooms, and to the narrowness of the piers. Other changes in dimensions and form were also motivated by convenience of use: a slight reduction in the height of tables and chairs ('such an apparently insignificant adjustment in the height (2–3 cm) makes the furniture much better adapted to serving human needs');[10] or a characteristic break in the back of a chair to support the back (the so called 'Akerblom' line after the Swedish hygienist who proposed this construction);[11] or, finally, in addition to movable furniture, built-in furniture including 'partition-cupboards', which, to economize on the small space allotted, very compactly combined several functions in a single large object. Their components often included fold-away beds, little tables, niches for radio sets, and suchlike. In this regard, as in many others, designers in the Baltic Republics led the way. By the end of the 1950s they had already progressed from a restrained stylization in the national, 'rustic' manner to strict, laconic models in the new style designed for mass production.

On the scale of the Soviet Union as a whole, this tendency manifested itself distinctly only in the closed exhibition of the results of the Second All-Union Competition for New Furniture held in Autumn 1961. The organization of this exhibition was noteworthy in itself. Fifty-seven apartments in the newly erected blocks in the Moscow suburb of Khoroshevo-Mnevniki were furnished with sets of furniture from the competition. It is characteristic that these models were not regarded as individual creations. They were proposed by the design and con-struction bureaux of *Sovnarkhozy* (Councils of the National Economy, local organs of economic administration introduced by Khrushchev), of the Moscow Higher Artistic-Industrial Institute, or of furniture factories. The point was not to display individual pieces, but to show the furnishing of the flat as a whole, including such necessary accessories as lighting, curtains, wallpaper, and prints on the wall. 'We need not only individual artistic objects but *an artistic ensemble of objects.* Here it is not so much the individual chair, table or cupboard that is a work of art, but the entire complex, *the interior of the home as a whole.*'[12]

The problem of how to integrate even a single old, inherited piece into such an ensemble was simply not discussed; life in the new flat was to begin as if from a *tabula rasa* in an entirely new environment. Only the narrowest scope was left for the amateur creativity of the consumer. His or her own taste was not trusted – the 'specialists' know best how one should live! Everyday needs were conceived as uniform, such that they could be totally generalized and anticipated. 'As our architects and designers (*dizainery*) are more and more able to satisfy man's daily needs on the basis of scientifically grounded norms, the sphere of amateur participation of the occupants of fitted apartments will grow more and more narrow. This process is legitimate and we should hardly try to hold it back.'[13] A converse tendency did also exist, however, toward the creation of flexible, multivariant constructions that allowed the apartment's occupants to put them together in various ways according to their own taste and requirements. Nevertheless, the arrangement of new furniture was, to a significant degree, predetermined by the components of the suite and the plan of the flat, which varied only slightly. Typically, one of the articles dedicated to the 1961 competition results, analysed the composition of items in the flats 'according to their specific functional purpose'.[14] The ensemble principle of furniture design fundamentally influenced the design of each separate item, depriving it of its independent image, perfection and self-sufficiency. Artistic quality now inhered only in the suite itself and not in its component parts, whether tables, chairs or shelves (Figure 5.3).

In accordance with the general principles of the new architecture, furniture designers exhibiting in 1961 rejected any moulded details such as cornices and plinths that crowned, delimited and generalized form. Objects lost their massivity and volume. 'Earlier, solid furniture was built on the basis of monolithic cubes, but now as the sum of separate sides, which is manifest in varying surface treatment and colour and in the appearance of narrow edges of panels on the front, etc.' The disappearance of details 'which lend forms monumentality and monolithicity, gives the impression that furniture is a kind of free space enclosed in a light envelope of separate facets.'[15]

The lightness of the furniture was further emphasized by the preference for pale rather than dark veneers, and the alternation of closed volumes with open or sometimes glazed alcoves with a coloured plastic surface. The geometric forms of solid pieces was taken up also by soft furniture for which layers of *porolon* (a porous synthetic material) or sponge rubber began to be used, mostly covered with smooth upholstery fabrics of quite strong, although sometimes also muted, colours.

Naturally, furniture of this sort, strictly geometric and light to the point of almost complete 'disembodiment', allowed for much closer interaction between individual items: they could be fitted tightly together as part of a single, usually asymmetrical, spatial-volumetric composition, where each item ceased to be perceived independently. Visually, the main elements of this composition were constituted by smaller sections, such as the contrast between projecting doors and open or glazed recesses, or the borders of surfaces of various colours and factures. One critic noted, 'often the tectonic and spatial boundaries do not coincide. For example, a cupboard is cut in half by a bright patch of colour'.[16]

However, it was permissible (and even recommended) to soften the new furniture's tendency to disembodiment and dry rationalism with contrasting decorative accessories. 'It has long been established that old decorative art objects, including folk arts and crafts and even contemporary folk handicraft can "live" happily among things that are contemporary in their purpose and external appearance. A Viatka toy, Ukrainian ceramics and Baltic hammered metalwork . . . can get along fine with the books on an "industrial" wall shelving unit. Strictly speaking, contemporary things on their own, without folk, handcrafted ones, can often seem somewhat dull.'[17]

Thus, even the designers and theorists who proselytized the contemporary style sensed a certain abstractness and aesthetic inadequacy in the new interior. But this did not weaken their resolve to work in this tendency, to which, they were convinced, the future belonged. 'All questions to do with the domestic interior must be addressed from the perspective of the future, taking account of the tendency of social development.'

The new stylistic tendencies were to be found also in textile design, at first in new patterns for curtain and upholstery fabrics for the new interior, and, subsequently, in dress fabrics. Textile design, an inherently decorative art form by its very purpose, had in the recent past been shackled by pseudo-realistic canons, which demanded a verisimilitude that was alien to its nature in respect of colour and form and which encouraged volumetric depiction, dry, meticulous drawing and fragmentary detail. The closeness of the pattern to its model in nature in the drawing of some coloured motif or other was considered the criterion of 'realism'.

Now, however, the decorative specificity of the textile pattern was recalled, as was its connection with the manufacture and surface of the cloth and with the space and rhythms of the contemporary interior or the cut of a garment and silhouette of the human figure. The patterns became more generalized, flat and no longer volumetric. Colour was also used more freely, leaving the former naturalistic colour far behind. It became open, fresh and, in accordance with the spirit of the time, relatively lighter. The rhythm of the patterns was enriched with a marked general tendency towards open compositions, free of mechanical repetitions and harsh symmetry.

In these searches for a new decorativeness one of the constant sources of inspiration was folk art. Motifs from traditional printed fabrics and *lubki* (woodblock prints), patterns of northern spindles, folk toys, or the blue-on-white patterns of tiles were frequently used in the fabrics of the Thaw. Folklore not only provided an arsenal of ready-made forms, but also set the stylistic keynote for artists and the measure for decorative abstraction, the planar flow of coloured patches, and the strong but harmonious colour scale.

Graphic devices grew more diverse. Harsh contours around areas of colour alternated with often undefined soft boundaries, and light, fluid drawing that preserved a sense of the quick, lively movement of the artist's hand, as if superimposed on this colour and almost independent of it. Not hiding the free mastery of this technique, but leaving it open to the viewer, the artist demonstrated the artistry and refinement inherent in the very technique of his work.

Bold, rapid drawing of this kind was usually figurative. But the loops, flourishes and intersection of lines in free flight across the surface could, in themselves, become an ornamental motif. Concrete figuration in textile patterns turned out to be only one possibility among many, and far from the preferred treatment in all cases. Alongside clear designs that set figurative or geometric, abstract motifs off against a contrasting ground, there also appeared quite a number of deliberately muted patterns that ran softly together. From deep below washes of close colour an undefined pattern glimmers which, since it cannot be fully made out, preserves a certain mystery.

The new, lighter, mobile-spatial ornamental system, while avoiding heavy naturalism, not only did not reject figuration but developed it in a new way. The stylized graphic manner allowed for a much freer use of developed figurative motifs without destroying the decorative nature of the textile. Landscapes, transformed but still clearly legible, appeared on curtain and even dress fabrics. Multi-storied urban buildings or old log cabins hove into view, piled up over each other in a complex rhythm. The surface of the cloth turned either into the expanse of a field, animated by trees and agricultural buildings, or into sparkling turquoise water with the white triangles of yachts. Still-life motifs were also widely used. The festive patterns of folk ceramics could be transferred to cloth either on their own or along with representations of the objects they embellish. The newly fashionable souvenir headscarves provided concrete pretexts for thematic or symbolic comp-ositions. Occasionally, stylized designs were also used in their compositions, although, as yet, quite timidly. These new tendencies were exemplified in the work of the young Moscow artists N. Zhovtis, A. Chertok, O. Chesnokova and others. As for furnishing fabrics, large and complex patterns were ousted by small-scale, elementary ones. Increasingly wide use was made of smooth fabrics whose artistic effect was based on their active, sometimes complicated facture. A light ripple of colour created by simply interweaving threads of two colours, was preferred to precise contours. Large expanses of such textured materials corresponded to a great degree to the laconic forms of the new furniture.

One characteristic expression of the new stylistic tendencies was the fashion that developed for expressive studio ceramics drawing on the traditions of village potters but which, at the same time, experimented freely with plastic form, colour, and the composition of the surface decoration. The simple forms of vases, mugs and dishes softly, sometimes even seemingly carelessly moulded from porous red clay, did not hide their relation to peasant earthenware pots and basins. In rugged fireclay, a rather coarse 'naturalness' of handling was emphasized. Dark, poured glazes of brown, blue-green and black flowed together into uneven colour areas sometimes contrasted with the matt tone of bare clay. Emphasis was placed on weight – a thick body, rounded rims, massive handles – and fluidity of outline, which represented the organic, the natural, and truth to the genuine qualities of materials. Alongside professional ceramicists, painters also made interesting experiments in this area. Small issues of decorative ware also appeared on sale, produced by semi-artisanal firms under the Art Fund.

Close on the heels of these studio ceramics, which were mainly one-off, experimental works for exhibition (and therefore somewhat irresponsible in their attitude to the utilitarian purpose of their applied form), there soon followed factory-made, predominantly mass-produced, glazed earthenware. Where, in the past, such ware had often tried to approximate the form and wealth of decorative detail of more expensive porcelain, towards the end of the 1950s a notable reorientation took place. The modernist principle of the age, that of striving for 'truth to material', made it necessary to find a generalized, laconic form of thicker bodies and soft edges that was more organic for earthenware. Thereby it came in some ways to approximate coarse majolica.

At this time a large group of young designers came to the biggest Russian earthenware factory, the Kalinin works at Konakovo (on the Upper Volga) (Figure

Figure 5.3 Detail of exhibition of Diploma work of graduates of artistic-industrial institutes: furniture, fabrics, ceramics. Leningrad, 1967.

5.4). In the course of a few years, along with a few of the senior craftsmen who had worked there for a long time, they fundamentally overhauled the range of the factory's production, to embody the hallmarks of the new style. They designed modest, democratic objects for everyday use, whose entire structure conveyed an image of bright and comfortable domestic life, rationally organized yet without intellectual coldness. Stylizations disappeared, but the distant relation of the new crockery to the traditions of folk ceramics was preserved, softening the functionalism of severe forms with the warmth of live, fluid contours. In the factory's numerous mass-produced editions, whose forms and decoration were created by

Figure 5.4 V. Filianskaia, Coffee Service. Earthenware. Kalinin factory, Konakovo, mid-1960s.

O. Belova, G. Sadikov, G. Beber, F. Krokhina and others, as well as by the more established designers including V. Filianskaia, A. Khilkheeva, I. Vasil'ev and N. Litvinenko, one could sense the rapid formation of a shared style of Konakovo rather than an individual hand, which made its products one of the most characteristic embodiments of the spirit of the times.

The modernization of porcelain was more problematic. This expensive and elegant material risked losing its artistic value along with the richness of its embellishment. However, a period of active form-creation had arrived: the need to activate and renew the plastic language of applied art was very acute. And this was demonstrated perhaps most vividly in porcelain and also in glass. 'One of the characteristic features of the contemporary style in decorative and applied art is the mass phenomenon of new forms of manufactured goods. Such familiar things as cups, glasses, lamps and vases, which for decades hardly changed, suddenly look completely different, in the rich diversity of ever newer forms', wrote one of the ardent propagandists of the new style, Nikita Voronov, in 1961. 'Only recently', he continued, 'the form of, for example, porcelain or glass was treated primarily as a vehicle for decoration, as a particular kind of ground for it. Today the independent aesthetic value of form is increasingly affirmed.'[18]

Porcelain decisively repudiated the customary classical tectonics that dismembered the neck of a Tula vessel from its body. It eschewed fragmentary detail and moulded forms, and avoided functional details such as handles and spouts that were not fused with the whole pot. The search was on for laconic silhouettes, flowing contours and fluid bends of the surface of a single synthetic form. Here again, East European experience, with which our artists were well acquainted, could help. The attenuated, slightly mannered plasticity of Czech porcelain or the more rational, constructive forms of German and especially of Polish ware were influential. In accordance with the changing spirit and style of the Thaw, the devices for decorating mass, everyday tableware became more inventive, freer and more artistic.

Of the country's many porcelain factories it was arguably the Leningrad Lomonosov Factory that played the most active part in these experiments. Curiously, the most principled work here was not that of young designers but of experienced ones who had long worked at the factory, such as Anna Leporskaia and E. Krimmer who were nearly sixty. The services, and especially vases from these years by Leporskaia, were distinguished by particularly clean and melodious soft lines. The self-contained plasticity of these vases rejected the painted decoration customary for porcelain, making it not only superfluous but sometimes a direct hindrance to perceiving the living elasticity of the form. Thus many of them were left white. Others, nevertheless, were decorated in the traditional way, some even by Leporskaia herself, but the form dictated a pattern that was as delicate and laconic as possible. Novel as the silhouette of Leporskaia's work was, it tended toward classicial balance and harmony. Krimmer's work was more witty and dynamic. He boldly changed the customary proportions of vessels – the relationship between upper and lower parts – and shifted the visual centre of gravity up or down. The silhouettes of his teapots were sometimes expressive, while the decoration boldly emphasized the plastic tensions of the form.

Thus, the decade of the Thaw signalled a decisive rupture with the aesthetics of everyday life of the preceding, Stalinist era, a purposeful search for new socio-aesthetic ideals, and a conscious attempt to form a contemporary style, both in 'pure' art and in the applied arts that organize real life. The style was characterized by the democratic simplicity and broad accessibility of mass-produced objects, lightness, constructiveness, rationalism and openness of form, a somewhat ascetic functionalism, and the visual manifestation of the materials used. Like all aspects of the culture of the Thaw it was, in spite of its programmatic democratism, thoroughly authoritarian. Concerned with satisfying the needs of ordinary people in their daily lives, and offering them an integral, rationally organized environment, it aspired to 'correct' their taste, and imposed its alternatives to old fashioned, 'philistine' concepts. Life had to be reorganized and regulated in accordance with the 'correct' formula – discovered at long last – and subordinated to the will and rational thinking of specialists. The short life of Thaw aesthetics was the measure of this programme's utopianism, yet it had time to exercise a considerable influence on the real living environment of the Soviet Union.

Translated by Susan E. Reid

Notes

1 *Vsesoiuznoe soveshchanie stroitelei. Sokrashchennyi stenograficheskii otchet*, (Moscow, 1955), p. 394.
   For an English translation of Khrushchev's speech to the All-Union Conference of Constructors, 7 December 1954, see Thomas P. Whitney, ed., *Khrushchev Speaks: Selected Speeches, Articles, and Press Conferences, 1949–1961* (Ann Arbor: University of Michigan Press, 1963) pp. 153–92. For differing interpretations of the impetus for modernization see Victor Buchli, *An Archaeology of Socialism* (Oxford: Berg, 1999); and essays by Victor Buchli, Catherine Cooke and Susan E. Reid in Reid, ed., *Design, Stalin and the Thaw,* special issue of *Journal of Design History,* vol. 10, no. 2, 1997. [Transl.]

2 *Vsesoiuznoe soveshchanie stroitelei*, p. 391.

3 Ibid., p. 392.

4 Ibid, p. 388.

5 Ibid., pp. 163–5.

6 G. Shemiakin, 'Problemy stilia v sovetskoi arkhitekture,' in *Problemy stilia v arkhitekture. Materialy soveshchaniia* (Moscow, 1964), p. 15.

7 *Programma Kommunisticheskoi partii Sovetskogo Soiuza* (Moscow, 1961), p. 94.

8 A. Riabushin, 'Zhilishche novogo tipa,' *Dekorativnoe iskusstvo SSSR* (henceforth *DI SSSR*), 1963, no. 2, p. 5.

9 Ibid.

10 L. Kamenskii, 'Mebel' vashei kvartiry,' *DI SSSR*, 1962, no. 1, p. 44.

11 L. Kamenskii, 'Ob udobstve mebeli,' *DI SSSR,* 1962, no. 7, p. 15.

12 N. Luppov, 'Novoe napravlenie utverdilos',' *DI SSSR,* 1962, no. 1, p. 9.

13 G. Liubimova, 'Ratsional'noe oborudovanie kvartiry,' *DI SSSR,* 1964, no. 6, p. 16.

14 L. Kamenskii, 'Mebel' v kompozitsii inter'era,' *DI SSSR,* 1962, no. 2, p. 28.

15 A. Chekalov, 'O kompozitsii inter'era,' *DI SSSR,* 1962, no. 2, p. 28.

16 Ibid.

17 N. Luppov, 'Novym zdaniiam – novyi inter'er,' in *Iskusstvo i byt*, vol. 1, (Moscow, 1963), p. 23.

18 N. Voronov, 'Kul'tura formy,' *DI SSSR,* 1961, no. 10, p. 37.

The Exhibition *Art of Socialist Countries,* Moscow 1958–9, and the Contemporary Style of Painting

Susan E. Reid

The exhibition *Art of Socialist Countries,* an unprecedented display of contemporary painting, sculpture and graphics from socialist states of Europe and Asia, opened in Moscow at the end of 1958. In this chapter I shall examine the exhibition's significance for destalinization in the official Soviet art world, focusing on the response of the Soviet public and art profession to their first comprehensive exposure to contemporary art from Central and Eastern Europe, and, in particular, to the unfamiliar modernist work shown in the Polish section. This was one of the formative experiences in the Khrushchev Thaw, and it brought to the surface long-suppressed fissures in the mythical unanimity of the Soviet people as well as divisions among the countries of the bloc over the appropriate nature of contemporary socialist culture. Central and East European art expanded the horizons of legitimate socialist art and provided corroboration for the arguments of Soviet reformists that socialist modernity required an artistic rapprochement with figurative modernism in the form of a 'contemporary style'. Through an analysis of comments in the exhibition's visitors' books, I shall argue that it also helped prepare some of the Soviet public and authorities to admit a range of modern styles as legitimate forms of socialist artistic expression. Perhaps most importantly, the differentiated popular consumption of this exhibition contributed to one of the central processes of the Thaw, the articulation of distinct social identities and re-emergence of civil society.

The Khrushchev regime's renunciation of Stalinist terror and coercion as means of governing both Soviet society and its satellites necessitated a degree of accommodation with pressures for change from the Soviet people and from its allies abroad. International tension eased somewhat in the mid-1950s as the principle of 'Peaceful Coexistence' moderated the Cold-War thesis of the 'Two Camps' promulgated in 1947. As diplomatic, scientific and cultural exchange revived after two decades of near autarky under Stalin, the sudden exposure of the Soviet public and its leadership to foreign cultures of both the socialist and capitalist camps had an important impact on the liberalization of artistic norms during the Thaw. Illustrated magazines from Eastern Europe were available at news stands. As Iurii Gerchuk recalls, 'Every decorative-painterly cover of the journal *Pol'sha* [Poland] behind a kiosk window seemed like a manifesto of new artistic possibilities. And for the "keepers" [of orthodoxy] the very word "Pol'sha" became an odious symbol of "modernism" infiltrating the country.'[1] Regarded with hostile suspicion by conservatives, they nevertheless found a receptive audience who welcomed their more 'Western' contents and modern design. While the most extreme experiments of the Russian avant-garde, suppressed under Stalin, only began to surface at the apogee of destalinization in 1961–2, Russian post-impressionism and French early modernist paintings in Soviet collections began to be restored to view from the mid-1950s, and a series of foreign exhibitions introduced the Soviet public to more recent developments in Western art.[2] In summer 1957, a year before *Art of Socialist Countries*, the Sixth World Festival of Youth and Students confronted the Moscow lay public and art professionals with a display of contemporary art by young socialist artists from around the world, some of whom worked in abstract expressionist, *informel* and surrealist modes. The festival acted as a rite of passage for disaffected Soviet artists who, from the late 1950s, became associated with the artistic underground.[3] It also made a deep impression on young artists such as Pavel Nikonov and critics such as Aleksandr Kamenskii, who subsequently became stalwarts of an emergent reformist wing within the official art world. Kamenskii urged tolerance towards the foreign art shown at the festival, for 'we cannot enter another monastery with our own code of practice.'[4] Nikonov had an epiphany there: 'In the West art was quite different. In our section everything was dead, some kind of tortured academicism. It had to be done differently. But how?'[5]

How to rejuvenate realist painting became the preoccupation of reformist artists and critics from the mid-1950s, when, for the first time since the 1920s, it became possible to begin to come to terms with the experience of modernization which the country had undergone since 1917.[6] Since Stalin's death, with the greater openness of debate that was enabled by the regime's renunciation of terror, divisions had surfaced in the Soviet art establishment between conservatives or Stalinists and those who sought to liberalize and modernize the parameters of socialist realism. The reformers – or modernizers, as we might call them – challenged the Stalinist dogma that realism required unambiguous narrative content and naturalistic verisimilitude and precluded any self-reflexive concern with form and artistic convention. In place of the almost exclusive paradigm of nineteenth-century Russian realism, they proposed that newly rehabilitated (but still highly contentious) aspects of early twentieth-century modernism, such as the colourism of *Bubnovyi valet* (The Knave of Diamonds) or the expressionism of OST (the Society of Easel Painters), provided more appropriate artistic models for post-war Soviet art.[7]

Between 1958 and 1962 modernizers debated the nature of contemporaneity, arguing that rapid progress and the advance of world communism effected corresponding transformations in human consciousness, which must in turn be reflected by the renewal, or modernization, of the language of art if it was adequately to express contemporary experience. For 'new times demand new forms'. In summer 1958, a few months before the opening of *Art of Socialist Countries,* aesthetician Nina Dmitrieva announced the advent of the 'contemporary style' *(sovremennyi stil'),* a modern period style embracing all aspects of visual culture. Its hallmarks were 'synthesis, laconicism and expression'.[8] Emphasizing formal innovation and specifically pictorial means of expression, her conception of a modern form of realism was inspired by the Brechtian synthesis of modernism and realism of the 1920s and 1930s, the heyday of international communism. Rejecting verisimilitude as the chief criterion of realism in favour of non-naturalistic, expressive formal devices, it was an attempt to recuperate the example of early modernism, indiscriminately condemned for 'formalism', 'subjectivism' and 'deformation' since the 1930s.[9] As the Soviet Union under Khrushchev abandoned 'socialism in one country' to reclaim leadership of the international socialist movement, reformist aestheticians presented the development of a contemporary style as the shared project of socialist artists throughout the world. It was surely quite legitimate, they contended, for the new international, socialist style to draw on an ecumenical range of twentieth-century, figurative models, foreign as well as Russian.[10] Thus, liberal novelist Iurii Nagibin proposed that the best examples of the 'extreme laconicism, simplification, and immediate expression of the contemporary style included Picasso's *Guernica* and the work of Diego Rivera.[11]

Even within the bloc, contacts with foreign artists and critics were still very limited and suspiciously guarded. Ideas from Central and Eastern Europe, where social and intellectual revolts had been endemic since Stalin's death, and where Stalinist aesthetics had never taken deep root, were potentially as corrosive as those from the capitalist world. (Typically, an exhibition of Polish art held in Moscow in 1952, shortly before his death, was presented to the Soviet public with a health warning about formalism.[12]) Reformers, however, sought such contacts hungrily, as a potentially fruitful source of rejuvenation for Soviet art. Dmitrieva's formulation of the contemporary style was foreshadowed, and probably influenced by, a discussion on 'Realism and Modernity' in the East German art journal *Bildende Kunst* in 1956.[13] The tradition of expressionism, which began to be recuperated in the German Democratic Republic in the mid-1950s, began to receive a more insightful and selectively favourable treatment in the Soviet Union. In summer 1958, the Moscow art press reviewed an exhibition of expressionist prints of the 1920s and 1930s by Otto Dix, George Grosz, Lea and Hans Grundig, Max Beckmann, and Käthe Kollwitz in terms that accorded closely with definitions of the contemporary style.[14] The work of those politically engaged artists substantiated the reformers' belief that formal devices associated with modernism were not inevitably the vehicle of bourgeois ideology, as Stalinists still objected, but could also serve the expression of contemporary 'socialist humanism'.[15] Indeed, in Poland, as Piotr Piotrowski recounts in this volume, modernism was even adopted as the official socialist aesthetic.

Soviet advocates of the contemporary style strategically invoked the official brag that the present age was one of 'scientific and technological revolution'. Space flight, atomic physics and cybernetics had so fundamentally transformed the nature of perception and cognition as to demand a commensurate revolution in the language of representation. Some went so far as to propose that stylistic devices associated with modernism, such as radical simplification and synthesis, bore a universal, deterministic correspondence to the technological era. They even broached the corollary that if the experience of scientific-technological modernity was shared by East and West, socialist and capitalist camps alike, it must therefore generate a common 'contemporary' or modern style, as the period style of the twentieth century.[16] This was dangerous ground and the implications were rarely explicitly articulated. For the possibility of any convergence between socialist contemporaneity and capitalist modernism directly contradicted current Soviet orthodoxy, according to which, although Peaceful Coexistence had reduced the threat of physical warfare, the ideological battle between the imperialist, capitalist camp and the anti-imperialistic, socialist camp would continue all the more intensely, as expressed in the worldwide struggle between modernism and realism.[17]

The ideologically suspect rapprochement of the contemporary style with modernism did not escape the attention of the guardians of orthodoxy. The storm burst on the eve of the opening of *Art of Socialist Countries*. On 4 December 1958 the Party section of the Moscow Artists' Union upbraided reformist critics for attempting to reconcile realism and modernism and, by extension, willing the convergence of socialism and capitalism.[18] The notion that the contemporary style was the inevitable product of industrial development was 'a loophole through which the decadent influences of cosmopolitan modernism can penetrate our art.'[19]

Conservatives also 'unmasked' the contemporary style's affinity with dangerous, 'revisionist' reinterpretations of Marxist-Leninist aesthetics proposed since the mid-1950s by East European and Western Marxists.[20] As a Central Committee letter made clear, the Communist Party of the Soviet Union (CPSU) held the ideological revisionism of the Polish and Hungarian intelligentsia responsible for the 1956 uprisings in those countries, and it was anxious to prevent it gaining followers among susceptible, 'politically immature' elements of the Soviet intelligentsia and youth.[21] From November 1957, under pressure from China, it adopted a hard line on revisionism within the bloc and began a vituperative press campaign against it.[22] An attack on revisionism published in the central art journal *Iskusstvo* (Art) in August 1958 denounced debates concerning 'contemporaneity', 'innovation', and the 'means of expression' as a mask, behind which revisionists promoted an anti-realist, bourgeois capitalist notion of art that was quite irreconcilable with socialist realism.[23] Polish and Hungarian revisionist aesthetics bore an uncomfortably close resemblance to the Soviet reformist discourse of the contemporary style. 'The Problem of Contemporaneity in Art is a Political Problem,' ominously read the title of an article in the conservative, Russian chauvinist art journal *Khudozhnik* (Artist). The author conflated Dmitrieva's demand for a modernized artistic language with the modernist notion of the autonomy of art, currently being proselytized, he alleged, by revisionists in Poland. For example, the journal *Pol'sha* (*Poland*), which was distributed in the USSR, had published an article entitled 'At the Exhibition of "Contemporary" [Art],' which assumed that in Poland the term 'contemporary' was widely understood to refer to 'pure geometric and non-geometric abstraction, non-figurative structures based on the factor of chance (*tachisme*), and also figurative art operating with broad, extended artistic metaphor' – in short, to modernism.[24] Revisionists such as Polish scholar Roman Zimand denied the Marxist-Leninist principle of art's cognitive role, proposing that the essence of art was 'not the reflection of actuality but its active deformation'. In Hungary, Georg Lukács – who, as Minister of Culture in Imre Nagy's government, was directly implicated in the revolution of 1956 – had allegedly substituted the subjective criterion of artistic sincerity for objective truth.[25]

The offensive against revisionism intensified towards the end of 1958 in preparation for the exhibition of *Art of Socialist Countries*, in order to counterbalance the Soviet people's increased exposure to information about foreign ideas, lifestyles and art.[26] The spectre of the uncoupling of socialism and realism in parts of the socialist camp and the unholy reconciliation with modernism loomed large over the exhibition's reception and over the domestic discussions of artistic rejuvenation with which it was closely associated.

The Exhibition *Art of Socialist Countries*

Art of Socialist Countries opened on 26 December 1958 in Moscow's Central Exhibition Hall or *Manezh*, at the epicentre of the Soviet empire. Bringing together examples of recent art from Eastern European and Asian socialist states in the shadow of the Kremlin, it was to dramatize Moscow's status as natural leader of a united socialist camp in its crusade to save the 'aesthetic values of humanity' from destruction by capitalism, and at the same time to proclaim the new, 'democratic', consensual basis of the post-Stalinist Soviet Union's control over its satellites.

The USSR Ministry of Culture's Fine Art section under Andrei Lebedev oversaw planning for the exhibition in collaboration with the USSR Artists' Union and with the equivalent bodies in each of the eleven other participating countries:

Albania, Bulgaria, Hungary, Poland, the German Democratic Republic, Romania, Czechoslovakia, China, North Korea, Vietnam, and Mongolia. Yugoslavia, which was included in the original plan, sent a letter in spring 1958 politely welcoming the initiative but declining to participate on the pretext that its programme for the year was already full.[27] The organization was to be based on fraternal cooperation, mutual respect and equality of the participating countries: not, that is, overtly dominated by the Soviet Union. Thus, the exhibition committee was 'demo-cratically' constituted of two delegates from each country's artistic organizations. However, it was chaired by a Russian, the elderly sculptor Sergei Konenkov, and it met in Moscow in March 1958 to endorse principles set out by the Soviet hosts. In accordance with the principle of equality, the work was to be displayed country by country in alphabetical order. Each country was responsible for selecting its own exhibits and for preparing the catalogue for its section, which gave the national curators a chance to defend potentially problematic works.[28] This strategy allowed the Soviet Union to appear to give free rein, while its guests took responsibility for putting together their sections with a weather eye on Moscow. On the whole, this may have made them more conservative than was necessary in the climate of the Thaw.[29]

In the course of preparations, delegates expressed the hope that international exhibitions of socialist art would become a regular, biennial event and would expand to include progressive artists from capitalist or post-colonial countries. The vision of a kind of socialist *biennale* was conceived as an answer to the major international exhibitions of the capitalist camp which promoted modernism and snubbed realism. As Konenkov noted in this context, 'Those who saw the exhibitions at the [Venice] *Biennale* and Brussels [1958 World Fair] will be convinced of the dead-end bourgeois art has entered.' The Czechoslovak representatives, seconded by the Romanians, proposed that the socialist exhibition be hosted by each country in turn.[30]

No one could doubt, however, that the first (and as it happened, the only one) should be held in Moscow. Although the decision was presented as spontaneous consensus, the location at the heart of the Soviet empire was fundamental to the exhibition's purpose.[31] As Sergei Gerasimov, President of the recently formed USSR Artists' Union, proclaimed, it was the first exhibition to be organized on neither a territorial nor a chronological basis, but on a 'shared, all-conquering progressive idea, the idea of socialism'.[32] For, as he had recently announced, 'The time has come to define the art of socialist realism on an *international* scale!'[33] Lebedev's official report stated its purpose, 'to manifest the success of socialist culture, its great humanist principles'.[34] According to Soviet critic Iurii Kolpinskii, this landmark exhibition initiated 'a new epoch in the development of world artistic culture', demonstrating that socialist realism was 'not the specific hallmark of Soviet art, but the shared truth of artistic culture throughout the socialist world.'[35]

The official Soviet position on the exhibition was to welcome diversity within unity of purpose, and to emphasize the varied and dynamic development of socialist art, in order to disprove, once and for all, Western accusations that in the Soviet bloc creative individuality and national identity were suppressed.[36] The unified method of socialist realism would take on diverse artistic forms in accordance with national artistic traditions.[37] While Soviet commentators sought to establish points of contact between the art of the participating countries on the basis of their shared 'ideological-political tasks of affirming the socialist order', they were careful to emphasize that shared goals did not imply uniformity or mechanical appropriation of Soviet models.[38] It was 'natural that in countries that have only begun to build socialism since the war the process of formation of socialist realist art is not yet complete', wrote Moscow art historian Nina Iavorskaia, citing approvingly the view expressed in the catalogues of various countries 'that their artists are mastering the method of socialist realism but coming to it by different paths'.[39] Thus, a Chinese painter such as Jiang Zhaohe might legitimately synthesize elements of traditional Chinese painting with those of European oil painting and murals.[40] 'Although on some specific questions there may be some disagreement among us', Gerasimov admitted in his speech for the exhibition opening, these differences would ultimately strengthen socialist art.[41]

While, for the reformers, the new internationalism implied that Soviet artists could and must learn from global, socialist experience, the conservative USSR Ministry of Culture organized the exhibition on the premise that the unity of the socialist camp was to be achieved on Soviet terms, under Soviet guidance. The President of the Romanian Artists' Union announced sycophantically, 'Soviet fine art as a whole ... is the model for determining the scale of the new art of the socialist order.'[42] The effect, however, was quite the opposite.

The USSR display gave little sense of the divisions and stylistic innovations in Soviet art since Stalin's death, despite the stipulation that the exhibition should reflect developments of the past five years. The selection committee feared to offend any member of the artistic elite by omitting them from such a prestigious international event.[43] Thus, the selection was dominated by geriatric academicians who had achieved their exalted status under Stalin. If it acknowledged that times had changed, it was at the level of theme alone, notably in the absence of icons promoting the Personality Cult.[44] Overloaded with mediocrity and 'lacking contemporaneity', the Soviet display appeared monotonous and anachronistic against the foil of international socialist art. Even the most loyal foreign delegates such as the Bulgarians could find little good to say about it. Professor Stanisław Teisseyre of Poland condemned the exhibition as a whole for the predominance of cold, academic, descriptive painting that neglected expressive treatment of form.[45] And, as Gerasimov confessed, viewers, too, criticized it for excessive descriptiveness and didacticism.[46]

If the Soviet Union was to preserve any credibility as leader of socialist culture it must urgently find ways to 'do it differently', as Nikonov put it. Soviet advocates of the contemporary style had often voiced similar views to those advanced by Teisseyre. As I have noted, the attempt to recuperate the use of expressive devices, often consciously derived from pre-war expressionism – including the licence to simplify, exaggerate, or even distort form, intensify colour and tonal contrasts, and flatten space – was a central part of their project. Hardliners, on the other hand, maintained that the elision of expressionism and realism was one of the most offensive heresies issuing from foreign revisionists.[47] Against their vituperative jeremiads, the reformers consciously sought corroboration in the exhibition that, as Iavorskaia declared, socialist and progressive artists throughout the world were united in the 'search for expressiveness'.[48] Prominent art historian German Nedoshivin adduced the work of Jiang Zhaohe, Romanian painter Corneliu Baba and German sculptor Fritz Cremer as 'convincing proof' that Soviet artists and critics must also embrace laconic expression, hyperbole, and stylization. Failure to do so would sever them from the great realist tradition of world socialist art.[49]

Reviewers specifically identified expressionism with the German Democratic Republic. Artists such as Cremer, Hans Grundig, Lea Grundig, Bernhard Kretzschmar and Theodor Rosenhauer (both the latter from the home of *die Brücke*, Dresden) had turned to expressionism as a means to deal with the horrors of fascism.[50] Cremer showed three tortured, emaciated figures from his 1958 Buchenwald monument in which he sacrificed naturalistic accuracy to express the struggle between life and death.[51] Iavorskaia and other reformists argued that this was a new, broadly accessible, expressive art, a contemporary, socialist hypostasis of the German 'national tradition', cleansed of the morbidity, despair, alienation and elitism with which earlier expressionism had responded to capitalism.[52] There was surprisingly little mention of expressionist deformation among the 166 visitors' comments relating to the German section of the exhibition. While many art professionals remained hostile to any trace of expressionist deformation, the public response seems, significantly for the reformist campaign, to have been either neutral or positive. As a report by the *Manezh* staff acknowledged, viewers 'understood Fritz Cremer's tragic sense, his expressivity and militant language', finding his work 'highly artistic, emotional and accessible at once'. 'In spite of the form of expressionism unfamiliar for our viewer, German art aroused a lively, active and correct reaction from visitors', who noted the 'contemporary character of German art'.[53]

The Polish Display

While Soviet viewers were mildly positive towards the German section, it was the Polish display that elicited by far the most written comments and ardent debate.

Eclipsing the exhibition as a whole, it became, for many, the sole objective of their visit. An American eyewitness, Nina Juviler, reported home: 'the display from Poland offered a striking contrast of semi-abstract works rendered in individual experimental styles (though more conservative, it might be noted, than those on view in Poland proper).'[54] In his chapter for this volume Piotr Piotrowski considers the Polish section of this exhibition from the Polish perspective, as an indication of the official endorsement of modernism in Poland in the late 1950s. Here I shall focus on Soviet reception of the Polish display. Just as Soviet theories about the contemporary style had more extreme parallels in Polish revisionist aesthetics, where the style of the modern age was explicitly identified with modernism, so, too, the Polish display provided some extreme examples of departures from socialist realist dogma and rapprochement with Western modernism, including even abstraction. By contrast, the expressive devices and synthetic reductions advocated by Soviet modernizers began to appear relatively moderate and acceptable.

Already by November 1958 it was clear to the Soviet authorities that both the Polish and Hungarian art establishments had taken rather too literally the principle of national sovereignty in selecting their sections, and had strayed intolerably far from even the elastic, post-Stalinist conception of realism as 'diversity within unity'. In his capacity as head of the USSR Ministry of Culture's Fine Art Section, the reactionary Andrei Lebedev wrote an anxious memorandum to his Minister, Nikolai Mikhailov, in early November. He had discovered, he wrote, that the Hungarian and Polish sections were to include 'formalist works', the presence of which would greatly undermine the significance of the exhibition by destroying the very unity it was intended to demonstrate. Soviet artists had been dispatched to Hungary and Poland 'to try to exercise "in a tactful way" a certain influence on the selection for the Hungarian and Polish sections'. But since this had not achieved the desired effect Lebedev now urged that the matter be taken up at the highest level of the Party, so grave were the political implications of the Poles' and Hungarians' maverick behaviour in the light of the uprisings two years earlier. The Ministry should ask the CPSU Central Committee to instruct the Central Committees of the Hungarian and Polish Parties to take direct control of their selections, lest 'the presence of a large number of works of a formalist nature' reduce the significance of the exhibition as a whole. As he emphasized in a letter to the Hungarian Socialist Workers' Party and Polish United Workers' Party (PUWP), 'The success of the exhibition will depend on how much the participating countries can achieve unity of ideological tendency and vividly express socialist ideology.'[55]

Whether the CPSU Central Committee ever responded to Lebedev's request to intervene remains to be established. However, on 11 November, Lebedev received ministerial authority to approach the Hungarian and Polish Central Committees over the necessity of selecting ideologically correct, realist works.[56] When the exhibition finally opened to the public the Hungarian display did not arouse any major outcry, which suggests that the curators may have submitted to pressure to observe the unwritten limits of 'diversity within unity'.[57] Alternatively, any residual misdemeanour on the Hungarians' part paled into insignificance beside the impudence of the Poles.

If the Polish Central Committee received Lebedev's injunction, it either refused to intervene in the professional affairs of the Polish curators, or failed to make the exhibition committee conform, possibly, as Piotrowski suggests, because Poland had moved so far beyond conservative Soviet models of socialist realism since 1956 that the curators no longer even had this option.[58] Whatever, the limitations of Moscow's control over Polish cultural life were evident. As a pre-emptive strike, the script of Minister Mikhailov's speech for the ceremonial opening of the exhibition, quite possibly written by Lebedev, was revised to include a stock tirade against revisionist treachery.[59]

Although the Polish regime had begun to impose stricter controls on cultural freedom under Władysław Gomułka, who had criticized elements in the Polish intelligentsia for 'ideological errors' in his recent address to the Third Congress of the PUWP, it had to walk a tightrope between excessively provoking Moscow on the one hand, and losing popular legitimacy at home. Its reprisals against revisionists after the 1956 uprising – in particular against the philosopher Leszek Kolakowski, whose 1957 essay 'Responsibility and History' upheld the value of independent moral judgement against Party discipline – risked irrevocably alienating the intelligentsia and youth.[60] Even propaganda chief Stefan Staszewski later admitted, 'Wherever it was possible to wriggle out of some act of servility we wriggled out of it. Above all we managed to wriggle out of a large part of the junk of Soviet socialist realist literature.'[61] An American journalist, Maurice Hindus, arriving in Warsaw from Moscow in 1958, was struck by the contrast in their cultural climates and, in particular, by the militant refusal of the Polish cultural authorities to submit – or be seen by their own people to submit – to Moscow's authority in cultural matters.[62]

Polish resentment at Soviet intervention in cultural affairs was acute at the end of 1958, following a blistering attack on Polish cultural life in the Leningrad literary journal *Zvezda* in July. The author, one A. Gozenpud, accused contemporary Polish culture of sharing the symptoms of decadence that afflicted Western modernism: 'loss of faith in man, nihilism, and the philosophy of despair'. He condemned Polish fascination with existentialism and psychoanalysis, which contradicted the official ideology of optimism and the omnipotence of the rational, conscious mind. In particular, he attacked the popular illustrated magazine *Przekrój* (*Profile*) for publishing an article on psychoanalysis discussing Adler's concept of the inferiority complex. Perhaps the most glaring instance of Poland's cultural degeneration and 'provincial kow-towing to the West', however, was more trivial but none the less telling: a series of colour reproductions of advertising labels of foreign airlines and hotels in Paris, London, New York, Rome, Casablanca, Montevideo and other capitals, which *Przekrój* had printed regularly since November 1957. The magazine advised its primarily female, adolescent readers to cut out and collect the stickers, glazing them with eggwhite. By affixing them to their suitcases they could pretend to have travelled widely and stayed in the best hotels.[63] The hotel labels were thus offered as vicarious compensation for what was a major source of dissatisfaction among Polish youth – the near impossibility of travel to the West. In an uncompromising Polish rebuttal to *Zvezda*'s criticisms, *Trybuna literacka,* the Party literary supplement, indicated to the Polish people – and to the Soviet leadership – that the PUWP and government would not bow to its pressure and that they opposed any policy of cultural autarky and ostracism.[64]

The Polish display stood out like a sore thumb. In the first place, it differed from the other sections in its individualistic emphasis on a few contrasting artists, each represented by a mini-retrospective. And as Lebedev had feared, it disrupted the facade of aesthetic and ideological consensus. It even cast doubt on the premise that realism was the inalienable artistic expression of socialism; or, conversely, it called in question whether Poland should rightfully be considered socialist. From a Polish perspective, however, it was a restrained and relatively conservative selection that attempted to present a quite broad cross section of Polish contemporary art, while downplaying the importance of abstraction at home, whose spread the Polish authorities were trying to contain at the time.[65] Thus it stopped short of the most controversial, Western-oriented developments, influenced by Parisian *art informel* and surrealism, such as the abstraction of Tadeusz Kantor, Tadeusz Brzozowski and Aleksander Kobzdej, with their concern for autonomous form and subjective experience.[66] While the curators could not honestly deny the importance of modernist tendencies altogether, they took care to counterbalance them by including also some work on ideologically impeccable themes of revolutionary struggle by Wojciech Weiss and Fejicjan Kowarski, whom Soviet critics accepted as continuators of the national traditions of nineteenth-century Polish realism.[67] Objectively, the selection was dominated by colourism and expressive or metaphorical forms of figurative art informed by early modernism. While Stalinists considered even this middle-of-the-road tendency formalist, it must have encouraged young Soviet artists associated with the contemporary style, such as Pavel Nikonov, Nikolai Andronov and Eduard Bragovskii, who regarded the 'painterly culture' of post-impressionism as a source of realism's rejuvenation. In Poland, unlike in Soviet Russia, colourism was firmly ensconced within the establishment. As Piotrowski points out, the selection committee, headed by Professor Juliusz Starzyński, did not consist of Young Turks, but included such respected figures as critic Zdisław Kępiński and the painter Jan Cybis, both advocates of post-impressionist colourism. Cybis' work was featured in the exhibition along with that of his fellow colourists Eugeniusz Eibisch and Wacław Taranczewski, whose *Still Life with Blue Vase* (1957, figure 6.1) was clearly indebted to Matisse and Picasso.[68] It seems clear that the curatorial team sought to avoid provoking Moscow's wrath while giving a relatively comprehensive and truthful account of Polish art, but had misjudged the gulf that had opened up between their conceptions of artistic destalinization.

Figure 6.1 Wacław Taranczewski, *Still Life with Blue Vase (and Shell) III*, oil on canvas, 1957, 80 × 100 cm. National Museum, Poznań.

The Soviet reformers would also be inspired and encouraged in their search for a more emotionally effective and metaphorical form of figurative art by the expressive painting and sculpture of Xawery Dunikowski. Dunikowski's work had been shown twice already in Moscow, and he was generally regarded as one of the more respectable Polish artists, albeit with reservations.[69] The reviewer in the popular Soviet magazine *Ogonek* argued that he was a realist of a new sort who could permit himself liberties with natural appearances in the interests of heightened expression.[70] Dunikowski was represented by works from various periods in a striking range of media and stylistic approaches, including an early series of monumental wood carvings, *Wawel Heads,* and a post-war cycle of expressionist

Figure 6.2 Xawery Dunikowski, *Grates*, from the cycle *Auschwitz*, oil on canvas, 1955, 180 × 170. Xawery Dunikowski Museum, Warsaw.

paintings, *Auschwitz* (1955, figure 6.2), concerning his own experience in the Nazi concentration camp. Departures from natural appearances in the *Auschwitz* cycle, the artist explained in Moscow, were necessary to express his 'cry from the soul' against fascism's unprecedented inhumanity, using the specific means of visual art. Even under an expanded definition of realism, however, not all his work was acceptable. Seven works were shown from his recent cycle, *Man in Space* (1958, figure 6.3), in which residual figuration was progressively stripped away to arrive, finally, at pure geometric abstraction. The work was dismissed by many as abstract, cubist and incomprehensible to the masses, although Dunikowski explained it as a search for a new form to express man's flight into the cosmos. His Soviet defenders – for defenders there were – took up the familiar argument, which

Figure 6.3 Xawery Dunikowski, *Man in Space (Cosmos)*, (sketch), tempera, oil on paper glued to cardboard, 1958, 52.5 × 39.5 cm. Xawery Dunikowski Museum, Warsaw.

accorded with the rhetoric of the contemporary style: space flight and the splitting of the atom had engendered a revolution in human perception that required a new, abstracted artistic language.[71]

A degree of flattening and abstracted forms was tolerable from the foreign guests which would yet be unacceptable from a Soviet artist, as for example, in the ink drawings of Professor of Graphic Art at the Warsaw Academy of Fine Arts, Tadeusz Kulisiewicz.[72] But the semi-abstract graphics of Halina Chrostowska and Jerzy Paneka and, above all, the paintings of Adam Marczyński (figure 6.4) – the only truly abstract works in the whole display – were quite indefensible.[73] In spite of the predominance of figurative styles, the widespread assessment of the Polish display was that it was dominated by abstraction, formalism and modernism; and for many of its opponents these were one and the same thing.[74]

Nina Iavorskaia, who was unusually knowledgeable of, and sympathetic towards, figurative modernism, attempted to explain and even justify 'the resurgence of formalism in Polish art as a reaction against the naturalistic tendency which appeared in the forties, not only in Poland but also in the art of other socialist countries.' Even she could not condone the rise of abstraction in work by Marczyński and other 'revisionists' who, 'under the guise of a struggle against naturalism waged a struggle with socialist realism.'[75] It was left to the Bulgarian

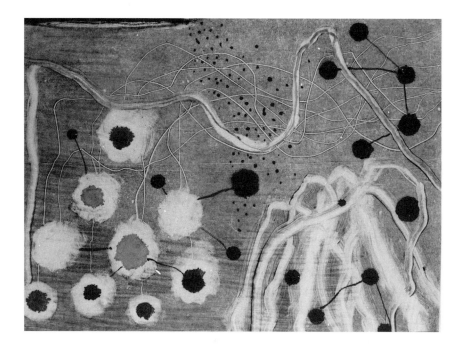

Figure 6.4 Adam Marczyński, *Spring*, 1956. National Museum, Krakow.

representatives Aleksandr Obretenov and Mara Tsoncheva to put the boot in at the international discussion of the exhibition held from 24 to 26 March 1959, allowing the Soviets to maintain their stance of tolerance.[76] The Polish abstract-ionists denied the very methods of socialist realism and even the significance of realist art, Tsoncheva accused. The Romanian delegate explained, 'For an artist who has adopted the method of socialist realism, the concept of contemporaneity is inseparable from the principle of *partiinost'* [party-mindedness] which defines art's purpose as a means of cognition and transformation of the world.'[77]

The Polish art historians Professors Starzyński and Teisseyre attempted to defend their selection in the press and at the formal discussion by pointing out how little of it was truly abstract, and by emphasizing that the new art was, in the tradition of all genuine *realism,* a response to contemporary life. Starzyński acknowledged unapologetically, however, that Polish art was influenced by 'close contact with the West, especially with French culture.'[78] Tsoncheva pounced on the Polish arguments for their proximity to bourgeois aesthetics, which represented modernity as a supra-ideological condition and modernism as its necessary expression. The turn towards pure, autonomous painting in contemporary Polish art, the concern with self-expression, painterly surface and form, rather than with accessible, realist content, could not even be defended as a rejuvenation of Polish national traditions, in the way expressionist elements were legitimated in German art. For the sources of contemporary Polish art lay not in any national traditions but in cosmopolitan modernist (*modernisticheskoe*) art, which abandoned real life for the absurdity of abstraction and pathological surrealism. 'We might ignore the "aggressive tone" of the Polish section as the chance selection dictated by the taste of the Polish organizers,' Tsoncheva went on, 'were it not for the whole series of responses to the exhibition in the Polish press in recent months', which went so far as to claim it a triumph for Polish art. The Poles' arrogant refusal to recant compounded the errors of their exhibition and was tantamount to a treacherous denial of socialist ideology and aesthetics.[79]

Viewers' Response to the Polish Section

The Polish press might well have been justified in claiming a Polish triumph if their measure was the sheer number of visitors and the volume of written and oral responses to their section. Nearly half a million viewers saw *Art of Socialist Countries,* the majority of whom, it was widely noted, tended to congregate in the Polish section. Indeed, many people queued for the show expressly to see with their own eyes the notorious offerings of the Poles. For the guardians of orthodoxy, their success – albeit scandalous – was a worrying and embarrassing state of affairs. The axiom that 'the people' was the final arbiter of artistic worth was the constant refrain of Soviet criticism and policy, and mass attendance at Soviet art exhibitions was routinely adduced as proof of the popular, national nature *(narodnost')* of socialist realism by contrast with the small, elite audience for modernist art in the West.[80] Unable to address this contradiction, hostile Soviet commentators merely insisted that the Polish art was 'incomprehensible to the people' and could not, therefore, be considered 'popular' *(narodnym)*.[81]

Although it was the exhibition's stated purpose to promote mutual knowledge and understanding within the bloc and contribute to 'the social-aesthetic education of millions of viewers', it was shown only in Moscow and was not toured to any other country, nor even to other Soviet cities.[82] How was a public raised on the narrow diet of nineteenth-century Russian realism and Stalinist academic naturalism to judge the alien inflections of socialist realism proffered under the slogan of 'diversity', not to mention the modernist distortions and abstractions smuggled in by the Poles?

Surprisingly, perhaps, not only did most viewers gravitate towards the Polish room, but many actively engaged with the work. As Juviler noted, the Polish display had a 'marked impact on its Russian audience: small groups of observers carried on excited conversations in front of the paintings and remarks could be overheard in praise of their freshness and imaginative qualities.'[83] Juviler's account, structured by Cold War prejudices, might be dismissed as the biased view of a Western observer. However, the hundreds of comments about the Polish art which dominated not only the visitors' books designated for the Polish section but also the general one for the whole exhibition, confirm that public response to it was neither indifferent nor uniformly hostile.

Visitors' books are, it must be emphasized, a problematic source of evidence: the entries can hardly be considered a candid or representative reflection of opinion, least of all in a culture of surveillance such as the Soviet Union. To engage in assessing their degree of sincerity is a fruitless task. Rather, comment-writing should be treated as a form of role-performance or self-alignment. This is so not only when the ritualistic language of the remarks suggest their authors are stooges obediently playing part in a campaign orchestrated against the exhibition, but also where the comments run boldly against the grain of orthodoxy and show signs of struggle to formulate a personal response. In the absence of sociological surveys of the Soviet art audience in this period one can only make informed guesses, on the internal evidence of the comments themselves, concerning what kinds of people wrote comments and with what motives; in what ways a consciousness of being watched or read affected what they wrote; and whom the writers hoped to impress by their displays of erudite taste and understanding, or, alternatively, their protestations of incomprehension. While many wrote as a form of self-affirmation or to edify their fellow viewers, some specifically addressed their comments to the Party or Komsomol.

Many were drawn to the Polish display like flies to a rotting corpse; the event provided an opportunity to experience themselves as part of the Soviet mass, participating in the ritual anathema of Polish decadence. However, there was also a significant number of comments that were ambivalent, open-minded or even positively enthusiastic, and which were quite remarkable in their outspoken defiance of orthodoxy. Soviet reports emphasized the varied composition of the public: workers, peasants, employees, soldiers, pensioners, artists, and foreigners. Although no firm conclusions can be drawn about the commentators' age or occupation, because they did not consistently provide this information (nor are gender differences possible to determine), there are indications that viewers' responses split along generational and occupational lines. Typically, a pensioner, proudly signing himself 'Party member since 1917', dismissed the paintings as 'daubing'. Meanwhile, many of those who identified themselves as students of Moscow institutes or as 'young people' made favourable comments or, at least, rejected the stock pejoratives and grappled to understand this unfamiliar art in their own terms. Thus, two 'students' declared Marczyński's abstract paintings 'especially amazing', and another confirmed that they 'interested young people predominantly'.[84] For such viewers, the exhibition provided a rare opportunity, inconceivable before 1956, to glimpse something like Western modernity refracted in the Polish prism, to debate cultural criteria in public, and to articulate a self-identity as part of an intellectual elite, distinguished from the philistine mass by cultural discernment and sophistication about foreign trends. Thus, it contributed to one of the most significant social processes of the Thaw: the collapse of Stalinist consensus and disaggregation of Soviet society into distinct interest groups and strata, most clearly manifested in the self-affirmation of the intelligentsia and the emergence of Western-oriented youth cultures defined through cultural and consumption choices.[85]

The hostile responses were, not surprisingly, highly repetitive, rote rehearsals of Cold War clichés the authors had imbibed from the mass media or Party meetings.[86] One writer admitted that he arrived already prejudiced against abstraction and that even his worst expectations were exceeded. Many equated departures from the familiar devices of Russian academic naturalism with political and social deviance. 'This art is not for us. Let the dying bourgeoisie have it', wrote a 'veteran of three wars'. Some refused to recognize it as art at all: it was a mockery; the work of monkeys and lunatics. One summed up: 'Burn them!'[87] Another accused Dunikowski of the political crime of revisionism:

> It is hard to believe Dunikowski is a materialist . . . the means with which he tries to embody his ideas are no use for it . . . symbols no-one understands. I don't know if Dunikowski considers himself a Marxist. First they attempted to revise Marxism; they were defeated. They went over into art, and here the revision of Marxist theory in this area is in full flame. Experiments reeking of bourgeois ideology![88]

A standard pattern followed by many of the negative comments was to stake a claim to first-hand knowledge of what Poland, its people and its art were truly like, and then to question the authenticity of the image presented: 'We don't find out anything new about the life and construction of socialism in Poland'; or worse, 'This is not Poland'. Not only did the art misrepresent contemporary Poland, or fail to represent it at all, but the selection of artists did not reflect the contemporary state of Polish art: 'Poland has other artists who, for some reason, haven't been shown.' Some attacked the Polish selectors, insinuating that they were divorced from their own people, in sway to the West, politically unreliable and even opposed to socialism, as the members of the intelligentsia responsible for the Polish unrest in 1956 had allegedly been. 'I was in Poland', one wrote. 'No, Polish art is not like this ... evidently the Artists' Union is headed by people who do not love genuine Polish [popular] art and are drawn to the bourgeois West in its worst examples.' Another ranted, 'Shame on the intelligentsia and organizers of this exhibition who monopolized the exhibition with abstract works. To most Soviet people it is clear that the abstract works are the delirium of individuals, a powerless protest against contemporary life in the socialist countries.' More elaborate conspiracy theories about the Polish exhibition were also put forward. It was part of a worldwide Masonic plot, one wrote, and the abstract work embodied the Masons' idealist motto, 'the flesh will rot'. The Masons, the writer went on to explain, were a secret political party, based in the US, which directed all the ostensibly autonomous political organizations of the capitalist world.[89] The Poles, in other words, were the agents of capitalism, attempting to undermine socialism from within. Their modernist, idealist display was a Trojan horse of bourgeois ideology.

If the authors of hostile comments attended the exhibition as a civic duty to confirm their prejudices and display their command of dogma, there were also a surprising number of open-minded and enthusiastic responses. 'The Poles are enjoying a "scandalous" success', one wrote with grudging respect. 'Why do none of the realist paintings arouse as much attention as Polish abstract painting?'[90] Even if they were unable to embrace the more extreme and unfamiliar works, they found much that was of interest in the Polish display. In spite of reactionary efforts to muddy distinctions and tar the whole exhibition with the brush of abstraction, many viewers were clearly capable of distinguishing between different styles and positively welcomed the range and diversity of the selection. Indeed, the comments demonstrated a level of discrimination and articulacy concerning aesthetic criteria that belied the continued insistence of reactionary critics that only a quasi-photographic naturalism could be loved and understood by the Russian people. 'Paintings should not be mere photographs,' one wrote. 'They must touch a person and make him think.' Viewers were prepared to accept work that was abstracted from reality and which employed expressive, non-naturalistic devices, provided these seemed justified by its content, as in Dunikowski's *Auschwitz* cycle. 'This irritated the eye and the mind, and made people think and perceive, not slide over the surface and admire beauty and craft as with the Vietnamese.' Students from Moscow State University and the Film Institute (VGIIK) also considered the *Auschwitz* cycle the best work in the show on account of its strength of expression. Another Moscow University student wrote a whole essay defending the right of all artistic tendencies to exist, including abstraction: abstraction was only bad if it was self-sufficient formal experiment, divorced from ideas and feelings.[91]

Some were already familiar with contemporary Polish art from reproductions in the journal *Pol'sha* and welcomed the opportunity to see it in the original. Others were disappointed by the Polish work, not because they rejected its westernized, modernist tendencies, but precisely because it was *not modernist enough*: they found it to be only a weak imitation, which discredited the Western prototypes. 'Great art is not the art of Poland but of France (Picasso[?]) and Spain (Salvador Dali).' 'If Tomaczewski does bad imitations of Matisse it doesn't follow that Matisse is bad', another reasoned.[92]

Some viewers returned several times and acknowledged that it was only through time and effort that they were gradually able to understand the Polish work. This admission contradicted the Stalinists' demagogic insistence that art should be transparent and immediately accessible to the masses. 'How sad that we don't help people to begin to think creatively when looking at a picture, but cultivate a view of a picture as an illustration or photograph, not requiring interpretation', one visitor lamented. 'The Poles are evidently able and like to think. We could do with learning this too.' Many seized the opportunity to vent their disgust at their compatriots' conformism, intellectual lethargy and refusal to engage with anything new and unfamiliar. 'Insults are not arguments', a student retorted to a CPSU veteran who had written 'so what – daubing!' 'Unfortunately, in our Union there are people who denigrate and curse everything . . . The Polish art moves one deeply . . . I respect Polish artists, many of whom experienced the German occupation. May people understand!' exclaimed another. 'The Polish room is a ray of light in the dark kingdom of socialist realism. Coming out of it, you feel that art is still developing . . . My advice is not to admit anyone who is not grown-up enough for it.' Similarly, a student wrote: 'The vivid, bright art of Poland is like a yellow line in the bog of realism.' Another viewer, who gave no occupation but was keen to parade his cosmopolitan erudition, dissociated himself from the herd, who 'don't understand the task of painting at all and especially of abstraction'. Citing Delacroix and Apollinaire to the effect that art should appeal as directly as possible to the subjective realm of emotions, he concluded by justifying unpopular art and the isolation of the creative intelligentsia from the masses: 'Never yet has an artist been fully understood by the middle-brow public, let alone by the majority.' A number of viewers expressed open admiration for anyone who, like the Poles, dared take risks in the name of artistic integrity. 'Thank you for your audacity' wrote a Moscow University student. 'There is a breed of people who can only listen to the kind of music they are used to', grumbled another. 'But you had the courage to paint such a picture . . . Fools risk nothing, sacrifice nothing, hiding behind the dependable back of official opinion. The same fools burnt Giordano. It is good that the pictures disturbed the fools to think a bit.'[93]

Others had more faith in the Soviet public's capacity to learn and broaden its aesthetic horizons, if only it were given regular exposure to a range of historical and contemporary tendencies through exhibitions and publications and were taught to understand 'difficult' art. Contrary to the 'two camps' orthodoxy that modernism, as the expression of bourgeois ideology, was incompatible with socialism, they believed that popular acceptance even of abstraction was only a matter of time and education. 'Abstract art has the right to exist! We are not educated to perceive these paintings, because we do not know the history of contemporary art . . . The future will show whether our viewer accepts this art. It seems to us that abstract-ionism can become an element in our art.' '[Abstraction] is in its experimental stage but gradually the viewer will begin to understand that [it] reflects our epoch. The future belongs to this tendency.' 'I hope this section will go some way towards helping to overcome conservatism in art', wrote, unusually, a pensioner and Party member; a student, meanwhile, expressed confidence that 'Further popularization of abstract painting will lead to further understanding.'[94]

Many of those who wrote comments objected to the condescending presumption of Stalinist art policy that they were incapable of understanding 'difficult art'. They thirsted for information, constructive discussion and intelligent explanation. 'You should not keep the viewers in ignorance all the time, inciting them to rumours, arguments and speculation', they complained, calling for accessible explanatory texts to be mounted next to the paintings. They also demanded better-informed consultants because some attendants allegedly refused to explain the problematic works, dismissing them as the 'personal impression of the artist.' Some viewers requested publication of articles on Polish art by Soviet art historians, or wished for popular lectures to explain abstract art. Others went so far as to call for the work of the early twentieth-century Russian avant-garde to be brought out from storage and put on public display at last so that they could comprehend the history of abstraction.[95]

The 'Struggle for the Viewer'

The 2,500 written comments by visitors to the *Art of Socialist Countries* were carefully analysed by the staff of the exhibition hall who prepared a report on the public response for the Ministry.[96] What uses were made of the visitors' remarks? It was common practice for conservatives to make selective readings of visitors' books in order to construct a *vox populi* that confirmed the status quo. Comments books also served as a safety valve and an early warning system to alert the authorities when action was needed to redress 'misconceptions'. But were they simply a means of giving people the impression that their opinion counted? Or did the cultural and political authorities respond to them? Could popular responses contribute to the process of destalinization?

Public interest in the Polish section clearly necessitated special measures. Four consultants were permanently detailed to it, under instruction to intervene actively in viewers' discussions and deliver Marxist-Leninist explanations of the formalist and abstract work. Their task was not only to disabuse young people with little knowledge of art history, but to counter the arguments of more formidable opponents.[97] A 'Party member since 1929' noted in the visitors' book that there were also self-appointed tour guides, whom he presumed to be students from Moscow institutes. They were always to be found near the Polish pictures, defending modernist art. 'What does the Moscow Komsomol Committee think of this?' he mused ominously.[98] Gallery staff, likewise, observed that the disputes that raged in front of the abstract works of Marczyński, Taranczewski and Chrostowska were invariably instigated by a small set of visitors, mainly students, who came daily to the exhibitions specially prepared with books, notes and reproductions, to passionately 'defend and propagandize abstract art'. 'These well-educated viewers demagogically exploit their knowledge of art history, aesthetics and philosophy to attract some of the visitors unfamiliar with these questions.' Some of these young men were identified as sons of prominent cultural figures such as the composer Bogoslavskii and director Vasil'ev.[99] They were, in other words, gilded youth from the upper echelons of the intelligentsia. This stereotype of the supporters of Polish modernism appears to have been widespread. Modernizers' attempts at innovation were routinely discredited by being conflated with the Westernized affectations in dress and behaviour of the *stiliagi*, the most prominent youth counterculture of the time. The emergence of the *stiliagi* in the post-war period, symptomatic of the process of social differentiation, was a source of much anxiety. They were constantly reviled in the press as a decadent, anti-Soviet 'social virus'.[100] One viewer, endorsing the preceding commentator's praise for Dunikowski, felt compelled to disclaim, 'I am not a *stiliaga* but I welcome and share your views on contemporary art.'[101] An article commissioned to dispel public fascination with the Polish display echoed the accusations made in the visitors' book and report. Entitled 'Abstract Painting and Pea Jackets', it insinuated that supporters of Polish modernism had sold their souls to the bourgeoisie to promote abstract art in return for 'far from abstract money'.

> There are always a lot of people in the Polish section arguing till hoarse, old and young, like debating clubs. But if you look closely you see, at the centre of each circle of

viewers, a young person dressed with cultivated nonchalance in a wide-shouldered, pea-green bouclé jacket with yellow spots; around his neck a less-than-clean silk cravat . . . Many have a beard like Levitan and a long nail on the little finger. They walk around stone-faced until they draw someone into an argument when they immediately turn into ardent propagandists of the 'new' art.

Thus characterizing them by their sartorial choices and comportment, the author type-cast the amateur guides as pretentious intellectuals who preyed on the innocence and susceptibility of young girls, one of whom reportedly exclaimed, 'I was blind but they have opened my eyes!' Echoing the Party veteran cited above, the author warned that this was a matter for the Komsomol to investigate, and called for active, communist counter-propaganda against these snobbish slaves to Western fashion and stooges of capitalism.[102]

The need to accommodate viewers' responses appears also, however, to have brought some concessions, advancing the cause of liberalization and greater freedom of information for which art-world reformers had pressed since the beginning of the Thaw. The administration of the Central Exhibition Hall supported viewers' proposals that modernist art be resurrected from museum basements; it was time to expose the history and origins of abstraction from the position of Marxism-Leninism. If the early twentieth-century Russian avant-garde's experiments in abstraction were shown to the Soviet people, they reasoned, this would corroborate the arguments of art historians that abstraction was a stage Russian art had long put behind it and had no need to repeat. In response to viewers' demands, exhibition guides (many of them advanced art students and professional art historians seconded from Moscow museums) were trained in the history and origins of abstract art by respected art historians. The administration also supported viewers' proposals that articles on abstract art should be printed, especially in publications for young people, who were clearly the most susceptible to the blandishments of Polish modernism.[103] If alien influences could no longer be suppressed, as under Stalin, they must be exposed in a controlled way, mediated by ideologically correct explanations: thus, the Soviet art press juxtaposed articles about the exhibition with articles unmasking the anti-rational, anti-humanist premises of abstraction.[104] This was part of a new strategy adopted in the Thaw and continued under Brezhnev. While the parameters of public discourse about art were still controlled, it was able to rise to a more informed and sophisticated level. Since the uses and meanings readers and viewers made of the new information proved impossible to predetermine – they might, for example, read critiques of abstraction against the grain – it also fuelled the formation of alternative and dissident communities of knowledge and understanding.

Many embraced the exhibition as a whole, and the Polish section in particular, as a seemingly sanctioned invitation to think critically and formulate their own positions on art. As Professor Teisseyre proposed at the formal discussion, it was the exhibition's great achievement that it engendered real debate among the audience.[105] In addition to the lively disputes in front of the works, especially Marczyński's, a kind of virtual discussion opened up within the visitors' books. Writers would respond to preceding comments, often to take issue, but sometimes with the euphoric recognition that they were not alone in their enthusiasm for what was only recently taboo. Although this dialogue was hindered, as one visitor objected, by the administration's practice of periodically removing the filled pages,[106] the visitors' books provided a space for an informal and surprisingly outspoken exchange of opinions such as could not appear in print.

Popular engagement with the exhibition, especially with the Polish display made a vital contribution to the process of maturation and differentiation of the Soviet audience. At a time when Khrushchev and other modernizers were in the ascendant in the Party, from 1959 to 1962, and were promising an enhanced role for popular initiative and participatory government, popular engagement of this kind could only assist the cause of artistic destalinization.[107] The argument that 'the aesthetic demands of the Soviet people' had matured significantly since socialist realism's inception in the 1930s was one of the legitimating premises of the contemporary style from the start.[108] Reformist critics such as Dmitrieva, Kamenskii, and Vladimir Kostin regarded the education of the viewer as an essential step towards official acceptance of the more metaphorical, synthetic and expressive form of realism they advocated. They insisted that the commandment that art be comprehensible to the people must be rethought in terms that both stressed the need for visual literacy – for 'to be a viewer is an art' – and placed an obligation on the viewer actively to engage with the work of art in the production of meaning, almost as a co-author.[109] This mutual relationship presupposed greater trust in the people's artistic and political judgement, a position the Party itself espoused as its official line from 1961, although it failed to apply it consistently in practice: 'It is necessary to trust the Soviet people, Soviet youth; it is necessary to entrust them more with . . . aesthetic evaluations, to put an end to the prejudiced mistrust and suspicion nourished at one time on the soil of the Personality Cult!'[110]

Exposure to the art of fraternal socialist countries, and especially to modernist tendencies from within the camp, contributed, then, to the central cultural processes of destalinization. By the time of the Twenty-Second Party Congress in 1961, the apogee of Khrushchevist populism, some elements of Soviet society had grown appreciably more open towards unfamiliar and 'difficult' styles. This was demonstrated in responses to the 1961 *All-Union Art Exhibition*, where the selection, hanging and lighting were all subjected to discerning popular critique.[111] Not only were the public more aesthetically sophisticated. So, too, were some of the ruling elite; contact with foreign cultures expanded their horizons and prepared them to endorse gradual innovations at home.[112] The diversity of socialist realism was enshrined in Khrushchev's new Party Programme in 1961.[113] In the backlash against the cultural Thaw that took place after 1962, the French revisionist Roger Garaudy's thesis of *Realism Without Shores* (1963) was temporarily blacklisted, and to the very last days of the Soviet empire, conservatives continued to rail against the heretical conception of 'realism as a rubber sack'.[114] Nevertheless, in the Brezhnevite 1970s, 'diversity,' 'complexity' and the concept of 'realism as an open system' became central tenets of liberal aesthetics.[115] Under Brezhnev, too, the existence of differentiated constituencies demanding different kinds of art, which had taken shape in response to the exhibition *Art of Socialist Countries*, was tacitly institutionalized.

Notes

1 Iurii Gerchuk, 'Iskusstvo "ottepeli" v poiskakh stilia', *Tvorchestvo,* no. 6 (1991) p. 28.

2 K. Sitnik, 'Vysokie traditsii. (Zametki o vystavke frantsuzskogo iskusstva)', *Iskusstvo,* no. 3 (1956), p. 40; and A. Pavlov, 'Novaia ekspozitsiia Muzeia izobrazitel'nogo iskusstva imeni A.S. Pushkina', *Iskusstvo,* no. 3 (1954) p. 76.

3 *Drugoe iskusstvo. Moskva 1956–76* (Moscow: Moskovskaia kollektsiia 1991).

4 A. Kamenskii, 'Razmyshleniia na festival'noi vystavke', *Moskovskii khudozhnik* (30 Aug 1957) p. 3.

5 Pavel Nikonov, 'Nemnogo o sebe', in *Pavel Nikonov,* exh. cat. (Moscow: Sovetskii khudozhnik, 1990) p. 69.

6 Compare Katerina Clark, *The Soviet Novel: History as Ritual* (Chicago: University of Chicago Press, 1985) p. 222.

7 L. Bubnova, 'V poiskakh ostrogo sovremennogo vyrazheniia,' *Moskovskii khudozhnik,* no. 15 (15 Aug 1958) p. 2.

8 N. Dmitrieva, 'K voprosu o sovremennom stile v zhivopisi', *Tvorchestvo,* no. 6 (1958) pp. 9–12; Editorial, 'Cherty sovremennogo stilia', *Tvorchestvo,* no. 10 (1958) p. 8; and 'Zerkalo epokhi. K diskussii o stile', *Tvorchestvo,* no. 12 (1959) pp. 9–11. See also B. Vipper, 'Neskol'ko tezisov k probleme stilia', *Tvorchestvo,* no. 9 (1962) pp. 11–12; and Iurii Gerchuk, 'Iskusstvo "ottepeli". 1954–1964', *Voprosy iskusstvoznaniia,* vol. 8, no. 1 (1996) p. 56. For more detail see my dissertation: Susan E. Reid, *Destalinization and the Remodernization of Soviet Art: The Search for a Contemporary Realism, 1953–1963*, Ph.D. diss., University of Pennsylvania, 1996.

9 Dmitrieva, 'K voprosu', p. 9; Aleksei Gastev, 'Dvizhenie k stil'iu', *Literaturnaia gazeta* (16 July 1960).

10 G. Nedoshivin, '40 let sovetskogo iskusstva', *Tvorchestvo,* no. 11 (1957) p. 6; and G. Nedoshivin 'Oshibochnaia kontseptsiia', *Tvorchestvo,* no. 5 (1959) p. 14. Contributions to the debate were translated and published in journals in the fraternal countries: 'Zerkalo epokhi', p. 9.

11 Iurii Nagibin, 'Chto sovremenno?' *Literaturnaia gazeta* (3 Dec 1960) p. 4. An exhibition of Pablo Picasso in the Pushkin Museum, Moscow 1956, organized by Il'ia Erenburg, was a formative cultural event. Vladimir Slepian, 'The Young vs. the Old', *Problems of Communism* (May–June 1962) pp. 56–7; and Igor Golomshtok, 'Unofficial Art in the Soviet Union,' in I. Golomshtok and A. Glezer, *Soviet Art in Exile* (New York: Random House, 1977) p. 89.

12 B. Sursis, 'Iskusstvo pol'skogo naroda,' *Iskusstvo,* no. 5 (1952), p. 20; Antoine Baudin, '"Why is Soviet Painting Hidden from Us?" Zhdanov Art and Its International Relations and Fallout, 1947–53', *South Atlantic Quarterly,* vol. 94, no. 3 (Summer 1995) p. 897.

13 Wolfgang Hütt, 'Realismus und Modernität. Impulsive Gedanken über ein notwendiges Thema,' *Bildende Kunst,* no. 10 (1956) p. 565; Martin Damus, *Malerei der DDR: Funktionen der bildenden Kunst im Realen Sozialismus,* (Hamburg: Rowohlt, 1991) p. 142.

14 I. Golomshtok, 'Vystavka nemetskoi grafiki,' *Moskovskii khudozhnik,* no. 14 (30 July 1958).

15 Dmitrieva, 'K voprosu', p. 10.

16 For example, G. Nisskii, 'Poiski formy,' *Moskovskii komsomolets* (9 April 1960) p. 4; Gastev, 'Dvizhenie k stil'iu'; and V. Turbin, *Tovarishch vremia i tovarishch iskusstvo* (Moscow: Iskusstvo, 1961).

17 Only on the pretext of a critique of modernism was any exploration of its relation to the contemporary style possible in the Soviet press, for example A. Kantor, 'O sovremennosti v iskusstve', *Iskusstvo,* no. 4 (1960) pp. 35–42.

18 'Khudozhniki obsuzhdaiut tezisy doklada N.S. Khrushcheva', *Moskovskii khudozhnik,* no. 22 (15 Dec 1958) p. 4. For objections to this position see A. Metchenko, 'Sotsialisticheskii realizm: rasshiriaiushchiesia vozmozhnosti i teoreticheskie spory', *Oktiabr',* no. 4 (1976) pp. 182–3.

19 D. A. Shmarinov (interview), *Moskovskii khudozhnik,* no. 22 (15 Dec 1958); Editorial, 'K novym uspekham sotsialisticheskogo realizma. Na pervom uchreditel'nom s'ezde khudozhnikov Russkoi Federatsii', *Iskusstvo,* no. 8 (1960) pp. 4–7.

20 See W. E. Griffith, 'The Decline and Fall of Revisionism in Eastern Europe', in L. Labedz, ed., *Revisionism: Essays on the History of Marxist Ideas* (London: George Allen & Unwin, 1962), p. 224; Vladimir Kusin, 'An Overview of East European Reformism', *Soviet Studies,* vol. 287, no. 3 (July, 1976) pp. 338–61.

21 'Ob usilenii politicheskoi raboty' (Dec 1956), cited by E. Iu. Zubkovo, *Obshchestvo i reformy, 1945–1964* (Moscow: Rossiia molodaia, 1993) pp. 154–5.

22 Carl A. Linden, *Khrushchev and the Soviet Leadership, 1957–1964* (Baltimore: The Johns Hopkins Press, 1966) pp. 56–7.

23 V. Skatershchikov, 'Krestovyi pokhod revizionistov protiv realizma', *Iskusstvo,* no. 8 (1958) pp. 5–8. N. Parsadanov condemned Henri Lefèbvre for charging that socialist realism mechanically appropriated the traditions of the past: N. Parsadanov, 'O novatorstve podlinnom i mnimom', *Tvorchestvo,* no. 11 (1958) p. 12.

24 'Zadachi khudozhestvennoi kritiki', *Tvorchestvo,* no. 12 (1959) p. 2; and M. Ovsiannikov, 'Problema sovremennosti v iskusstve – problema politicheskaia', *Khudozhnik,* no. 9 (1959) p. 2.

25 Skatershchikov, 'Krestovyi pokhod', pp. 6–7. Revisionist concepts of expression were also critiqued by O. Sopotsinskii, 'O vyrazitel'nosti podlinnoi i mnimoi', *Iskusstvo,* no. 10 (1959).

26 'Teoriiu blizhe k praktike!' *Iskusstvo,* no. 9 (1958) p. 4. A conference 'Against Contemporary Revisionism in Art and Art History' was held on the eve of the opening, 22–23 Dec 1958: RGALI (Russian State Archive for Literature and Art), f. 2465, op. 1, ed. khr. 354–7; and a vicious attack on revisionism appeared in *Literaturnaia gazeta* (28 Dec 1958).

27 RGALI f. 2329, op. 4, ed. khr. 994, ll. 19, 47 (planning meetings for exhibition *Art of Socialist Countries,* 25 Feb–30 Mar 1958).

28 RGALI f. 2329, op. 4, ed. khr. 994, ll. 9, 14; RGALI f. 2329, op. 4, ed. khr. 998, l. 16 (meeting of exhibition committee, 22 Dec 1958); and RGALI f. 2329, op. 4, ed. khr. 999, ll. 21–22 (documents on organization of exhibition *Art of Socialist Countries*). The allocation of space was also to be 'democratic'. In the event, a single catalogue was published in Moscow in an edition of 10,000, compiled from materials provided by the participating countries. E.S. Melikadze, ed., *Vystavka proizvedenii izobrazitel'nogo iskusstva sotsialist-icheskikh stran. Katalog* (Moscow: Sovetskii khudozhnik, 1958).

29 On self-censorship see Miklós Haraszti, *The Velvet Prison: Artists under State Socialism* (New York: Basic Books, 1987).

30 RGALI f. 2329, op. 4, ed. khr. 994, ll. 4, 12.

31 RGALI f. 2329, op. 4, ed. khr. 994, l. 3; and compare Karel Pokorny, 'Edinstvo i druzhba!' *Iskusstvo,* no. 12 (1958), reprinted in *Khudozhnik i sovremennost',* (Moscow: AKh SSSR, 1960) p. 108.

32 S. V. Gerasimov, 'Iskusstvo stran sotsializma', *Tvorchestvo,* no. 12 (1958) p. 1. A total of 2945 works were shown, including 799 painting, 527 sculpture, 1472 graphics and 147 examples of applied arts. RGALI f. 2329, op. 4, ed. khr. 998, l. 16.

33 S. Gerasimov, 'Otchetno-vybornoe sobranie MOSSKha,' *Moskovskii khud-ozhnik*, no. 1 (Jan 1959).

34 RGALI f. 2329, op. 4, ed. khr. 999, l. 21.

35 Iu. Kolpinskii, 'Khudozhniki dvenadsati stran,' *Iskusstvo*, no. 6 (1959) p. 13.

36 RGALI f. 2329, op. 4, ed. khr. 1000, l. 5 (N. A. Mikhailov, USSR Minister of Culture, speech at opening of exhibition, 26 Dec 1958); Melikadze, *Vystavka* (n.p.); and RGALI f. 2943, op. 1, ed. khr. 2978, l. 1 (protocol of meeting of criticism section of MOSKh, 13 Nov 1959).

37 Iu. Kolpinskii, 'Edinstvo sotsialisticheskogo metoda i mnogoobrazie natsional'-nykh form', *Sovetskaia kul'tura* (15 Jan 1959); Kolpinskii, 'Khudozhniki,' 13; N. Zhukov, 'Iskusstvo i sovremennost'. Razdum'ia na vystavke', *Literaturnaia gazeta* (17 Jan 1959); and RGALI f. 2329, op. 4, ed. khr. 999, l. 63. The 'diversity' of socialist realism was the line taken at the Second and Third Congresses of Soviet Writers in 1954 and 1959 respectively. See V. Shcherbina, 'Preds'ezdovskaia tribuna. O khudozhestvennom raznoobrazii', *Literaturnaia gazeta* (14 Oct 1958). On the significance of the concept of diversity or multiplicity for official art see also D. Sarab'ianov, 'K voprosu o tvorcheskom mnogoobrazii sovetskogo iskusstva,' *Voprosy estetiki*, vol. 3 (Moscow, 1960) pp. 25–45; and A. Morozov, *Aspekty istorii sovetskogo izobrazitel'nogo iskusstva, 1960–1980-kh godov, Avtoreferat*, (Moscow State University, 1988).

38 N. Iavorskaia, 'Poiski vyrazitel'nosti', *Tvorchestvo*, no. 3 (Jan 1959) p. 11; Kolpinskii, 'Khudozhniki,' p. 14; Sergei Gerasimov, 'Otchetno-vybornoe sobranie MOSSKha', *Moskovskii khudozhnik*, no. 1 (Jan. 1959); and 'Iskusstvo i deistvitel'nost'. Obsuzhdenie vystavki proizvedenii izobrazitel'nogo iskusstva sotsialisticheskikh stran', *Tvorchestvo*, no. 5 (1959) p. 2.

39 Iavorskaia, 'Poiski', p. 10.

40 Dmitrieva, 'K voprosu', p. 10; Zhukov, 'Iskusstvo'; and RGALI f. 2329, op. 4, ed. khr. 1005, ll. 26–9.

41 RGALI f. 2329, op. 4, ed. khr. 1000, l. 10.

42 Ion Zhalia, 'Fakel gumanizma v iskusstve', *Moskovskii khudozhnik*, nos. 23–24 (25 Dec 1958), p. 5.

43 RGALI f. 2329, op. 4, ed. khr. 997, ll. 13–19 (meeting of exhibition committee of Soviet section); E.S. Melikadze, ed., *Vystavka proizvedenii izobrazitel'nogo iskusstva sotsialisticheskikh stran. Katalog* (Moscow: Sovetskii khudozhnik, 1958–9). A very similar selection was made for exhibitions sent abroad, for example to the Royal Academy, London, in 1959: see 'Russian and Soviet Painting at the Royal Academy', *The Studio*, vol. 157 (April 1959) pp. 115–8; and see N. Malakhov, *Otechestvennoe iskusstvo na vystavkakh za rubezhom* (Moscow: Izobrazitel'noe iskusstvo, 1980).

44 RGALI f. 2329, op. 4, ed. khr. 996, l. 9. Recent stylistic innovations associated with the contemporary style were represented only by a few relatively

unproblematic tokens which doubled up as representatives of the national republics, such as Azerbaijani Tair Salakhov's *To the Watch,* and Latvian Edgar Iltner's *The Men Return,* 1958. RGALI f. 2329, op. 4, ed. khr. 885 (provisional list of Soviet exhibits).

45 RGALI f. 2329, op. 4, ed. khr. 1005, ll. 67–9.

46 RGALI f. 2329, op. 4, ed. khr. 1005, l. 20.

47 Skatershchikov accused the East German journal *Bildende Kunst* of declaring expressionism the true realism of contemporaneity: 'Krestovyi pokhod', p. 6.

48 Iavorskaia, 'Poiski vyrazitel'nosti', p. 11.

49 Nedoshivin, 'Oshibochnaia kontseptsiia', p. 15; and 'Iskusstvo i deistvitel'nost', *Tvorchestvo,* no. 5 (1959) p. 2.

50 Kolpinskii, 'Khudozhniki', p. 15. On art in the GDR see Damus, *Malerei der DDR*; and Gerhard Pommeranz Liedtke, 'New Ways in German Art: the situation and prospects in the German Democratic Republic', *The Studio,* vol. 127, no. 790 (Jan 1959) pp. 1–11.

51 A. Tikhomirov, 'Iskusstvo 12 stran', *Ogonek,* no. 6 (1959) p. 16.

52 Iavorskaia, 'Poiski', p. 9.

53 RGALI f. 2329, op. 4, ed. khr. 1001, ll. 24–25.

54 Nina Juviler, 'Art and Artists in the USSR. Forbidden Fruit', *Problems of Communism,* vol. 11, no. 3 (May–June 1962) p. 51.

55 RGALI f. 2329, op. 4, ed. khr. 999, ll. 12–16 (draft). Lebedev was an indefatigable foe of liberalization. See A. Lebedev, 'Slovo s pred's'ezdovskoi tribuny', *Iskusstvo,* no. 6 (1956) pp. 7–8.

56 RGALI f. 2329, op. 4, ed. khr. 999, l. 18.

57 Hungarian delegate Nora Aradi took a conciliatory line at the discussion, condemning the emergence of revisionist, subjectivist aesthetics in the 1956 'counter-revolution'. RGALI f. 2329, op. 4, ed. khr. 1005, l. 11.

58 Piotr Piotrowski, 'The "Thaw"', in Piotrowski, ed., *Odwilż: sztuka ok. 1956 r.,* (Poznań: Muzeum Narodowe, 1996) p. 244.

59 RGALI f. 2329, op. 4, ed. khr. 1000, l. 7.

60 Interview with Stefan Staszewski, in Teresa Toranska, *'Them': Stalin's Polish Puppets,* transl. A. Kolakowska (New York: Harper & Row, 1987) p. 191. Kolakowski's essay was published in *Nowa kultura* (22 Sep 1957); see K. Reyman and H. Singer, 'The Origins and Significance of East European Revisionism', in Labedz, *Revisionism,* p. 216.

61 Toranska, *Them,* p. 141.

62 Maurice Hindus, *House Without a Roof: Russia after Forty-three Years of Revolution* (London: Victor Gollancz, 1962) p. 511.

63 A. Gozenpud, 'O neverii v cheloveka, o nigilizme i "filosofii" otchaianiia', *Zvezda* (July 1958) pp. 195–214. The article on Adler appeared in *Przekrój* no. 653 (13 Oct 1957).

64 Hindus, *House,* pp. 510–12.

65 Piotrowski, 'The "Thaw"', p. 243.

66 The selection differed significantly from those presented to Western audiences, eg. Aleksander Wojciechowski, 'Polish Art: the younger figurative painters', *The Studio,* vol. 157 (Feb 1959) pp. 33–41; Juliusz Starzyński, 'Quatre peintres polonais d'aujourd'hui', *Quadrum,* no. 7 (1960) pp. 123–34; and Peter Selz, *15 Polish Painters,* exh. cat. (New York, MOMA, 1961).

67 RGALI f. 2329, op. 4, ed. khr. 1001, ll. 42–3.

68 See Selz, *15 Polish Painters,* p. 2; and Piotrowski, 'The "Thaw"', p. 244. Eibisch had openly opposed the imposition of socialist realism in Poland: Toranska, *Them,* p. 141.

69 RGALI f. 2329, op. 4, ed. khr. 1005, ll. 22–3.

70 Tikhomirov, 'Iskusstvo 12 stran.'

71 RGALI f. 2329, op. 4, ed. khr. 1000, ll. 35, 41; and RGALI f. 2329, op. 4, ed. khr. 1001, ll. 44–5.

72 Kolpinskii, 'Khudozhniki dvenadtsati stran', p. 14.

73 RGALI f. 2329, op. 4, ed. khr. 1005, ll. 43.

74 Tikhomirov, 'Iskusstvo 12 stran'; Zhukov, 'Iskusstvo i sovremennost''.

75 Iavorskaia, 'Poiski vyrazitel'nosti', p. 8.

76 RGALI f. 2329, op. 4, ed. khr. 1005, ll. 38–48; 'Iskusstvo i deistvitel'nost'', pp. 3–4; and compare Piotrowski, 'The "Thaw"', p. 243.

77 RGALI f. 2329, op. 4, ed. khr. 1005, l. 72.

78 RGALI f. 2329, op. 4, ed. khr. 1001, l. 45; and 'Iskusstvo i deistvitel'nost'', p. 3. Starzyński's speech is missing from the archive file of the discussion, perhaps extracted for KGB scrutiny: RGALI f. 2329, op. 4, ed. khr. 1005.

79 RGALI f. 2329, op. 4, ed. khr. 1005, ll. 38–48.

80 Tikhomirov, 'Iskusstvo,' 16; Zhukov, 'Iskusstvo.'

81 RGALI f. 2329, op. 4, ed. khr. 1003, l. 6.

82 RGALI f. 2329, op. 4, ed. khr. 998, l. 17.

83 Juviler, 'Art and Artists', p. 51.

84 RGALI f. 2329, op. 4, ed. khr. 1002, l. 77 (general visitors' book for *Art of Socialist Countries,* 27 Dec 1958–22 Mar 1959); and RGALI f. 2329, op. 4, ed. khr. 1003, l. 12 (visitors' book for Polish section, Jan–Feb 1959).

85 For further detail see Susan E. Reid, 'De-Stalinisation in the Moscow Art Profession,' in Ian Thatcher, ed., *Regime and Society in Twentieth-Century Russia* (Basingstoke: Macmillan, 1999), pp. 146–84; and Susan E. Reid, 'Destalinization and Taste, 1953–1963,' *Journal of Design History,* vol. 10, no. 2 (Spring 1997) pp. 177–201.

86 The exhibition was popularized by radio, television and short documentary films, as well as through journal articles and reproductions. RGALI f. 2329, op. 4, ed. khr. 1000, l. 51.

87 RGALI f. 2329, op. 4, ed. khr. 1002, ll. 4, 26; and RGALI f. 2329, op. 4, ed. khr. 1003, l. 6.

88 RGALI f. 2329, op. 4, ed. khr. 1003, l. 27.

89 RGALI f. 2329, op. 4, ed. khr. 1000, l. 22-29; RGALI f. 2329, op. 4, ed. khr. 1003, l. 24, 4; and RGALI f. 2329, op. 4, ed. khr. 1002, l. 85.

90 RGALI f. 2329, op. 4, ed. khr. 1002, l. 50.

91 RGALI f. 2329, op. 4, ed. khr. 1000, l. 32; RGALI f. 2329, op. 4, ed. khr. 1003, l. 28, 17, 8; and RGALI f. 2329, op. 4, ed. khr. 1002, l. 23.

92 RGALI f. 2329, op. 4, ed. khr. 1003, l. 18, 1; and RGALI f. 2329, op. 4, ed. khr. 1002, l. 22.

93 RGALI f. 2329, op. 4, ed. khr. 1003, l. 34, 12, 9-10, 4, 14, 16, 5.

94 RGALI f. 2329, op. 4, ed. khr. 1003, l. 37, 44, 20, 22.

95 RGALI f. 2329, op. 4, ed. khr. 1003, l. 2, 32; RGALI f. 2329, op. 4, ed. khr. 1002, l. 9, 13, 30, 46-7, 71; and RGALI f. 2329, op. 4, ed. khr. 1001, l. 48.

96 RGALI f. 2329, op. 4, ed. khr. 1001 (gallery report on conduct of the exhibition, 19 May 1959).

97 RGALI f. 2329, op. 4, ed. khr. 1001, ll. 3–4.

98 RGALI f. 2329, op. 4, ed. khr. 1002, l. 72.

99 RGALI f. 2329, op. 4, ed. khr. 1001, l. 47.

100 For example, I. Gorin, 'Zhivopis', skul'ptura i grafika na stranitsakh zhurnala "Iunost'", *Iskusstvo,* no. 8 (1962) p. 74. See also Zubkovo, *Obshchestvo i reformy,* p. 150.

101 RGALI f. 2329, op. 4, ed. khr. 1003: ll. 9–10.

102 RGALI f. 2329, op. 4, ed. khr. 1000, ll. 33-36 (typescript of article by V. Larionov, 'Abstract painting and pea jackets').

103 RGALI f. 2329, op. 4, ed. khr. 1001, l. 48.

104 An article by Igor Golomshtok, '"Otrkytiie" tashizma', unmasking abstract expressionism and *tachisme,* was printed immediately after N. Voronov's article on the exhibition in *Tvorchestvo,* no. 9 (1959) pp. 23–4. See also V. Prokof'ev, 'Chto takoe siurrealizm?' *Tvorchestvo,* no. 7 (1959) pp. 23–4, which was preceded by an editorial explanation that the journal received many letters requesting information about Western art; and S. Mozhniagun, 'Estetika abstraktsionizma porochna', *Iskusstvo,* no. 9 (1958) pp. 13–18. The need for serious art-historical analysis of contemporary capitalist art was emphasized by an editorial, 'Khudozhestvennoi kritike - neoslablennoe vnimanie!' *Iskusstvo,* no. 12 (1959) p. 6.

105 RGALI f. 2329, op. 4, ed. khr. 1005, ll. 67-9; RGALI f. 2329, op. 4, ed. khr. 1003, l. 4,12; and RGALI f. 2329, op. 4, ed. khr. 1002, l. 15.

106 RGALI f. 2329, op. 4, ed. khr. 1003, l. 34.

107 Editorial, 'Kommunizm i iskusstvo', *Kommunist,* no. 8 (1961) pp. 3–10.

108 'Zerkalo epokhi', pp. 9–11.

109 A. Kamenskii, *Zriteliu ob iskusstve* (Moscow, 1959); Ernst Neizvestnyi, 'Otkryvat' novoe!' *Iskusstvo,* no. 10 (1962) pp. 9–10; and V. Kostin, *Iazyk izobrazitel'nogo iskusstva* (Moscow: Znanie, 1965), p. 3. See Reid, 'Destalinization and Taste.'

110 I. Matsa, 'O zhivykh traditsiiakh v sovetskoi zhivopisi', *Tvorchestvo,* no. 8 (1962) p. 7; and O. Roitenberg, 'Chitateliu nado doveriat'', *Tvorchestvo,* no. 1 (1963) pp. 18–19.

111 RGALI f. 2329, op. 4, ed. khr. 1375 (visitors' book for RSFSR section of *All-Union Art Exhibition,* 1961).

112 Even within the fundamentally conservative USSR Academy of Arts, 'As early as the Khrushchev period, "modernists", subtly shadowing the changing tastes of the Party elite, were beginning to emerge in official painting.' K. Kor, 'Jubilee Reflections on the Academy of Arts', *A-Ya,* no. 7 (1986) p. 56.

113 G. Hodnett, ed., *Resolutions and Decisions of the Communist Party of the Soviet Union,* vol. 4 (University of Toronto Press, 1974), p. 256; and see D. Sarab'ianov, 'K voprosu o tvorcheskom mnogoobrazii sovetskogo iskusstva', *Voprosy estetiki,* vol. 3 (1960) pp. 25–45; and A. Mikhailov, 'Mnogoobrazie v iskusstve sotsialisticheskogo realizma', *Kommunist,* no. 7 (1964) pp. 86–96.

114 B. V. Vishniakov, 'Ob odnoi kontseptsii iskusstva 1960–1980-kh godov', *Puti tvorchestva i kritika* (Moscow: Izobrazitel'noe iskusstvo, 1990), p. 13; Jochen-Ulrich Peters, 'Réalisme sans rivages? Zur diskussion über den sozialistichen Realismus in der Sowjetunion seit 1956,' *Zeitschrift für slavische Philologie,* vol. 37 (1974) pp. 291–324.

115 Morozov, *Aspekty istorii*; Metchenko, 'Sotsialisticheskii realizm'; D. Markov, *Problemy teorii sotsialisticheskogo realizma* (Moscow, 1978). Prominent art historians under Brezhnev elaborated an inclusive international 'revolutionary style'. G. Nedoshivin, *Teoreticheskie problemy sovremennogo izobrazitel'-nogo iskusstva* (Moscow, 1972), pp. 123–4; A. Morozov, 'Sovetskoe iskusstvo 60-kh godov i opyt "novogo realizma"', *Sovetskoe iskusstvoznanie,* vol. 25 (Moscow: Sovetskii khudozhnik, 1989) pp. 42–3; and compare Richard Hiepe, *Die Kunst der neuen Klasse* (Vienna: C. Bertelsmann Verlag, 1973), published in Russian as *Iskusstvo novogo klassa* (Moscow: Progress, 1978).

−7−

Modernism and Socialist Culture: Polish Art in the Late 1950s
Piotr Piotrowski

The changes that followed Khrushchev's 'secret speech' in February 1956 were not experienced synchronously in Eastern and Central Europe. Destalinization, or what was known as 'the Thaw', took on quite different faces in each Central European country both in terms of politics and culture. In Romania and the German Democratic Republic only a few people at the very top of the Party knew about Khrushchev's 'secret speech', whereas in Poland it was distributed like a bestseller warning of an impending political earthquake. In fact, the political and cultural tremors were felt very rapidly. After street demonstrations and shootings in Poznań in June, Władysław Gomułka seized power in October 1956. As a pre-war communist and legendary prisoner of the Stalinist regime, Gomułka embodied the workers' and intellectuals' hope for a better future and, during the early years of his rule – the late 1950s, he fulfilled (more or less) such expectations. Poland at that time experienced a wide range of Western and modernizing influences. In comparison with other countries in the Soviet bloc, art and culture, philosophy and literature were relatively free there.[1] In Hungary, the period after the Uprising in 1956 until the mid-1960s was one of police repression and cultural depression. In Czechoslovakia, political reforms began to be introduced from around 1963. They were preceded, however, by a revival of forms of modernist culture (albeit one experienced not in the public sphere but in private studios as exemplified in the two famous 1960 Prague exhibitions of art, *Confrontations*). In Romania a limited kind of political and cultural Thaw began in 1965. It was led, paradoxically, by Nicolae Ceauşescu, who later became a bloody dictator. In contrast, the Thaw failed to take hold in Bulgaria and the GDR: instead, these countries experienced what might be described as 'Stalinist destalinization.'[2]

It would seem that Poland after 1956 was in a unique situation. Here the Thaw in art and culture, and in the visual arts in particular, began earlier than in the other Central European countries. Moreover, it did not have a dissident or alternative character. It is true that the 'freedoms' of the Thaw allowed hitherto proscribed conceptions of modernist art and its role to be discussed, but abstraction in painting and other forms of modernist practice cannot be neatly characterized as oppositional.

The Thaw, I will suggest, marked the demise of the Polish *avant garde* and the triumph of modernism if these two terms, as they have functioned in European and American culture since the 1930s, can be treated antithetically.[3] In Poland, the tension between the tradition of the avant-garde and modernism had appeared already in the 1930s and resurfaced in the post-war decades. In general terms, I define the avant-garde as an approach which aims at situating art in the context of reality and, by various means as well as for various ideological reasons, tries to overcome those barriers that separate art from events and circumstances beyond the walls of the museum and gallery. From this perspective we can distinguish a number of variants: utopian art practices such as Soviet constructivism and productivism in the 1920s; critical art practices such as Berlin dadaism; as well as transgressive art practices such as French surrealism which interpreted the crossing of the boundaries of consciousness in terms of social revolution. By contrast, modernism, as a concept, refers to the tendency to separate art from everyday social and political practice: it proclaims autonomous art as that which finds its place in reality by following the principle of independence, though not necessarily of isolation. In fact, autonomy becomes a form of 'engagement' in the processes constituting modern civilization. Polish debates and the ascending currents within art practice during and after the Thaw confirmed the tendency towards the autonomy of modern art, understanding 'commitment' in a peculiarly modernist way that was neither utopian nor critical but could be taken as 'commitment' to modern civilization in general terms of progress, freedom, etc.[4] Modernism, in this context, can be understood as a retreat from the political engagement of the historic avant-garde. As this chapter demonstrates, in the late 1950s, modernism became an element of official cultural strategy and, as such, defined the future course of art in the People's Republic of Poland.

An Exhibition in Moscow

At the end of 1958, *The Art of Socialist Countries*, an exhibition of the art of twelve communist countries, opened in Moscow. In addition to the hosts, the artists of the Soviet Union, delegations from Albania, Bulgaria, China, Czechoslovakia, North Korea, Mongolia, the GDR, Romania, Hungary, Vietnam and Poland took part in the exhibition. Polish art was represented by a selection of art works prepared by a team under the supervision of Professor Juliusz Starzyński. However, the Polish section differed markedly from those representing the other 'people's democracies', a fact that, as Susan E. Reid records in her chapter in this book, appears to be the reason why it attracted an unusual level of curiosity on the part of visitors, artists and members of other delegations. In the opinion of many observers, the difference lay in the strong modernist character of these works, all the more conspicuous by being shown in the context of stylistically uniform socialist realist art of the other national expositions. Naturally, the ensuing tension was political rather than artistic. Thus the defensive position adopted by the chairman of the Polish delegation, Starzyński, in the face of criticism was drawn from political discourse:

> The art of twelve socialist countries shown at the exhibition in Moscow does not and cannot present a uniform picture. The reasons for this should be sought in history; in the various conditions of social and economic development which cause differences in consciousness and have influenced the present artistic situation in each country in specific ways.[5]

In other words, the chairman of the Polish delegation spoke for the right to pursue the 'national road to socialist culture', which, in this context, was to include the right to refer to the tradition of modern art. He claimed that art derives from a concrete material background, always conditioned by the social context in which it emerges and functions. Socialist culture did not, therefore, have to be uniform throughout the 'camp': on the contrary, it could not logically be so. Poland's development, Starzyński argued, was conditioned by its own traditions and needs, and this explained why contemporary Polish culture was different from that of other socialist countries. In the fervent discussions held in Moscow, the organisers of the Polish exhibition, using the phraseology derived from the so-called Marxist-Leninist philosophy of culture – the rhetorical somersaults that apparently should have convinced all of the legitimacy of the exhibition – failed to persuade the other delegates who upheld the orthodoxy that 'progressive' artists always express themselves in realistic forms, while all modernist art is nothing but reaction.[6]

The Moscow exhibition is introduced here as a *pars pro toto* of the complicated situation of Polish culture in the late 1950s both at home and abroad. It should be emphasized that the Polish exposition in Moscow was attacked for its modernism and, to make matters even worse, abstraction, incompatible with the doctrines of socialist realism. What is more, its organizers acted on an assumption that the art they should show in Moscow was, precisely, modernist art. However, both the organizers and the critics of the Polish display shared extremely subjective impressions: for actually it was not dominated by abstraction but by the painting of the so called colourists or post-impressionists, together with works displaying expressive or allusive forms of realism. If abstract art, the most contentious form of modernism (exemplified, for example, in the paintings of Adam Marczyński), was present at all, it only had a marginal place in the Polish selection. What is remarkable is that a single vein of modern art turned out to hold greatest interest for the Moscow audience (Figure 7.1). 'The number of viewers in the Polish department', according to its designer, Andrzej Pawłowski, 'was so large that on the second day after opening the exhibition to the public our Soviet consultant

Figure 7.1 Adam Marczyński, *Composition*, oil on canvas, 1957, 75.5 × 104 cms, National Museum in Poznań.

asked for a permission to place protective ropes around certain exhibits such as the paintings by Adam Marczyński.'[7] Of all the artistic styles exhibited at the Moscow exhibition (expressionist, post-impressionist, abstract, etc.), abstraction was identified by the audience and other participants to be the epitome of modern art. However, let me ask a question: would it have been possible for the Polish delegation to mount a display of socialist realism? I do not think so. In 1958 a complete return to the dominant poetics of the early 1950s was almost inconceivable in Poland. The course of political and cultural reform after Stalin's death in 1953 (including changes in the leadership of the Party in 1956) had acquired such force that it was irreversible. Thus communist authorities in the field of culture were forced not only to accept modernism but even to employ it as their own strategy as *The Art of Socialist Countries* exhibition in Moscow shows.

The Thaw in Poland

It is important to define the Thaw in terms of the historiography of Polish art.[8] In the literature on the subject and particularly in popular books dealing with the recent history of Polish art, destalinization is conventionally considered to have begun with the *National Exhibition of Young Art (Ogólnopolska Wystawa Młodej Plastyki)*, usually referred to as the *Arsenał*, which opened in Warsaw in July 1955. The *Arsenał* reflected a general mood of artistic freedom and the rejection of socialist realism. However, the work had more to do with a tradition of expressionism and social comment than with modernist practice as I will define it below. It is more accurate to identify the first expression of rigorous modernist tendencies in the *Exhibition of Pictures (Wystawa Obrazów)* held in the Artists's House on Łobzowska Street in Cracow in November 1955, commonly referred to as the 'Exhibition of the Nine' because of the number of participating painters (Tadeusz Brzozowski, Maria Jarema, Tadeusz Kantor, Jadwiga Maziarska, Kazimierz Mikulski, Jerzy Nowosielski, Erna Rosenstein, Jerzy Skarzyński and Jonasz Stern). The exposition was fairly small and its catalogue modest, yet its significance today seems enormous. It is here in Cracow, in that first public manifestation of modernist art after socialist realism, that one should locate the threshold of the Thaw in the visual arts. The paintings on display revived a current of artistic poetics exemplified in the so-called 'first' *Exhibition of Modern Art (Wystawa Sztuki Nowoczesnej)* held in Cracow between December 1948 and January 1949. Two subsequent exhibitions of modern art in Warsaw, the *Second* and *Third Exhibition of Modern Art* held in 1957 and 1959, as well as the celebrated *March Salons (Salony Marcowe)* at Zakopane had their roots in the 'Exhibition of the Nine.'[9]

The *Second Exhibition of Modern Art* (1957) is particularly noteworthy as it can be interpreted as the apogee of modernism during the Thaw. The size of the exhibition and the prestige of its participants, combined with distinct dominance of modernist poetics, made it the most significant manifestation of contemporary art on the Polish artistic scene of the late 1950s. The exhibition also provoked polemical disputes, of which the most crucial seems to have been the confrontation of two attitudes or traditions of Polish modernism, revealed in a debate between Mieczysław Porębski and Julian Przyboś. Porębski, a leading art historian, was closely involved in the promotion of modern art both in his role as co-editor of *Przegląd Artystyczny* and as organizer of exhibitions of contemporary art. In 1957 Przyboś published an article in a weekly, *Przegląd Kulturalny*, maliciously entitled 'Abstract art – how to get out of it?' (*Sztuka abstrakcyjna – jak z niej wyjść?*).[10] Przyboś, a poet closely connected to the Polish constructivist avant-garde of the 1920s and 1930s, argued for rigorous, deliberate and intellectual art that would be 'non-objective' rather than 'abstract'. Following the tradition of Kazimir Malevich and Piet Mondrian as well as the Poles, Władysław Strzemiński and Henryk Stażewski, he held a view of art based on the timeless language of construction, the idiom of the concrete, whereas, in abstraction, he perceived only a 'slovenliness' of composition that ignored the rules of representation as well as a superficial fascination with Western fads. Przyboś argued that Poland had developed its own modernist tradition: Polish constructivism had made an original contribution to modern artistic culture and as such should be an inspiration for contemporary art. His arguments were somewhat reinforced by the 1957 exhibition of the classic Polish avant-garde in the gallery of Denise Réné in Paris, *Précurseurs de l'art abstrait en Pologne*, which restated Polish achievements in the history of modern European art. Porębski's rejoinder, an article entitled 'How not to get out', claimed that the *tachiste* painting of the late 1950s was a manifestation of another generation, very different from the now classic idiom of constructivist art and, as such, it could not be just ignored in the artistic landscape of the present.[11]

Another participant in this discussion was Tadeusz Kantor, even though he did not address Przyboś and Porębski directly (Figure 7.2). A major figure in Polish culture in the post-war period, Kantor was a painter, writer and theatre director. Under an embargo issued by Stalinist authorities in the early 1950s, he had been refused opportunities to exhibit his art and made his living as a theatre designer in Cracow. One of the most outstanding advocates and practitioners of post-war modernism who advanced and adapted the *Informel* in Poland, he had been a visitor to the galleries and studios of existentialist Paris in 1947 and in 1955. His article entitled, 'Abstraction is Dead – Long Live Abstraction!' published in a supplement to *Zycie Literackie*, proved to be as significant as the statements by Przyboś and Porębski.[12] As if referring to Przyboś, he wrote that geometrical abstraction in the period of classic constructivism and the great movement of the transformation of artistic language ensued from the need to measure the world with the instrument of rationality. The intellect was the main tool by which man understands reality, and art must, therefore, became subject to the intellectual rigour of production.

Figure 7.2 Tadeusz Kantor, *Amarapura*, oil on canvas, 1957, 100 × 120 cms, , National Museum in Poznań.

He invoked the art of Mondrian as being particularly relevant in this early context. By the mid 1950s, however, after some decades of 'twentieth-century' experiences, intellect had not proven to be a sufficient instrument of knowledge. In the modern world there were many forces that transcended intellectual cognition, not; including the forces of the absurd, elementary energy, rebellion, negation and irrationalism. We are unable to account for the world in terms of reason alone, Kantor argued, and so we have to use other instruments such as imagination, instinct or emotion. The artist referred to the examples of dadaism and surrealism as trends that rejected the intellect as an instrument for describing the world in favour of the imagination and irrationalism (though not abandoning their cognitive functions but, on the contrary, revealing many unknown dimensions of reality). Introduced by dadaism and surrealism, the techniques of 'automatism' and 'chance' as methods in the process of creation as well as in the recognition of reality, made it possible to discover new aspects of reality that were crucial in contemporary life as well as in art. *Matière* or material, a key term in Kantor's aesthetic discourse, was valued as an element that, by employing artistic techniques based on chance, could be structured. 'Chance' was a much more appropriate artistic tool than geometry as it had been employed by the classic pre-war avant-garde. His ambition to comprehend material by means of the intellect was exemplified by the contemporary tendencies of *tachisme* or *art informel*. In conclusion to his 1957 essay, Kantor wrote:

> Art is a kind of comprehension of life. Abstract art based on geometry, which has already yielded thousands of works, is today the equivalent of scholastic life. Confined by the rigours of construction, complete with its beginning and end, calculated and stiff, it has produced an image of life pedantically strung on a chain of causes and effects. The contemporary idea of life is more complicated. The art of today, just like life, is concerned with meanings that can never be fully known. We are watching its movement which can be rationally governed to an extent. That movement, action, the art of today, is an attempt not to render, produce or record but to be its own result. The point is no more to imitate anything, either an object or imagined reality. The painting is creation itself and a manifestation of life; it becomes its own continuation. This is a completely new concept of work and new aesthetics.[13]

The debate between Przyboś, Porębski and Kantor was to some extent an argument between different generations. But it was also a conflict between two different traditions of modernist thinking about the place of art in the contemporary world: one derived from the heritage of constructivism, and the other from surrealism in general and, in the immediate Polish context, from the *First Exhibition of Modern Art* of 1948–9. In the mid-1950s, the latter tradition was the more prominent.[14] In the following decade, however, the tradition of constructivism began to play an increasingly important role in Polish art. In particular, it was promoted in exhibitions displayed at the El Gallery in Elbląg, run by Gerhard Kwiatkowski, which developed specific notions of spatial forms, and the Foksal Gallery in Warsaw where the problematic of artistic self-analysis, derived in part from the heritage of constructivism, seems to have been crucial.

Freedom and the Autonomy of Art

The year of that discussion, 1957, saw dynamic developments within modern art. It is noteworthy that in 1957 the Cracow Group was established or, rather, reactivated. No doubt, the revived Group was much changed. Its members included Kantor and also Jerzy Nowosielski, for whom the measure of art was much deeper than history, a figure who was not just a modernist but a mystic;[15] and Maria Jarema, active in the so-called First Cracow Group of the late 1940s and the pre-war 'artistic as well as socially radical Left.'[16] After the war, Jarema maintained both her ideological commitment and her predilection for modernism. There were others including Tadeusz Brzozowski, who developed a painterly practice of 'defiguration' (a term coined by Porębski), a method leading to the 'violation of form' in which figurative suggestions were included – in a spirit of contradiction – only as the titles of abstract paintings.[17] It was without doubt Kantor who animated the whole group. His significant role in the reception of the *informel* in Poland can be seen in the joint exhibition held with Jarema in the Warsaw *Po Prostu* salon (1956), organized just after his return from Paris.

After Kantor – who splashed colour or, in fact, paint, impulsively and spontaneously onto the canvas – one can observe developments in Polish painting which stressed 'the experience of texture and material rather than of gesture', as Porębski put it.[18] In the Cracow Group, the best example of an artist more concerned with texture than with gesture was Jadwiga Maziarska. Her paintings, incorporating such materials as gravel, rocks, plaster, and wax, were called simply 'the art of material', or *la peinture de matière*.[19] Outside the group, one should mention such

Figure 7.3 Zbigniew Tymoszewski, *Postać z księżycem*, oil on canvas, 1962, 200 × 128 cms, National Museum in Poznań.

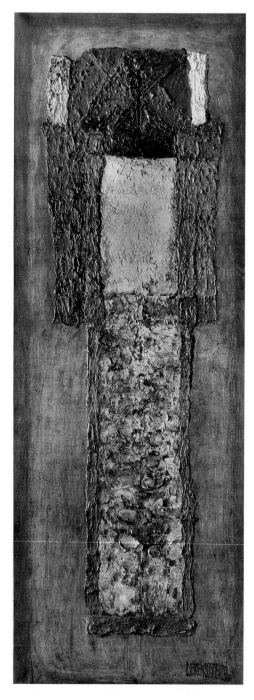

Figure 7.4 Jan Lebenstein, *Figure*, oil on canvas, 1957, 130 × 45.5 cms, National Museum in Poznań.

artists as Zbigniew Tymoszewski, Rajmund Ziemski, Aleksander Kobzdej, and Jan Lebenstein who combined his interest in the matter of paint with the 'ideogram of the human figure' composed according to 'a peculiar geometry.'[20] (Figure 7.4) At the Paris Biennial of 1959, Lebenstein was awarded the *Grand Prix de la Ville de Paris*, a moment that marked the climax of international interest in Polish modernist art of the late 1950s.

The two main elements in the discourse of artists and critics in the late 1950s in Poland were the terms 'freedom' and 'autonomy'. Freedom was articulated both at the level of individual experience, according to existentialist philosophy, and – in a wider context – at the communal level of society. But the cafes of Warsaw, Cracow, and Lublin were not identical to those on the Boulevard Saint-Germain. In Poland, freedom was by no means self-evident (nor was it in Paris, but that is a different problem): it was pitted against a real power system which had at its disposal a well-developed network of institutions and equivocal rhetoric. The autonomous work of art was counterposed to that which was subject to indoctrination. The claim made for 'abstraction', which in modernist discourse acquired a mythical quality by its opposition to 'realism', was that it was autonomous and free: what is more, it was taken as a manifestation of freedom in general.[21] This was, in fact, the defence offered by Kantor when accused of isolationism from historical reality.[22] With similar intent, Aleksander Wojciechowski, another critic writing in *Przegląd Artystyczny*, offered the view that the 'commitment' of abstract art was to the processes shaping contemporary civilization.[23]

The Thaw and After

After 1956 the return to the practice of propaganda art, to socialist realism, was inconceivable. Until the very end of the system in 1989, Polish artists were to enjoy liberties that – at least for a much longer period of time – were not available to artists in other countries of the Soviet bloc.[24] These facts are beyond this discussion, although they may yet require justification and systematic comparative studies. Still, let us now address the question of the artistic consequences of the Thaw and its significance for further developments in Polish art. My reflections will address three points.

First, the Thaw probably marked the demise of the avant-garde and the triumph of modernism if, as I have already suggested, these two terms can be treated antithetically. Polish debates and the ascending currents within art practice during and after the Thaw confirmed the tendency towards the autonomy of modern art, understanding 'commitment' in a particularly modernist way which was neither utopian nor critical but could be taken as 'commitment' to modern civilization in general terms of progress, freedom, and so forth.[25] This paradigm in the history of the art after the Thaw stemmed not only from the general developments in

European and American artistic culture, but also from the local, historical premises. To put it in simple terms, the brutality and force with which the Stalinist regime implemented the doctrine of socialist realism – a form of art that in its ideological aspect declared commitment to the processes of political and social transformation – triggered totally opposite tendencies in Polish art after 1956, directly proportional to the intensity of the socialist realist campaign. Thaw and post-Thaw modernism in Polish art was rooted in the fear of direct commitment, which, in most general terms, was unambiguously associated with socialist realism. In one way – following the principle of *á rebours* – the strong emphasis on the autonomy of the work of art throughout the period after the Thaw may be interpreted as a kind of 'revenge on socialist realism'.[26] The most common line of reasoning was that autonomous art meant free art, and that artistic freedom was the most valuable gain of the Thaw. Whether that freedom was complete or fabricated and whether it implied the right to choose any artistic form or to express one's attitude towards the world in any chosen manner, is a separate problem. I have no doubt that the Polish regime after 1956 continued to be concerned about the spread of such freedoms and, for that reason, maintained the institution of censorship as well as its interest in the kinds of self-censorship practised by artists. What I mean by this is the reluctance of Polish artists to adopt the kinds of subversive practices developed in the West in their art; especially those practices of social and political critique that questioned culture and power structures in general.[27] It is notable that when Tadeusz Kantor and other Polish modernists visited Paris, they paid no attention to the subversive forms of art directly involved in a critique of the power system (such as the *art brut* of Dubuffet, the works of the Cobra group, or the practices of the Situationists), but only to the phenomena accepted by the establishment (the *informel* and *la peinture de metière*).[28]

Second, if socialist realism and modernism are bound together in this paradox, another paradox is connected to the relationship of modernism and colourism, or post-impressionism. The painting of the *informel* – or, broadly speaking, abstraction – may have stemmed (in most general terms, for the details of this picture are not that clear) from a critique of any kind of mimetism and traditionalism, including colourism derived from the reception of impressionism and from the painting of the pre-war Polish colourists living in Paris. Kantor, for example, wrote quite explicitly that abstract art was the only adequate expression of modern times.[29] At the same time, however, interest in the painter's gesture and, consequently, in the whole repertoire of painting (such as surface, colour, paint, texture) triggered in Poland not only a 'second youth' for colourism but, more generally speaking, also fostered a cult of pictorial values of which the colourists were the most distinct exponents. The cult of pictorialism and aestheticism was characteristic of the methods of education in the academies of fine arts where many post-impressionists were professors. More importantly, it stunted discourses of art criticism which might have stimulated those kinds of art rooted in a critique of modernism.[30] Accordingly, this discourse has been responsible for the lack of critical and artistic categories in the mass media and the press after the Thaw. Although there have been some exceptions, the results of that process, especially in the discourses of the daily press and in the practice of museums, can be perceived even today.

Third and finally, as a result of its stress on the autonomy of art and its emphasis on pictorial values, the modernist approach ruled out critical art directly involved in politics and the social context – those forms of art which focus on 'here and now' rather than stressing the enigmatic, universal artistic values. In the modernist way of thinking, critical art is alien and has no place in the space of culture. This attitude has had serious consequences, including the conservatism of Polish artistic culture of the last few decades which has prevented art from becoming an arena of debates about its own time or the moral and political problems of society. The modernized communist system that emerged after the Thaw tolerated enclaves of 'freedom' from direct control but only on condition that 'free' individuals would not criticize the power system. In this context, modernist ideology was convenient for the authorities because it virtually prevented artists from developing a political critique of the regime. This conception of art was especially important during the so-called Gierek decade (in the 1970s). Paradoxically, Polish revolutionary art of the Thaw in the late 1950s, which seemed to oppose communist power, became a conservative tradition supporting modernizing post-Stalinist regimes.

Notes

1 See the comparative study related to the issue in my essay 'Modernism and Totalitarianism. The Thaw and Informel Painting in Central Europe, 1955–1965', in *Artium Quaestiones*, vol. X, Adam Mickiewicz University Press, Poznań (in press).

2 M. Damus, *Malerei in der DDR. Funktionen der bildenden Kunst im Realen Sozialismus* (Reibeck bei Hamburg 1991) p. 123 nn.

3 Cf. P. Bürger, *Theory of the Avant-Garde* (Minneapolis: 1984); H. Foster, *Recodings. Art, Spectacle, Cultural Politics* (Seattle: Bay View Press, 1985); A. Huyssen, *After the Great Divide. Modernism, Mass Culture, Postmodernism* (Bloomington: Indiana University Press, 1986).

4 A. Wojciechowski, 'Sztuka zaangazowana', *Przegląd Artystyczny*, no. 1 (1959).

5 'Dyskusja nad wystawa sztuki krajów socjalistycznych', *Zycie Literackie*, no. 14 (1959).

6 'Jeszcze o dyskusji nad wystawa sztuk plastycznych krajów socjalistycznych', *Zycie Literackie*, no. 15 (1959) (*Plastyka*, the art supplement, no. 32).

7 'Wystawa polska w Moskwie. Rozmowa z inż. arch. Andrzejem Pawłowskim, projektantem ekspozycji działu polskiego na wystawie sztuki krajów socjalistycznych w Moskwie', *Zycie Literackie*, no. 5 (1959) (*Plastyka*, the art supplement, no. 30).

8 Cf. *Odwilż Sztuka ok. 1956*, ed. P. Piotrowski, (Poznań: Muzeum Narodowe 1996).

9 The 1948–49 exhibition can also be taken as the origin of the revival of the Cracow Group in 1957 as well as the establishment of the Krzysztofory Gallery (which held its inaugural exhibition in June 1958).

10 J. Przyboś, 'Sztuka abstrakcyjna – jak z niej wyjść?', *Przegląd Kulturalny*, no. 45 (1957).

11 M. Por bski, 'Jak nie wychodzi', *Przegląd Kulturalny*, no. 45 (1957).

12 T. Kantor, 'Abstrakcja umar a – niech zyje abstrakcja', *Zycie Literackie*, no. 50 (1957) [*Plastyka*, the art supplement, no. 16].

13 Ibid.

14 In the 1960s this tradition was largely replaced by metaphorical painting exemplified by the works exhibited at the *Metaphors* exhibition shown at the Zachęta Gallery in Warsaw in December 1962.

15 Cf. A. Kostolowski and W. Nowaczyk, eds, *Jerzy Nowosielski* (Poznań: Muzeum Narodowe, 1993).

16 M. Sobieraj, 'Maria Jarema,' in A. Ryszkiewicz, ed., *Współczesna sztuka polska* (Warsaw, 1981); cf. J. Chrobak, ed., *Maria Jarema*, (Cracow, 1988); J. Chrobak, ed., *Maria Jarema (wspomnienia i komentarze)* (Cracow: 1992).

17 M. Porębski, 'Tadeusz Brzozowski', in I. Moderska, ed., *Tadeusz Brzozowski. Obrazy i rysunki* (Poznan: Muzeum Narodowe, 1974).

18 K. Czerni, *Nie tylko o sztuce. Rozmowy z profesorem Mieczysławem Porębskim* (Wrocław: 1999) p. 105.

19 A. Kostolowski, 'Uwagi o malarstwie Jadwigi Maziarskiej' in J. Chrobak, ed., *Jadwiga Maziarska* (Cracow: 1991).

20 W. Baraniewski, 'O 'figurach' Jana Lebensteina' in M. Kurasiak and T. Rostkowska, eds, *Jan Lebenstein* (Warsaw: Zachęta Gallery, 1992).

21 Cf. P. Piotrowski, 'Filozofia gestu' in *Sztuka polska po roku 1945* (Warsaw: 1987).

22 Kantor, 'Abstrakcja umarła . . .,'.

23 A. Wojciechowski, 'Sztuka zaangazowana', *Przegląd Artystyczny*, no. 1 (1959).

24 M. Haraszti, *The Velvet Prison. Artists under State Socialism* (New York: New Republic, 1987).

25 Wojciechowski, 'Sztuka zaangazowana,'.

26 T. Nyczek, 'Zemsta socrealizmu', *Sztuka*, no. 1 (1981).

27 An interesting example of the way in which Polish art of the 1960s and 1970s was deprived of its critical significance is its 'desexualization.' Cf. P. Leszkowicz, 'Ucieczka od erotyki. Seks jako strategia sztuki krytycznej. Szkic o polskiej sztuce krytycznej w latach 1960–1980. Władza-sztuka-seks' in *Sztuka a erotyka* (Warsaw: 1995).

28 A. Markowska, *Druga Grupa Krakowska*, typescript in the Institute of Arts of the Polish Academy of Sciences (Warsaw: nd).

29 Kantor, 'Abstrakcja umarła . . .'.

30 M. Lisiewicz, 'Kontestacja czy kontynuacja. Szkic o polskiej sztuce i krytyce lat 60' in *Magazyn Sztuki*, vol. 1, no. 5 (1995).

−8−

Socialist Realism's Self-Reference?
Cartoons on Art, c. 1950
Katarzyna Murawska-Muthesius

This chapter is an attempt to look at socialist realist art through its own eyes: the cartoons on the theme of art that were published in satirical journals and in the daily press of the people's democracies around 1950. Cartoons, capable of 'telescoping a whole chain of ideas in one pregnant image',[1] were given great significance as vehicles of communication and opinion-making by the new state apparatuses. Cartoons on art should thus enable us to look at the ways in which the visual culture of socialist realism explained itself. This will be a glimpse from within the system, endeavouring to see through an entirety by examining its distorted image as reflected in the magic mirror that itself forms part of this entirety and, moreover, whose distortions are controlled by it. In other words, it will be an exercise in describing a culture within the confines of its own language, or through the strategies of its self-advertisement, or, to put it in yet another way, through its patterns of self-reference. But, is it plausible to seek traces of self-reference in what should simply be called instances of 'totalitarian propaganda'? It is still a common assumption that socialist realism was a blunt and passive monolith fed by politicians, rejecting individualism for the sake of collectivism, and therefore incompatible with, or deprived of, the freedom of self-analysis.[2] This is contrasted with modernism whose self-referential disposition has been discussed widely (including analysis through the prism of cartoons on modern art).[3] This article will nevertheless venture into testing the strategems and limits of this particular kind of self-reference in socialist realist visual culture that can be read from its cartoons on art.

Cartoons on art have been used as points of departure for studying problems of visual perception and representation, including the discussion of cartoons as 'metapictures' that are 'capable of reflection on themselves' and thus provide second-order discourses on issues of imaging.[4] This chapter, examining cartoons of the Stalinist period, will have to be built on slightly different premises – it will refer to images that talk not directly about themselves, but about other images which are contemporary to them. It will discuss the ways in which pictures made by artists, mainly by painters, were commented upon, or, as it were, 'censored' by having been caricatured within the pictures made by the professional cartoonists. It is of more than marginal importance here that cartoonists, sharing the status of an artistic profession, were, at the same time, in a position to set themselves apart from the area of 'pure art' and of 'high art' and to perform the role of critic. Thus the self-reference attributable to cartoons referring to art is curtailed by the ambiguity of the cartoonists' self-identification. Moreover, their double status of acting both inside and outside of 'pure art' is enhanced by the specificity of the medium, which transgresses the purely visual level of communication, by also embracing words as an inherent element. In effect, the cartoons in question express attitudes towards art not only by visualizing but also by verbalizing it. The cartoon on socialist realist art is seen as both a one-way as well as a two-level discourse between a 'speech-aided' cartoonist and a mute artist. At the visual level, the discourse is performed between the outer and inner image, the actual image of the cartoon and the image(s) contained within it. Having been contextualized and explained by its title, caption and inserted words, the discourse joins in with the heated debates of the politically engaged art criticism of the time. In other words, rather than serving as particular vehicles of self-reference, socialist realist cartoons on art might be read as pictorialized versions of socialist realist art criticism, as 'texts' that have been summarized into persuasive pictures and whose main task is to unmask the impropriety of the picture within. The inner image is shown as a culprit, but the outer image provides the rationale of the charge, occasionally hinting at scope for improvement. Although the outer image is usually helped with words, it attempts to visualize the objectives of the cultural politics of Stalinism: the battle against formalism, against '*l'art pour l'art*', and for political involvement of art and artists (who are constantly rebuked for not 'catching up' with the speed of the building of the New World). It is significant, however, that all those admonitions could also have been directed against the cartoonists themselves, who were not immune either from accusations of formalism or from evading contemporary arguments in their subject matter. Examining the relationship between the condemned image inside the cartoon, and the outer image of the cartoon itself, we do not only have to trace the identity of the condemned image within, but also the affiliation of the outer image.

Hence we must ask: in what ways are those objectives, the abstract concepts of cultural policies, translated into images by the cartoonist? Which iconographical patterns from the stock of cartoonists' armory do they turn to? What kind of intertextual discourses do they engage in? How closely are they related to verbal art criticism? Is there any gap between the iconic and the verbal messages of the cartoon? What is their ranking within socialist realist cartoon genre? To which audiences do the cartoons on art appeal? Is a non-political reading of Stalinist cartoons on art at all possible? The list of the questions could be much longer, and by no means all of them can be tackled here.

One of the major difficulties is the virtual lack of Western research on cartoons of the peoples' democracies post-1945. Occasionally employed as 'visual evidence' in studies on the culture and aesthetics of Stalinism, they have not attracted much attention as regards the specificity of their own medium. In the Western literature devoted to political cartoons, East European examples appear very sparingly: they are nearly exclusively Soviet and examined under the banner of totalitarianism. What is stressed is their total subordination to the objectives of state propaganda, as well as the strong contrast between the biting, or 'punitive' characterization of enemies, driven to generate hatred rather than simple laughter, and the pale idealization of the leaders and allies at home (sometimes dismissed as not belonging to the language of caricature at all) which at its best is dressed as a '*druzheskii sharzh*', friendly and mild criticism.[5] What has not been addressed are the further characteristics and the borders of this separate class of 'cartoons of socialist countries', or of 'Stalinist' cartoons as distinguished from the 'Western' ones. Are the criteria of the customary assessment, such as innovative modernism versus retrograde socialist realism, at all applicable here? No less important is the question as to how 'Stalinist cartoons' differ from country to country.

Soviet and East European writings on their own political cartoons are impressive, especially throughout the 1950s, when caricature was firmly entrenched in the role of the 'ideological weapon of class struggle, which reacts rapidly to political moves of the class enemy, mocks his habits and unmasks the falseness of his philosophy'.[6] Soviet political caricature, as the model of ideological commitment in realist form, a kind of a counterpart of the unequalled superiority of Soviet socialist realist painting, was widely disseminated across Eastern Europe by way of the numerous travelling exhibitions, as well as in luxurious albums of Soviet masters of political cartoons, such as the Kukryniksy and Boris Efimov. They were published in many languages in thousands of copies, thus contributing to the wide spread of the visualized Cold-War rhetoric, with their pictorialized invectives such as 'imperialist warmonger' and others.[7] There were also large retrospective exhibitions of caricatures of individual 'brotherly countries', as well as congresses devoted to political satire, organized in Warsaw, Berlin, Bucharest, and other East European capitals.[8] On the other hand, cartoonists were often severely criticized for their lack of the right kind of political commitment, for their 'careless humour', irresponsible punning, and altogether for the cultivation of the sinful traditions of the reactionary bourgeois caricature, with its aestheticism, schematism and disregard of the realistic detail and of psychological characterization. The progressiveness of a political cartoon of the early 1950s was measured primarily against the 'daring to express the unrelenting hatred against the class enemy'.[9] Particularly interesting are those Soviet sources that throw light on the complex process of devising a political cartoon, which, apart from the necessity of its collective approval by the editorial board, would often involve cooperation between cartoonist and the so called 'themist' – the person who works out the concept and caption, and sometimes even the whole composition, leaving the artist as mere executant.[10]

Despite the attention given to caricature in the people's democracies, their cartoons on art have never been really dealt with because they do not appear to fall into the category of the political. However, the majority of cartoons on art cannot be read today without understanding a political background, or the politico/ cultural catchphrases of the day. Moreover, they usually refer to particular events such as large exhibitions or important announcements following the meetings of cultural bodies of the state. On a par with other cartoons, they were published in the daily press, in cultural periodicals and in satirical magazines which could vary considerably in respect of their audiences.[11] Their more serious and more artful variant, the satirical print, would occasionally make its appearance also in art journals, read by professionals only.[12] The common strategy, applied in cartoons on art as much as in all others, was to manoeuver between the new discourses of cultural politics and art criticism in the particular country and the available stock of cartoonists patterns. Among the 'hottest' issues around 1950 were 'dehumanization', corruption and the 'class hostility' of formalism. The visual- ization of those verbal denunciations, however, created several problems for cartoonists, especially in those countries that put a rigorous ban on the 'contam- inated' art. Interestingly, those few cartoons that would include the outlawed imagery would revert to the old clichés of the aggressively anti-modernist cartoons thriving in the West from the end of the nineteenth century onwards, condemning modernism for its moral depravation, or even insanity.[13] As regards the artists in the cartoonists' own yard, a constant theme was their social and political isolationism, their detachment from reality and the sin of 'staying behind', for which a standardized image of the artist as an eccentric was particularly suitable. He would often be shown as an older man (practically never a woman) in outmoded or bohemian clothes, sitting at the easel and painting, typically, still-lifes, or old- style rural scenes, instead of the newly-built towns, or tractors ploughing fields.[14] A variant would be an artist who attempts to feign ideological content of his otherwise empty works by changing their titles, or inserting some political details, such as a Party newspaper.[15] At the end of the Stalinist period, which would fall with different speed in different countries, cartoonists would identify more with artists than with their censors, and would move towards criticism of overcentralized cultural politics, with its 'lists of subjects' and 'ready recipes'. A common form became a comic strip, narrating stages of a total transformation of a work under the pressure of the absurd interventions of the commissioning bodies, and resulting in its ultimate rejection.[16] The much publicized attack by Khrushchev on the over-indulgence of Stalinist architecture resulted in the virtual flood of the cartoons all over Eastern Europe, ridiculing the sumptuous, over-monumental, and over-decorative buildings.[17] Significantly, however, the cartoons that visualized highly professional debates regarding specific demands of socialist realist method, and especially those that illustrated the existent or 'ideal' socialist realist images, were few in number and not evenly spread across Eastern Europe. They appeared mostly in the Soviet Union, where particular issues of socialist realism, such as the emphasis on psychological characterization which would enable the public to 'read mental biography' of the people represented – were most widely discussed.[18]

Not even pretending to offer, at this stage of research, a comprehensive study of East Europeans cartoons on art, I will focus on the analysis of one cartoon only, which seems particularly significant for the Polish scene around 1950. Belonging to the anti-formalist group, and rich in intertextual references, it appears typical in the way it turns to the schemes of political cartooning, as well as remarkable for the manner it exemplifies the dilemma of the 'socialist realist self-reference', by addressing the issue of realism yet evading its visualization at the same time.

The small cartoon by Jantar under the heading 'At the First All Poland Exhibition of Art' (Figure 8.1) provides a striking, if rather coarse, summary of the message

Figure 8.1 Jantar [Ernest Petrajtis], '-Now We Are Painting Real People!', *Mucha*, 1950.

of the exhibition: the battle against formalism, which was the prime agenda of the cultural politics of the time.[19] The exhibition, held at the National Museum in Warsaw in spring of 1950, was acclaimed widely by its organizers and the press as the 'battle for socialist realism' and its primacy of content and the contemporary subject matter. It was aiming to channel Polish art away from the 'cul-de-sac of formalism', from abstraction and post-impressionism, the exponents of hostile ideology which had been harassing it before and in the aftermath of World War Two, and were still detectable in the works of some artists.[20] The cartoon, accordingly, shows a grotesque creature being kicked out of the exhibition by an anonymous figure. The creature is depicted in great detail as composed haphazardly of many geometric segments, while the body of its oppressor is hidden from sight by the wall, and all we can see is his leg delivering the kick. The two pictures that can be seen on display in the room from which the automaton is thrown away represent people, and one of them portrays somebody with a pick. The caption, 'Now we are painting real people!' helps to establish the cartoon's rights or wrongs. The 'futurist' figure stands for the 'condemned image' in the cartoon, and is unmasked by the invisible man as an intruder who has stepped out from the wrong kind of painting into the exhibition. It represents the wrong subject matter, avoiding the 'real people'. The 'futurist figure' represents all that was meant to be eradicated: the detachment of artists from reality, the unwillingness to express 'humanist content of our days', and the 'formalist aesthetics of the rotting capitalism, which transformed humans into a dead composition of prisms and cones'.[21] In general terms, the identity of the 'futurist man' can be contextualized within the then-vilified works of Polish constructivism and avant-garde of the inter-war period; it does not, however, point to any particular composition. In terms of the exhibition scenario, the 'futurist man' may be related to the group of works which were sent by Polish artists living in France and, according to the leading Soviet painter Aleksandr Gerasimov writing in *Przegląd Artystyczny*, had to be confined to a separate room to visualize the 'unsuitability of the degenerate, formalist methods to describe the new reality'.[22]

The identity of the hidden man is, however, much more enigmatic. The 'realistic' manner in which his trouser leg and his shoe are drawn, as well as his rough behaviour, characterize him as a categorical opponent of the 'futurist figure'. It is unclear, nonetheless, whether he stands for a rival image or whether he is a human. If the latter, we are then left guessing whether he is an artist, the curator in charge who has sieved the works sent for the exhibition, an art critic, or a cultural officer in the state apparatus. Or, perhaps, he is all rolled in one, or even, in a more general sense, the 'real man', representative of the 'new nation', who gives vent to his anger against his class enemy. If, however, he should be taken as a rival image, another inner image within the cartoon, he must have stepped from one of the approved paintings of the exhibition which focus on the theme of the 'contemporary real man'. He is a winner whilst his opponent is a loser in much the same way as socialist realism triumphs over formalism.

Another puzzling fact is that we cannot see the 'winning image' properly and, thus, learn little about the requirements of the socialist realist method apart from the erroneous perception that it is meant to record reality faithfully down to the pattern on the fabric of his trousers. In this case the caption 'Now we are painting real people!', which must have been uttered by the 'winning image', would be a curious example of a purely verbal self-reference on the part of the image, the resolution which declares intentions about images verbally, and yet avoids defining them further visually. The same evasiveness as regards 'how' to paint, and not only 'what' to paint, shines through the role allocated here to the two pictures on the wall, surely the 'approved images' within the cartoon. Correspondingly, their correctness has been measured solely and somewhat perfunctorily against their presumed subject matter, the 'real people'. The 'correct pictures' do not constitute in any way the main concern of the cartoonist: they are small and unremarkable and cannot possibly offer any visual explanation to the caption. The cartoon tells us what socialist realism is going to fight against, but is much less precise as to what it is going to fight for, or rather how it is going to achieve the aim. We can see the enemy very well, but it is, as yet, too early to see the winner.[23]

Certainly, one factor here is that cartoons are meant to chase enemies rather than praise winners. Nonetheless, we can also assume that this evasiveness is caused by the fact that the latter were still hard to find in the process of implanting socialist realism on the soil of Polish art. Describing only the enemy and stressing in his cartoon the 'battle with the old', Jantar follows the main argument of the exhibition, the focus on the repudiation of the old values rather than on the recognition of the new ones. The organizers and art critics publicly admitted their reservations towards the exhibited works. By emphasizing the difficulties accompanying the break-through from the Old to the New Order, they were trying to justify the shortcomings of the exhibits, which at that point were evaluated as merely '*intended* [my italics] as the works of socialist realism' and considered 'not entirely free from the remnants of the past'. They explained that the artists 'make them in the conditions of a pressure from foreign and hostile ideology, of sharp class struggle, inflamed sometimes by an intrusion from outside'.[24] Notably, they devoted considerable attention to those 'dangerous' influences, virtually staging the 'battle between the Old and the New' by including in the exhibition the above mentioned 'degenerate formalist' works by Polish émigré artists.

Having discussed so far aspects of the identity of the 'inner images' of the cartoon, we must now turn to their mutual relationship and to their associations with the 'outer image', as well as the affiliations of the latter, which contain more ambiguities. Consciously or not, Jantar's cartoon engages in the old anti-modernist discourse, falling into a wider category of anti-modernist cartoons which have ridiculed the new ways of representation – some of them emphasizing political aspects, and, paradoxically in this context, the leftist affiliation of modern art. Especially significant would be here a comparison with Bernard Partridge's satire 'For this relief not too much thanks' (*Punch*, 3 June 1925) (Figure 8.2) which

Figure 8.2 Bernard Partridge, 'For this relief not much thanks', *Punch*, 2 June 1925.

unmasks Epstein's *Rima*, the public sculpture much despised by the contemporary British audience as an example of 'Bolshevism' in art: while *Rima* is whispering 'Kamerad' to the Piccadilly *Eros*, the latter, undaunted, aims towards her modernist body with a non-amourous arrow ('I think not!'). An anti-modernist cartoon produced under another totalitarian system, the much-reproduced *The Sculptor of Germany* by O. Garvens (*Kladderadatsch*, vol. 49 (1933) p. 7), while associating modernism with Jewishness, does not shy away from giving the correct image of the 'real man', whose triumphant body is being modelled by Hitler himself from the same clay as had been used for some 'chaotic' composition of a sculptor who would at that time have been considered to be Jewish-looking.[25] As mentioned earlier, the anti-formalist cartoons of Stalinism can be seen as a special variant of cartoons on modern art. Simplifying the point, we may say that if the anti-modernist cartoons recorded modern art's 'formal shortcomings' in the eyes of the public, Stalinism would be concerned with its inadequacy in the eyes of the State.

Above all, Jantar's cartoon is linked to Marxist-Leninist political iconography and is based upon various patterns used in agitprop caricatures and posters to express the act of getting rid of the remnants of the Old Order. The act of kicking as a signifier for implementing social justice often appeared in Bolshevik visual propaganda, namely in the ROSTA Windows, satirical images addressed to the widest and often illiterate audience in Russia in the early 1920s.[26] Jantar's kicking leg can be read within this code as a synecdoche of the angered new nation, of the 'real people', thus confirming that the message of the cartoon transgresses the level of cultural argument onto the level of class struggle. The images of the gigantic working man's arm raising victorious banners, or strangling, smashing, and getting rid of capitalists were also a common sight in Polish political posters and in many title-page cartoons around 1950. The significant difference between that code and Jantar's cartoon is the fact that the capitalists' figures escaping in panic would be always miniaturized.

Jantar's image can be also discussed within another political cartoon scheme, this time visualizing the class struggle as an act of literally sweeping the enemies away, which, notably, has been used in the context of various battles in the field of socialist realist visual culture. Its 'origin' can be traced back to the well-known Bolshevik poster by Victor N. Deni, *Comrade Lenin Cleans the World of Filth* (1922, Figure 8.3),[27] in which Lenin with a large broom purges the globe of oppressive classes: royalty, capitalists and clergy. The scheme had since been applied to various occasions, including campaigns against the petit-bourgeois taste in home decoration in which a young man uses a broom against the 'domestic trash': porcelain figurines of dancers, monkeys and elephants (1928).[28] Significantly for us, it reappears also in another Polish cartoon, by Baro, in the context of the same First All-Poland Exhibition of Art, which was printed a few weeks earlier and must have served as one of the stimuli for Jantar's composition (Figure

Figure 8.3 Viktor N. Deni, 'Comrade Lenin Cleans the World of Filth', poster, 1922.

8.4).[29] The broom is compared there to a large painter's brush – its owner, standing in a doorframe, chases away a surrealist painting. The picture, in a decorative frame and comparatively small, is also given anthropomorphic features, the running legs and one eye. Baro consciously and rather faithfully adopts Deni's scheme, retaining all the major compositional features: the proportion of the winner to the loser, the direction of the sweep from top to bottom, as well as the rhetoric of political purge suggested by the caption, 'Spring Cleaning' which refers, otherwise, to the timing of the exhibition. Jantar, in turn, seems to have been inspired primarily by Baro's image, borrowing from it the general idea of expelling the non-

Figure 8.4 Baro (Karol Baraniecki), 'Spring Cleaning', *Szpilki*, 1950.

representational works of art from the exhibition. He re-worked it and gave it a fresh appearance by replacing the act of 'sweeping off' by that of 'kicking out'. He 'lost', however, the original relationship between the protagonists and complicated it considerably by blurring their identity and, what is more, he introduced a 'new' caption which added to the simple concept of removing the Old a more complex task of building the world anew.

Having traced the various affiliations of the 'outer image' of Jantar's cartoon, we can see clearly in what ways it breaks with the appropriate codes of signification.

His gravest 'error' is, of course, that the 'futurist man' was made too big: he equals his adversary in size, hence he is made equally important. Furthermore, he is described in too much detail, which only makes him interesting, individual and memorable, arresting the attention of the reader not less than that of the draughtsman. Even worse, the 'futurist monster' is not abominable enough and therefore does not generate strong antipathy as it should have done according to the rules of the 'progressive political cartoon'.[30] On the contrary, he may even evoke some compassion among the readers, because he is shown visibly scared: his eyes wide open, forehead frowned, his hands and legs fighting to catch balance. We see how he turns his head trying to identify its oppressor, and, if it not had not been for the caption, we may find it difficult to decide where to locate our sympathies in this confrontation: with the poor victimized creature and against the anonymous brute, or vice versa. For all those reasons the 'futurist man' cannot be easily dismissed and forgotten as one of those miserable pygmies that escape from below the steps of the marching giant of the New World.

While the first reading of Jantar's cartoon seems clear, namely the battle against formalism, which is linked to the imperative of class struggle, the second reading, informed by examining pictorial discourses, reveals confusing discrepancies within the dialogue between the 'inner' and the 'outer' image, as well as the gap between the verbal and iconic message. The cartoon 'says' and 'pictures' different things. When speaking, it looks into the future, when picturing, it focuses on the past. While the caption is a 'positive' (though vague) declaration, the image is 'negative' and evasive. Jantar's attempt to mythologize the new cultural policy as an act of exorcism, as the expelling of evil spirits of modernism, failed because he was not able to keep within the rigid cultural code of political cartooning. He transgressed it by devoting too much attention to his depiction of the Evil. The memorability of the 'condemned' image may, in fact, betray the 'formalist ballast' carried by the author himself and, moreover, may account for the fact that the cartoon was allocated only an inferior place in the journal, having been inserted at the bottom of a page into a single column of unrelated text.[31] The cartoon has been forgotten for many decades, but its ambiguity offers a different point of view of the uneasy ways in which policies of socialist realism of the early 1950s were perceived in Poland, including cartoonists who were expected to make them simple. Distortions and ambiguities can help us to see the strategies much better than their flawless displays.

There is yet another way in which we can read the *Now We Are Painting Real People* cartoon, as well as *Spring Cleaning* by Baro. Both of them can be seen not only as encapsulating the cultural politics that overshadowed the First All Poland Exhibition, but, in more general terms, as a 'forecast' of the policy of rehanging galleries in major Polish museums in the early 1950s.[32] The introduction of socialist realism into their displays of contemporary art was accompanied by a boisterous charge against exhibiting modernism and the avant-garde of the interwar period. In 1952, the National Museum in Warsaw opened its new National Gallery of Polish Art, with the two last rooms taken up by the works from the First and Second All Poland Exhibitions. As it appears from the debates, the 'methods of display' of the interwar modernism in the preceding rooms became a major headache for museum curators and the burning issue for the cultural officers of the Ministry. While curators and museum directors were defending the integrity of their collections, the officers severely criticized their lack of social responsibility, demanding a sharp selection that would eliminate all 'manneristic novelties' and would give assent only to the works which 'express humanist values'. Moreover, the selection should not leave the visitor in any doubt 'that there is a distinct caesura between yesterday and today', and that 'the interwar period is a minor phenomenon in our art'.[33] Particularly interesting here is the case of the Museum of Fine Arts in Łódź which in October 1950 locked up its collection of Polish constructivism and of European avant-garde and even plastered over the neo-plasticist decor of one of the rooms designed by Władysław Strzemiński, a leading constructivist in the inter-war years, to display nineteenth-century realism.[34]

Jantar's cartoon appears to offer a strikingly accurate visual herald of this process, and in this museological context it was to lead an afterlife by playing a part in yet another intertextual dialogue between cartoonists. Typical of the vicissitudes of socialist realism in Poland, only a few years later the same museums rearranged their displays yet again, and on the wave of the 1956 Thaw they restored modernism to the galleries and relegated the so called 'socrealizm' to store rooms. But even before this 'second' reshuffle another cartoonist, Jerzy Zaruba, also 'predicted it'. He did so by borrowing the same scheme that had been introduced to the repertory of Polish 'cartoons-on-art' by Baro and Jantar, and applied it 'the other way round', using the 'anti-formalist' scheme to an 'anti-socialist realist' cartoon. His cartoon was a hot comment on the XIX Session of the Culture and Arts Council, which took place in Warsaw in March 1956, and referred to the speech by literary critic Jan Kott attacking the 'administrative canonization of the mythology of socialist realism'. The speech was printed on the first page of the *Przegląd Kulturalny* (vol. 5, no 14, [4–11 April 1956]), the cultural weekly that was controlled by the same Council, with Zaruba's cartoon inserted prominently in the middle of the text (Figure 8.5). The lack of a caption suggests that the image is elucidated by the whole speech and that it attempts a summary of it. The leading intellectuals' bold attack on state cultural policies is metaphorized as the scene of the spring cleaning in the yard of the Ministry of Art and Culture – a carpet marked with the Ministry's initials *MKiS* is energetically 'beaten' by two figures, Jan Kott and his ally in front of Minister Włodzimierz Sokorski, who now winks at the events. The rubbish bin (*śmietnik*) in front reveals that the old books and official decrees, such as 'Our battle against formalism' or 'Art meets collective farming'

Figure 8.5 Jerzy Zaruba, cartoon in *Przegl¹d Kulturalny*, 1956.

have been dumped, and the radicality of the change is further stressed by the scene in the background where modernist and socialist realist paintings exchange places in museums' collections (*Zbiory*) and their stores or junk rooms (*Rupieciarnia*).

The tone of Kott's speech was accusative and solemn, condemning the 'dangerous mythology' which, amongst others, led to identifying a modernist painting with the class enemy;[35] in effect Kott condemned the message of Jantar's cartoon. Zaruba's drawing, by contrast, is pervaded by a light-hearted spirit, and deprived entirely of political fervour. He consciously refers to the earlier cartoons, retaining even the *Spring Cleaning* framework used by Baro; however, he replaces the acts of 'sweeping off', or of 'kicking out' by the much milder juxtaposition between 'going in and out', as well as 'up and down' the stairs. Nonetheless, he makes no attempt to vilify the enemy, since both of the 'inner images' of Zaruba's cartoon, roughly of the same size, are characterized in a somewhat patronizing way. The essence of socialist realism is now reduced to an optimistic, 'poster-like' image of a tractor, while modernism is represented by a surrealist composition with an 'existentialist', sad and rather overblown profile, and a violin. In fact, the 'inner images' do not fight with each other, but are manoeuvered 'in' and 'out' by, to use the Polish expression, 'technical staff'. One cannot help noticing that the decisions are now taken by 'intelligentsia' (in glasses), which reinstalls in the public collections the art of its own class. While Jantar's cartoon was meant to be seriously triumphalist, taking a political stand to criticize art for being 'class hostile', Zaruba merely laughs at 'cultural politics', not attempting to differentiate between 'good' and 'bad' art, or between 'us' and 'them'. If Jantar's cartoon was an attempt of a 'punitive satire' that would bite the enemy, Zaruba's drawing belongs to the category of *druzheskii sharzh*, distancing itself quietly from both its 'inner images'. Significantly, the tractor is not a threatening attribute of the 'dangerous mythology', but, rather, a laughable epitaph to the 'collective madness', short in duration and already overcome, comical in itself because it appears foreign to the context of museum collections.

The comparison of those two cartoons, one quoting the other, helps us to realize again that Jantar, while confused over the 'rules' of political cartooning, demonstrated an intuitive awareness of the course of art policy in Poland. We may even see in the cartoon *Now We Are Painting Real People*, an overall and accurate diagnosis of the state of Polish socialist realism as a whole, and in this way, a striking example of socialist realist evasive self-reference. The 'pro-socialist realist' image reflects on socialist realist imagery by focusing on the imaging of its opponent and shying away from picturing itself. In Poland, modernism turned out to be a far more 'dangerous' disposition, a far bigger threat than it had been expected, while socialist realism, never convincingly defined and always formulated against the Soviet matrix, was, all in all, a short-lived episode of the turbulent reception of an external frame of mind. Never internalized as Poland's own, socialist realism was always marked as the property of the Other, be it represented as the goal of reaching the lofty Soviet/Internationalist ideal by its supporters, or an unwanted imposition of an occupiers' language by its opponents. Given the fresh memory of the more than century-long Russification of Poland, which ended in 1918, the arguments of its opponents, though silent or silenced, had a still 'unmeasured' resonance with the Polish audience. In spite of the efforts of the Party's ideological apparatus and the initial support given to socialist realism by a number of left-oriented artists and intellectuals wanting to change the world, it did not put down roots in socialist Poland. Rather, it was seen within the trope that was chosen by Jantar for his cartoon – as acting from behind the border, as hiding behind the wall – and it was rarely talked about other than in terms of simple subject matter: 'those pictures of Stakhanovites and tractors'.[36]

Notes

1 Ernst H. Gombrich, *Meditations on a Hobby Horse and the Other Essays on the Theory of Art* (London: Phaidon Press, 1962) p.130.

2 Tomasik has proposed locating recent Western studies on socialist realist culture in two categories: 'totalitarian' versus 'total'. While the first embraces those works that assess it as a foreign product, as a negation of culture and a rupture of traditions which can only be described from outside, the second is willing to negotiate its links with traditions, to stress the active role of artists as its makers, and favours approaches describing Stalinism through its own language. See Wojciech Tomasik, 'Totalitarna czy totalna' (*Kultura stalinowska w świetle współ czesnych opracowań)' in Konteksty*, vol. 51 (1997), nos 1–2, pp. 105–17.

3 W.J.T. Mitchell, 'Metapictures', in W.J.T. Mitchell, *Picture Theory* (Chicago and London: University of Chicago Press, 1994) pp. 35–82.

4 Mitchell, *Picture Theory* and Gombrich, *Meditations on a Hobby Horse*, pp. 3–8.

5 By far, the most informative Western book on Soviet political cartoons is by Milenkovitch who discussed the cartoons published in *Pravda* and *Izvestia* in order to 'enhance our understanding of Soviet propaganda technics', as material for a preventive Sovietology. Michael M. Milenkovitch, *The View From Red Square. A Critique of Cartoons from Pravda and Izvestia, 1947–1964* (New York and Buenos Aires: 1966) p. v. See also Charles Press, *The Political Cartoon* (London and Toronto: Associated University Press, 1981) pp. 52–3,106–8,145–7; for the recent literature see Sophie Coeurè, 'Le dessin satirique soviétique' in W. Berelowitch and Laurent Gervereau, eds., *Russie-URSS 1914–1991. Changement du regards*, ex. cat., Musée d'histoire contemporaine de la Bibliothéque de Documentation Internationale Contemporaine, (Paris: 1991) pp. 118–23; and Claire Mouradian, 'Les peuples de l'Empire russe et soviétique à travers les caricatures: des nations en quête d'images', in M. Godet (ed.), *De Russie et d'ailleurs. Feux croisés sur l'histoire. Pour Marc Ferro*, Paris, 1995, pp. 83–95. The differentiation between the 'punitive' and 'laughing' cartoons was proposed by Coupe, albeit not in the context of Soviet cartoons. See W.A. Coupe, 'Observations on a Theory of Political Caricature' in *Comparative Studies in Society and History*, vol. 11 (1969) pp. 79–95.

6 Tadeusz Borowski, 'O postępowych i wstecznych tradcjach karykatury politycznej', Przegląd Artystyczny nos 7/9, 10/12 (1950); Kukryniksy in Milenkovitch, *The View From Red Square*, p. 12.

7 Boris Efimov, *Za prochnyi mir, protiv podzhigatelei voiny. Risunki* (Moscow: Izdatel'stvo Iskusstvo, 1950); Kukryniksy, *Bredovye 'anglo-amerikanizatory'. Risunki* (Moscow: 1951).

8 For instance, Jan Szeląg [Z. Mitzner], *Polska karykatura polityczna* (Warsaw: 1951); S. Collillieux (ed.), *Karykatura oraż walki o pokój. Zbiór prac karykaturzystów rumuńskich* (Warsaw: Wydawnictwo MON, 1952) [translation from Romanian]; *Wystawa karykatury polskiej*, exh. cat., Arsenał (Warsaw: 1953), introduction by Z. Mitzner; *Deutsche Karikaturenausstellung*, exh. cat.,

Zentral Haus der DSF (Berlin: 1954); see also H. Olbrich, K. Haese, U. Horn, L. Lang, and G. Piltz, *Sozialistische deutsche Karikatur. Von den Anfängen bis zum Gegenwart (1848–1978)* (Berlin: Eulenspiegel Verlag, 1978); Hanna Górska, Eryk Lipiński, *Z dziejów karykatury polskiej* (Warsaw: PWN, 1977); Jan Koźbiel, *Gorąca zimna wojna. Polska satyra polityczna 1944–1956*, exh. cat., Muzeum Karykatury (Warsaw: 1987); Jan Koźbiel, 'Satyra polityczna w Polsce', in *Almanach satyry polskiej* (Warsaw: c. 1990).

9 Borowski, 'O postępowych i wstecznych tradycjach karykatury politycznej', pp. 54–9; Jan Lenica, 'O karykaturze słów kilka', *Nowa Kultura*, no. 31 (1950); Zbigniew Lengren, 'Kilka uwag na temat rysunku satyrycznego', *Przegląd Artystyczny*, no. 2, (1951) pp. 49–52.

10 Borowski, 'O postępowych i wstecznych tradycjach karykatury politycznej', pp. 56–7; Boris Efimov, *Osnovy ponimania karikatury*, (Moscow: 1961) pp. 49-54; I.P. Abramskij, *Smekh silnykh. O khudozhnikakh zhurnala 'Krokodil'* (Moscow: 1977) pp. 292–7.

11 *Krokodil* in USSR, *Mucha* and *Szpilki* in Poland; *Ulenspiegel* and *Frischer Wind*, later *Eulenspiegel* in GDR; *Ludas Matyi* in Hungary; *Dikobraz* in Czechoslovakia.

12 Tomasz Gleb, 'Ailing Art', *Przegląd Artystyczny*, no. 2 (1953) p. 72. The print is overtly critical of socialist realism with its over-institutionalization, the emptiness of its slogans and recipes and the inadequate methods of cultural politics that only aggravate the poor condition of art.

13 An interesting example of an attack on a foreign culture without visualizing it is the *Poisoner* by William Gropper, in which, under the heading 'American kitsch floods the art of Western Europe' (1949), 'kitsch' is shown as an oily and poisonous liquid being pumped out from a large tank over Western Europe by a fat Wall Street capitalist (*Szpilki*, no 42 [16 October 1949] p. 3). For a later example of an anti-formalist Soviet cartoon, see, J. Semenov, 'In the Western Museum', *Krokodil* (20 May 1961) p.13, or the two cartoons published on the occasion of the Manezh exhibition of 1962 (*Pravda*, 3 and 4 December 1962). On anti-modernist cartoons in the West, see George Melly and J.R. Glaves-Smith, *A Child of Six Could Do It! Cartoons on Modern Art*, exh. cat., The Tate Gallery (London: 1973).

14 For example, J. Zaruba, 'A Painter at Harvest-Time', *Szpilki*, no. 27 (2 July 1950); K. Klamann, K. Schrader, *Frischer Wind*, no. 5 (1953).

15 Ha-Ga, *Szpilki*, no. 50 (18 December 1951).

16 'A Sad Story', *Krokodil*: (30 April 1954), reproduced in *Szpilki*, no. 24 (13 June 1954).

17 L. Zachorski, 'A Voice in the Discussion About Architecture', *Szpilki* (1 March 1955); *Krokodil* (10 January 1961); *Krokodil*, (28 February 1961); *Krokodil*, (20 May 1961).

18 For example, J. Uzbiakov, 'In the Poster Department of the Publishing House "Iskusstvo"', *Krokodil*: (20 August 1950). On Soviet art criticism see Matthew Cullerne Bown, *Socialist Realist Painting* (New Haven and London: Yale University Press, 1998) in particular pp. 264–6.

19 Ernest Petrajtis, pseudonym: Jantar, *Mucha*, no. 13 (16 April 1950) p. 6.

20 Juliusz Starzyński, introduction in *I Ogólnopolska Wystawa Plastyki*, exh. cat., National Museum in Warsaw (Warsaw: 1950) pp. 7–13; Urszula Pomorska, 'O prasie przed- i powystawowej', *Przegląd Artystyczny*, nos 5/6 (1950) pp. 63–4.

21 Juliusz Krajewski, 'I Ogólnopolska Wystawa Plastyki', *Przegląd Artystyczny*, nos 5/6 (1950) pp. 18–22, p. 19.

22 Aleksandr Gerasimov, 'Sztuki plastyczne demokratycznej Polski', *Przegląd Artystyczny*, 1950, nos 5/6, pp. 24 (reprinted from *Kul'tura i zhizn'*, 11 May 1950). Interestingly, the show was treated with silence by the Polish professional press.

23 'The common fault of all cartoonists is the difficulty of drawing a positive hero – the man of labour of our days, caused by the unsufficient acquaintance with reality [. . .].' Lenica, 'O karykaturze słów kilka'.

24 Starzyński, *I Ogólnopolska Wystawa Plastyki*, exh. cat., pp. 12–13.

25 Melly and Glaves-Smith, *A Child of Six Could Do It!*, nos 38, 45.

26 Stephen White, *The Bolshevik Poster* (New Haven and London: Yale University Press, 1988) nos 4.4, 4.5, 5.14., 5.21. See also a poster by Khvostenko-Khovstov in L.V. Vladich, *Ukrainskij politichnij plakat / The Ukrainian Political Poster* (Kiev: 1981) no. 2.

27 Deni's poster was based upon a newspaper cartoon by Mikhail Cheremnykh (1918; see White, *The Bolshevik Poster*, pp. 56–7, no. 3.32). Deni repeated the same scheme in another poster on the Red Army victories over the Nazis in 1943 (see Peter Paret, Berth Irwin Lewis, Paul Paret, *Persuasive Images. Posters of War and Revolution from the Hoover Institution Archives*, Princeton NJ: Princeton University Press, 1992, no. 236). The scheme reveals a clear iconographical affiliation to Christian theme of the expulsion of the Philistines from the Temple.

28 Karen Kettering, '"Ever more cosy and comfortable" Stalinism and the Soviet Domestic Interior', *Journal of Design History*, vol. 10, no. 2, (1997) pp. 119–35, pp. 123–4.

29 Piotr Labużek, pseudonym: Baro, 'Spring Cleaning', *Szpilki*, no. 13 (26 March 1950) p. 11.

30 Borowski, 'O postępowych i wstecznych tradycjach karykatury politycznej'.

31 The author seemed to feel more secure in the field of verbalizing rather than visualizing and he soon became better known as an author of songs. Górska and Lipiński, *Z dziejów karykatury polskiej*, p. 261.

32 K. Murawska-Muthesius, 'The Case of the Man of Marble, or, The Rise and Fall and Rise of Socialist Realism in Polish Museums', in W. Reinink, J. Stumpel (eds.) *Memory and Oblivion.* Proceedings of the XXIXth International Congress of History of Art, Amsterdam, 1996 (Dordrecht: Kluwer Academic Publishers, 1999) pp. 905–12.

33 Wanda Załuska, 'Malarstwo współczesne w galeriach muzealnych', *Muzealnictwo*, II, (1953) p. 8.

34 *Kolekcja sztuki XX w. w Muzeum Sztuki w Łodzi*, exh. cat., Galeria Zachęta (Warsaw: 1991) p. 12.

35 In fact, Kott talked here about a painting in the 'post-impressionist manner' (Jan Kott, 'Mitologia i realizm', *Przegląd Kulturalny*, vol. 5, no. 14 (1956)).

36 For attempts to explain the radical rejection of socialist realism in Poland see Crowley's analysis of the negative response to the Soviet Palace of Culture in Warsaw as not being invested with 'popular' memory (David Crowley, 'People's Warsaw/Popular Warsaw' in *Journal of Design History*, vol. 10, no. 2 (1997) pp. 203–23); see Murawska-Muthesius on the failed attempts of museum curators to trace the roots of socialist realism in the nineteenth-century Polish painting (Katarzyna Murawska-Muthesius, 'A "new body" for the "new nation" and the search for its prototypes. A chapter in the advancement of socialist realism in Poland, 1949–1955' in Francis Ames-Lewis and Piotr Paszkiewicz, (eds.), *Art and Politics* (Warsaw: Insytut Sztuki PAN, 1999) pp. 171–86); see Antoine Baudin on the difficulties with the dissemination of the Soviet model of socialist realism in Poland in his '"Why is Soviet Painting Hidden from Us." Zhdanov Art and Its International Relations and Fallout, 1947–53', in T. Lahusen, E. Dobrenko (eds), *Socialist Realism without Shores* (Durham and London: Duke University Press, 1997) pp. 227–56; as well as Polish critical studies of socialist realism written in the 1980s (Waldemar Baraniewski, 'Wobec realizmu socjalistycznego' in *Sztuka polska po 1945 roku* (Warsaw: Państwowe Wydawnictwo Naukowe, 1987) and Wojciech Włodarczyk, *Socrealizm. sztuka polska w latach 1950–1954* (Paris: Libella, 1986).

–9–

Veils, *Shalvari*, and Matters of Dress: Unravelling the Fabric of Women's Lives in Communist Bulgaria

Mary Neuburger

'Socialism can not be built from behind a veil.' Or so proclaimed Boris Nikolov, a regional secretary of the Bulgarian Communist Party (BCP) in the 1950s.[1] Nikolov, a missionary of BCP values in the northeastern Bulgarian provinces, found himself stationed in a district heavily populated by Muslim Turks, the largest of Bulgaria's minority populations. Turks who are concentrated in rural areas of Northeastern and Southeastern Bulgaria, and Pomaks (Bulgarian-speaking Muslims) who live in compact enclaves along the Southern border, have inhabited the geographical and social margins of Bulgarian society since 1878, when Bulgaria gained political autonomy from the Ottoman Empire.[2] Since the late nineteenth century, but particularly in the communist period (1944–89), Bulgarian bureaucrats and intellectuals have confronted the Muslim fringe in various ways, with evolving theories and practices about what these populations represent and how they should or should not be integrated into Bulgarian society writ large. Like other negotiators of Bulgarian national identity before and after him, Nikolov cast his gaze onto the problem of Muslim women as caretakers of cultural difference and hence barriers to communist-driven modernization and national integration.

Bulgaria, insecurely teetering on the edge of the continent, went to extreme lengths to express its Marxist modernity in European terms, which by definition necessitated a negation of Bulgaria's five centuries under Ottoman rule. The Muslim margins had attracted attention from the centre of the modernizing Bulgarian state throughout the twentieth century, spawning projects aimed at re-shaping Muslim material culture in the image of a modern Bulgarian national ideal. The veil and other Turco-Muslim women's garments were at times central to twentieth-century Bulgarian efforts to confront difference at the hidden and often obstinate periphery, particularly in the communist period. Clothing reform, aimed primarily at Muslim women, was an arena in which Bulgarian bureaucrats and intellectuals pondered and negotiated Bulgaria's place between 'East' and 'West', Europe and Asia, the past and the future. As a result, Muslim women's garment choice became politicized, a mark of defiance or loyalty to the state and the nation. Both before and during the communist period, draping 'oriental' garments seemed incompatible with concepts of Bulgaria as modern and European. As the Bulgarian state attempted to eliminate material vestiges of the Ottoman past, the Muslim women of Bulgaria challenged state power subtly but pointedly as it seeped into the fabric of their lives.

A vast literature on dress has emerged in the past few decades, which tries to answer questions about the multiple meanings assigned to clothing. Engaging theoretical questions on material and consumer culture, this literature generally has an empirical focus on the industrialized 'West' and, to a lesser extent, on its former colonies.[3] Among other issues raised, numerous authors have advanced the assumption that clothing is one dimension of material culture that is a most extraordinary indicator if not a catalyst for social and cultural change. As Grant McCracken explores, apparel choices are a communicative device through which 'social change is contemplated, proposed, initiated, enforced and denied'.[4] Furthermore, he and others have explored how, in various contexts, in the midst of various power relations, dress has assumed the role of an 'instrument of attempted domination' as well as 'an armory of resistance and protest'.[5] As is often the case, the former Eastern bloc, the so-called 'Second World', has been largely left out of this new current of scholarship.[6] Yet some important questions and conclusions have come out of the existing literature that may shed light on the perhaps less dynamic, but not less complex, realm of material culture in Eastern Europe under communism.

To what extent has clothing, its production, consumption, and display, been a catalyst for social or political change, a base of everyday resistance or, alternatively, an agent of domination in Eastern Europe? In particular, as pertains to the communist period, when production and consumption of garments were under severe constraints, and when unofficial economies and activities left behind few records, how can we ascertain the meaning of clothes? In this context, it is precisely in regard to the ways and means of such attempted control, and to the interstices of state control, that a more nuanced exploration of the changes in production and consumption of material culture is possible and desirable. The diversity of economic and cultural conditions across Eastern Europe (as well as the Soviet Union) demands an exploration of particular contexts, where divergent historical legacies and cultural complexities played their role in the most dramatic social and political experiments in the twentieth century. Just as the dynamics of material culture, its consumption and production, drove social change in the West, there is a growing recognition that within the Eastern bloc, shortages, demands and unofficial activities in the realm of material culture may well have been instrumental in bringing down the system. Slavenka Drakulic, for example, aptly recognized how the seemingly trivial nuts and bolts of everyday life, 'how people ate and dressed', were permeated with political meaning in communist societies; to her this was what mattered on a daily basis, especially in women's lives.[7]

All dimensions of material culture were politicized in one way or another in the period of communist rule in Eastern Europe. Communism, after all, was a material ideology. It was about material conditions, material factors, and material transformations. Above all, communist regimes sought to transform society by remaking material culture. Dress and all it symbolized was one of the most basic and intimate arenas in which the various battles of the communist state were fought and over which identity and loyalty were negotiated. Dress was about image, and in the communist period the 'new man' and the 'new woman' were carefully constructed images. The socialist person was expected to dress for success, that is, the building of a bright new communist future. The politics of dress in Bulgaria in the communist period (1944–89) provides a fertile ground for exploring some of the nuances of state policy and the various forms of resistance it provoked in the very personal, and yet very political realm of clothing. Bulgaria is probably the least-studied East European country, besides Albania, in part, because of the erroneous assumption that since Bulgaria was 'the most loyal satellite' there are no nuances worth exploring in the Bulgarian experience under communism. But the Bulgaro–Muslim encounter under communism was one area in which certain deviations from the Soviet model were apparent as pre-communist legacies were clearly brought to bear. Although Yugoslavia and the Soviet Union also had domestic encounters with Islam, their federal nature and much larger populations of Muslims necessitated a more compromising relationship with Muslims within. While both these states did try to modernize Islam and even de-veil Muslim women, Bulgaria had the most dramatic and far-reaching confrontation with its Muslim minorities in the period in question. That is, the Bulgarian state went the furthest in its attempts to integrate Muslims completely into the Bulgarian 'socialist nation'.

Marxism-Leninism in the Bulgarian context (perhaps more than anywhere else in Eastern Europe) was tightly intertwined with a complex and dual confrontation, at once with the imperialist 'West' and the backward 'East'. Bulgaria, like the rest of Eastern Europe, was critical of Western Europe and the US in Marxist terms, explicitly rejecting Western imperialism and consumerism. Communist Bulgaria, however, did not forsake its own Europeanness and, in fact, like Western Europe, associated out-of-control consumerism with the US, rather than West European culture *per se*.[8] Although, like the rest of the bloc, Bulgaria had to pay lip service to spreading communism to the colonial 'East', it gradually went to war against the 'oriental' within. These battles, and their underlying themes and concepts, were brought to bear in campaigns aimed at directing and controlling the garment choices of Muslim women in Bulgaria. Far from hapless victims, these women developed strategies of everyday resistance that undermined state efforts to enforce material conformity.

Clothing had always been one of the critical arenas in which the Europeanization of Bulgarian society proceeded. What began as a more spontaneous process among Bulgarian Christians in the nineteenth and early twentieth centuries would only later become a state-directed programme targeting Muslim difference. After Bulgaria gained its independence from the Ottomans in the 1877–8 Russo–Turkish War the Europeanization of men and women's fashion followed, a continuation of earlier nineteenth-century trends. Bulgarian thinkers began to assimilate European clothing as a part of fashioning a national identity on the ruins of an Ottoman past, now increasingly understood as a 500-year 'Ottoman yoke' that held Bulgaria back from the general currents of European experience. For Turks and Pomaks left behind in the receding tide of Ottoman influence, Turco-Ottoman clothes remained the norm both in the depleted urban areas and in the still-vital Muslim countryside. As Western influence grew and Ottoman influence waned after 1878 – although less so among the considerable Muslim minorities left on Bulgaria soil – there was a general flood of criticism of all 'foreign' influences in all aspects of Bulgarian life. In their place there was a pointed search for the native, that is, *Bulgarskoto* (Bulgarianness). The Bulgarian folk costume, and, in particular, women's dress, seemed to represent a pure repository of the Bulgarian national spirit in this period. Historians, geographers and ethnographers went on elaborate expeditions to map the regional variations in Bulgarian folk costumes all of which held national meaning.[9] But, just as Bulgarian commentators began to lament the contamination of Bulgarian cities by 'foreign' (here European) influences, so the rural reservoir of purity was seemingly sullied only by the presence of 'oriental' garments. In this period, it was the wearing of the 'veil' by the Pomak population of Southern Bulgaria, as well as in Thrace and Macedonia, that seemed most disturbing to Bulgarian ethnographers, who set out scientifically to 'prove' the 'Bulgarianness' of this purportedly 'Turkified' and 'Islamicized' group.[10] Although it is doubtful that rural women in the Balkans were heavily veiled in this period, any scarf tied in a different fashion could be conceptualized as a 'veil' by the Bulgarian social scientist, undoubtedly influenced by West European discourse on the veil as ultimate manifestation of the 'Orient'. The seemingly illegitimate presence of the veil on the heads of Pomak women became a focus of academic study and obsession, as it was viewed as not *narodno* (native) but *chuzhdo* (foreign).[11]

Pomaks, were increasingly conceptualized in the historical and ethnographic literature as 'victims' rather than perpetrators of Ottoman crimes. This was in stark contrast to the way the Bulgarian academy viewed Turks, that is, as collaborators with the Ottoman overlords. This differentiation was based on historical and ethnographic studies which had determined that Pomaks were presumably forcibly 'Islamicized Bulgarians'.[12] Thus the focus was on their victimization rather than collusion. It was in the context of Pomak-as-victim that 'liberation' was first contemplated. In the post-war period the 'Turkish masses' would also be re-cast as victims and it was only then that they, too, would be subject to the kinds of modernizing campaigns that targeted only Pomaks in the pre-1944 period. Hence, dress reform and other modernizing measures were never conceived as punishment, but rather as 'liberation.'

A key part of the pre-war 'liberation' of Pomaks from presumed 'foreign' occupation took the form of an assault on material vestiges of the Ottoman past. During the First Balkan war of 1912–13, as Bulgarian armies advanced southwards to fight the Ottoman Empire, they brought an entourage of Orthodox priests who carried out forced conversions of some 200,000 Pomaks (but not Turks) on and across Bulgaria's southern border. On the heels of these conversions, Pomaks were given Bulgarian names, and the fez, turban and 'veil' were replaced with Bulgarian hats and scarves.[13] This incursion into Pomak villages caused a mass migration of Pomaks from Bulgarian territories and large numbers of Pomaks demonstrated on the streets, re-donning the fez and the veil and spontaneously re-Islamicizing.[14] Although the fez also, clearly had significance in this Bulgarian war on Islam among Pomaks, the veil was increasingly the larger 'problem' for Bulgarian modernizers.

Although the Balkan War measures were reversed in 1914, by the late 1930s, dramatic campaigns to reform Pomak clothes re-surfaced, this time orchestrated by a small segment of the Pomak community itself (Figure 9.1) The *Rodina* (homeland) movement, founded in 1937 in Smolian by a handful of Pomaks, articulated its primary goal as the diffusing of 'Bulgarianness' to their 'misguided' Pomak brothers and sisters, who prevalently identified with the Turks (only just beginning to discover their own Turkishness). De-veiling campaigns were one of the central arenas of activity for the movement, although de-fezzing was also a continued area of concern. Initially, *Rodina* launched a clothing reform campaign that was entirely voluntary, executed through the mass distribution of appeals such as this one:

> The time has come . . . The future is ours . . . We appeal to all the Bulgaro-Mohammedans from the Rhodope region to break with centuries of darkness and ignorance; the men must, once and for all, throw off the foreign hat, the fez, and replace it with a Bulgarian national hat, and women shed the black veil (*bulo*) and mantle (*feredje*) as signs of slavery and inhumanity, and replace them with Bulgarian national clothes.[15]

With the outbreak of the Second World War, however, these appeals had the power of the state behind them as the *Rodina* project expanded rapidly into the occupied territories of Thrace and Macedonia. *Rodina* leaders set out to 'establish general order' in these 'newly liberated territories' through the de-veiling of Pomak women. By 1943 the government had passed the 'law on clothes' which codified the

Figure 9.1 These pictures of a 'veiled' (left) and a 'deveiled' woman were juxtaposed in *Rodina* appeals to Pomak women in the 1930s and 1940s and appeared in Petur Marinov, ed., *Sbornik Rodina*, vol. 3 (Smolian: Izdanie na "Rodina", 1940). The captions read 'The clothing of the past – the sign of slavery, violence, and inhumanity' (left) and 'The clothing of the future – the sign of freedom, heath, and national consciousness.'

rejection of 'foreign' clothing; the veil (as well as the fez) were temporarily shed once more.[16] These clothing reform campaigns, again aimed at both men and women, were abandoned and reversed at the end of the war with the change of regime. They were labelled as 'Fascist' by the communist regime, and numerous *Rodina* members were imprisoned or pushed from positions of responsibility by 1947. This occurred in spite of the fact that most *Rodina* members, who were enthusiastic about the modernizing essence of the new regime, were ready and willing to take part in the building of socialism.

After World War Two, the Bulgarian state inscribed meaning on the everyday, and specifically women's dress, with a new intensity and new theoretical and practical tools of enforcement. In general, the new image of the Bulgarian woman mimicked the high-Stalinist and new Eastern bloc image of woman as amalgam of worker, peasant and soldier, as producer and reproducer. By propagating such images, communist states set out to emancipate women from their bourgeois past and activate them as participants in the economy and politics. These states thereby endeavoured to penetrate the perceived fortress of the domestic sphere. For it was in the home that the younger generation could be exposed to the influence of women, the presumed guardians of the gate. The state had the complicated task of diverting women from their assumed role as trustees of tradition and, instead, reconstructing their image and essence in the socialist spirit. The communist world stressed women's history of oppression and hence their seemingly natural role as ultimate proletariat.[17] In line with Soviet theorists, Balkan communists conceptualized Muslim women as more oppressed than their Christian counterparts both by feudal and bourgeois-capitalist society and by the Muslim patriarchy (presumed more onerous than the Christian one).[18] In the post-war period, 'liberation' again would provide the rationale for Bulgarian penetration into Muslim women's lives.

Paradigms of the Bulgarian pre-communist past provided a subtext that melded well with modernizing, Soviet-imposed concepts of the socialist woman. Bulgarian theoreticians and bureaucrats cut their new images of women and women's dress out of the same cloth as pre-communist conceptual frameworks, albeit with Marxist-Leninist patterns. Bulgarian nationalist discourse on backwardness and progress, East and West, and the expunging of an onerous Ottoman past was readily compatible with the theory and practice of socialist modernization. Dress and other visible material remnants of the Ottoman past had long been targets of state programmes for the Europeanization of Bulgaria. The communist regime was even more insistent about the need for conformity in the realm of material culture in Bulgaria, which was perceived more than ever as an indicator of social progress. If the women of Bulgaria, no matter what their ethnic background, dressed in a modern way, then they would be modern in the eyes of the Bulgarian state (and the outside world).

Women, with their heavily scarved (or veiled) hair and peasant garb, were considered to be the bastion of material backwardness. In Bulgaria, as elsewhere, traditional women of the majority as well as minority groups were enticed to mimic idealized images of the socialist equivalent of the semi-androgynous, American 'Gibson girl', with simple dresses and hairdos and smaller, less traditional scarves tied over their hair. Often subtle folk themes were integrated into this new mode of dress, and hence folk attire was not rejected wholesale as long as it was sanitized, modernized and generally relegated to folk ensembles and ethnographic museums.[19] In a sense, communist states imposed 'socialist realism' in fashion, especially as women across the bloc became urbanized and purchased factory-produced garments; clothing other than the simple, proper, communist style was simply not available in state-run stores. This process seemed to proceed more quickly and naturally with Bulgarian women in the urban milieu, who tended to conform more readily to idealized socialist images of women. Significantly, the generic modern costume was increasingly equated with socialist Bulgarianness. For minority women in Bulgaria and elsewhere, the price of this 'progress' in fashion was much greater and the rewards less enticing. Their invitation to modernity, it became increasingly clear, was couched in terms of a socialist melting pot or assimilation into the socialist majority. For Muslim women in Bulgaria, the promise of socialist modernity, which by the late 1950s was clearly synonymous with uncompromising Bulgarianness, could not lure them from their rural Turkish and Pomak enclaves. Muslims in Bulgaria remained primarily rural throughout this period in contrast to Bulgarian populations that rapidly urbanized. In the rural context, large numbers of Muslim women resisted the state campaigns to shed their 'oriental' garments.

The veil and, for the first time, *shalvari* (baggy Turkish trousers) became the linchpins in communist campaigns to build a homogeneous, socialist, material culture on a putatively Bulgarian foundation. However erroneous the definition of the veil might have been, discourse on the veil makes a certain amount of sense in the general framework of subverting patriarchy and moving towards 'socialist progress'. The campaigns against *shalvari*, however, at a time when women in the West were just beginning to wear trousers as a liberating mode of dress is ironic. Emancipationist women in nineteenth-century Britain and America had actually begun an ill-fated movement for women to don 'Turkish trousers' as a way of liberating women from their burdensome heavy skirts. Amelia Bloomer, after whom the baggy pantaloons (bloomers) they wore were named, had taken 'oriental' pantaloons as a model and had justified the new fashion both in terms of comfort and practicality and by pointing out that even 'oriental women' were allowed to wear such garments.[20] In the communist period in Bulgaria, *shalvari* were suddenly seen as an affront (along with the veil) to the Bulgarian nation and its communist future. The political meaning behind *shalvari* had been laid bare in early BCP documents. One BCP report from the 1947 elections, for example, comments on how Turkish women had been slow in the voting booths because they 'hid their opposition ballots in the folds of their *shalvari*'.[21] Like the veil, *shalvari* seemed to be part of an impenetrable barrier between Muslim women and the state, something that hid or reshaped their supposedly true Bulgaro-European essence.

Initially, the Bulgarian Communist Party had to move fairly gradually in its endeavour to stamp out the remaining vestiges of the Ottoman past, as well as in its efforts to put the state in control of all production and consumption of material culture. In the immediate post-war period there was an awareness among communist cadres in the provinces that Muslim support for the Party was severely lacking or, at best, tentative. Specifically, Party agitators in the provinces recorded the existence of local anxieties about communist intentions to 'de-veil' Muslim women.[22] This apparent fear of an assault on local dress practices was probably a result of uncertainty brought by a new regime with a radical ideology, the legacy of pre-communist de-veiling campaigns, and power shifts within the Turkish community itself. Whereas, before the war, the Bulgarian regime had supported conservative Muslim elements in the fairly autonomous Turco-Muslim institutions, the communists had purged such 'fascist' elements in favour of so-called 'Young Turks', who tended to have modernizing, Attaturkian sensibilities that melded well with communist plans for modernization. In spite of BCP support for the 'Young Turks', de-veiling began as a strong suggestion rather than an order from on high. There was no real, urgent campaign in the Bulgarian or Turkish press in the immediate post-war period. On the contrary, 'veiled' women were occasionally shown in the press as willing participants in the new project of building socialism (Figure 9.2). On one occasion in 1946 in the southern Bulgarian town of Haskovo, the communist-dominated coalition government, the so-called Fatherland Front, actually ordered the provisioning of cloth specifically for the making of veils for local Muslim women.[23] The veil and women's garb were a low priority on the immediate agenda of the fledgling communist regime which had to build its base of power slowly and steadily. In the late 1940s and early 1950s the Communist Party focused its efforts on mobilizing the population, and in particular women, into the Bulgarian work force. Initially it was the carrot, not the stick, that was

Figure 9.2 This is one of many such images from the early post-war period of a 'veiled' Muslim in a public space participating in the 'building of socialism'. Here the anonymous Muslim woman is marching in a public parade (clearly out-numbered by Muslim men) to celebrate "July 9" while holding a small girl. *Yeni Isik* (9 July 1951).

used to lure women into newly created positions of responsibility in Party committees and economic endeavours.

From the very beginning of the post-war period *Yeni Isik*, the Turkish-language organ of the BCP, and other mainstream Bulgarian communist newspapers depicted Muslim women as 'liberated' copies of idealized socialist women, equal citizens of the People's Republic of Bulgaria (Figure 9.4). These representations of Muslim women as modern were scattered across the pages of the BCP-generated Turkish press, interspersed with more traditional images of Muslim women with hair fully

Figure 9.3 This photograph from a refugee camp on the Bulgar-Turkish border (after the expulsions of 1951) shows two women (left) in the typical costume for rural Turks and Muslims more generally, baggy Turkish trousers (*shalvari*) and variations on head scarves that would have been interpreted as 'veils'. From Huey Kostanick, *Turkish Resettlement of Bulgarian Turks: 1950–53* (Berkeley: University of California Press, 1957).

covered (and in *shalvari*) but fully participating in the building of socialism. It was important, at least initially, not to alienate or exclude any Muslim women from socialist society; on the contrary they were to be mobilized into the state economy regardless of garment choice. But as the building of socialism gained momentum in the late 1950s, the diversity of images of Muslim women faded into a monolith of socialist sameness, with veiled and *shalvari*-clad women appearing only as objects of ridicule and pity.

Birleşik Amerika, Çin cumhuriyeti Fransa'dan müte lef arasında Barış iktedilmesi için

Sovyetler Birliği, İngiltere ve şekkil Beş dev antlaşması imzalıyorum

Figure 9.4 This is a typical image of a Turkish woman from *Yeni Isik* (17 April 1951) as worker, mother, and political actor, here, signing a petition for peace.

Suspicions about the true loyalties of Bulgarian Turks were heightened as Cold War tensions settled over the Balkans after Turkey made clear its intention to join NATO in 1950; Eastern and Western threats to Bulgarian security became intertwined with a new intensity. As a direct result, the BCP engineered the expulsion of approximately 140,000 Turkish-speaking Muslims from Bulgaria in 1950–1, an action that targeted allegedly disloyal Turkish elements (Figure 9.3). At the 1951 Party Plenum in the wake of the exodus, the BCP made public the decision for the 'faster raising of the ideological, political, cultural, and economic level' of the Turkish and Pomak populations, a programme in which the 'veil' was afforded a special place.[24]

It was not until the famous April Plenum of 1956, however, that Bulgarian leader Todor Zhivkov consolidated personal power and began to assert a rapid plan of action for Bulgarian society in general and Bulgaria's Muslim populations in particular. The link between socialist progress and nationalist homogenization in Bulgaria became increasingly clear as ethnic categories were taken off the Bulgarian census. 'Special rights' and institutions for minorities came under fire in this period and suffered gradual erosion while the Party increasingly used nationalist rhetoric to build legitimacy at home. This Bulgarian brand of 'national communism' was perhaps most akin to the openly Romanian nationalist tactics of Nicolae Ceausescu, with its attendant anti-Hungarian campaign, although without the anti-Soviet dimension. In the wake of Khrushchev's de-stalinization there was a need throughout the bloc to bolster legitimacy as the Stalinist past was so harshly criticized. In spite of the hard line taken against the Hungarian revolution of 1956, Khrushchev made it clear that, to a large extent, he would tolerate separate 'roads to socialism' within the bloc.

The so-called 'April Line', the cornerstone of the Bulgarian 'road to socialism', articulated at the 1956 Plenum, called for an accelerated drive towards 'progress' in all realms of socialist development. In a direct emulation of communist projects in China, the BCP pushed forward an all-encompassing plan for rapid economic development and a 'cultural revolution' that targeted Muslim minorities in the Bulgarian hinterland. Because of their more 'backwards' economic and cultural circumstances, Muslim populations and their material culture, in particular, became designated targets of the BCP's economic and cultural measures in what they called the 'Great Leap Forward' of 1958–60. Facts and figures on de-veiling were consistently held up as the definitive indicator of the success of these measures in the provinces.[25] As a result of the apparent successes of the 'cultural revolution' the BCP was triumphant about their noteworthy achievements, reporting that Muslim women had broken 'the bonds of fanaticism and almost all women are wearing beautiful, light, comfortable, European clothes'.[26] Party-organized *zhenotdeli* (women's committees) were the primary force behind dress-reform campaigns of the late 1950s 'cultural revolution'. These committees recruited Muslim women, when possible, and organized intensive 'explanatory sessions' and even door-to-door visits. *Zhenotdeli* propaganda sessions often included testimonials of Muslim women who had embraced dresses (that is, shed their *shalvari*) and cast off their veils. As one such re-dressed Muslim woman expressed it, 'I've begun to feel like a person . . . in nothing do I differ from my Bulgarian female comrades.'[27] Muslim leaders were also instructed to go from village to village preaching the gospel of de-veiling to their flocks.[28] The message of the 'de-veiled' Muslim woman cited above was echoed at a conference of Muslim leaders in the aftermath of the 'cultural revolution' where one delegate proudly declared, 'Now, wherever you go there is no difference, and you can't even tell who is a Turk and who is a Bulgarian . . . The Turkish woman is freed from her centuries-old black veil.'[29] Although these testimonials focus on Bulgarian-flavoured socialist sameness, it is important to note that women were appealed to in Marxist terms on the basis of progress, civilization, and a bright utopian future.

When such appeals rang hollow for large portions of the Muslim female masses the Bulgarian state had to employ new tactics, both suggestive and coercive, to bring Muslim women into the fold of socialist modernity. One approach was to assert more control over the distribution of clothing in Muslim districts, as Muslim women began to be directly supplied with the proper garb of the new socialist woman. With this in mind, by 1960 cooperative farms in Muslim districts began to take money directly out of the wages of female Muslim members and 'advance' dresses against their salaries.[30] Muslim women, who generally sewed their own *shalvari* and veils in this period, had apparently complained that they could not afford the more onerous costs of factory sewn dresses. To avoid such excuses the state simply made the consumer choice for Muslim women; dresses would be supplied in lieu of a portion of their salaries in many cases. Officially, the results were astounding as reports from the provinces in 1960 claimed that 100 per cent de-veiling and shedding of *shalvari* by Muslim women had been achieved in certain locales in a single week or in a matter of months.[31] In conjunction with this approach, sewing brigades were sent into Islamic regions to liquidate the problems of veils and *shalvari*. According to one local report, with the sewing of 900 dresses in Razgrad in eleven days, the Great Leap Forward was achieved.[32] To the communists directing the campaign, coerced supply seemed to solve the issue of lack of demand faster than a revolution in consciousness. Yet, in spite of glowing reports from the provinces the problem apparently continued or resurfaced throughout the Muslim provinces and the need to re-dress Muslim women remained on the BCP agenda. If Muslim women would not respond to all-out coercion then perhaps they could be won over to socialist modernity through their sense of fashion and beauty.

The Party's shift in tactics coincided with the subtle shift towards appealing to and satisfying the consumer needs of populations across the bloc, often in conjunction with asserting a 'national path to socialism'. This shift towards socialist consumerism in the 1960s and 1970s was linked to the crisis of legitimacy that had rocked the foundations of the bloc since 1953. Many East European regimes had begun slowly to turn their efforts towards bolstering the standard of living for their citizens, mostly through Western credits, as a way of keeping the masses satisfied, but without openly embracing consumerism, still deemed part of the decadent capitalist world. Unfortunately for the bloc, they took out loans they could never pay and they opened a Pandora's box they could never close. A powerful underground market grew in strength to meet unfulfilled consumer expectations, a 'second economy' that played a powerful role in undermining the official economy.[33] Analysts of gender in Eastern Europe have even suggested that women's consumer needs, in particular, were critical in fuelling popular opposition in the more overt protest movements of East Central Europe that are often credited with the fall of the system.[34] Muslim women, in contrast, were not demanding consumer goods, but refusing to consume. Although their protests were less overt, their behaviour may still have proved erosive to the efficacy and hence legitimacy of the system as a whole. Bulgaria, along with Romania, was one of the most hesitant members of the bloc in terms of playing with the fire of consumerism and foreign debt in the 1960s and 1970s. Still, this period witnessed a subtle shift in BCP tactics in its ongoing campaigns to achieve social and ethnic levelling through conformity of dress. Some very nuanced appeals to the population's consumer sensibilities seem to have seeped into BCP writings in general, including clothing campaigns aimed at Muslim women.

The regime's use of fashion, which became a larger part of the public appeals to Muslim women by the 1960s and 1970s, might have been linked to the general assumption that women were inherently more materialistic than men; the regime presumably could be most effective by pandering to their sensibilities as 'material girls'. The BCP had already made a conceptual link between socialism and fashion for the women of Bulgaria in one of the official women's magazines *Lada* (Harmony). *Lada* was devoted solely to fashion and 'everyday culture' (*bitova kultura*) and was filled with drawings and, later, photographs of fashion models in 'modern' attire. Inside its front cover, *Lada* launched its appeals to women's sense of fashion and beauty, which it applauded, linking it to the building of socialism:

> *Lada* will become your friend. It will help you to chose your clothes – for work, everyday, and holidays: with their beautiful appearance people show that they respect themselves love and admire others . . . *Lada* will endeavour to raise consciousness about all that is beautiful for the builders of a new life.[35]

Beauty, which was coterminous with modern Europeanized sensibilities, was raised to the level of a socialist virtue. Clearly, fashion and socialism were not like oil and water, as might be imagined. For Bulgarian women, this was a seeming concession that the Bulgarian state extended to their existing consumer needs, a socialist rationalization for shopping and vanity. For Muslim women, on the other hand, a demand had to be created for modern European fashion, both in terms of its utility and beauty.

By the 1960s, while bureaucratic and academic discourse on the veil and *shalvari* still contained its harsh polemic, the state increasingly appealed to women on a more practical, if not consumer-oriented level. As early as 1960, lectures and presentations aimed at Turkish and Pomak women stressed the need to discard 'out of date, expensive, old clothes' such as the veil and *shalvari* for 'cheaper, more hygienic and practical dresses.'[36] The new emphasis on price, comfort and hygiene went beyond past discussions of such clothes as representative of a patriarchal, despotic, if not 'foreign' past. Instead, in multiple Muslim districts Party functionaries suggested that local officials organize 'fashion shows' to encourage the Europeanization of Turkish dress.[37] One such 'fashion revue' advertised in *Yeni Isik* in 1975 promised displays of 'clothes throughout the centuries', with *shalvari* exhibited as belonging to a past epoch. In contrast, the spokesman for the fashion show asserted that, 'In our time clothes are light, comfortable, hygienic, and beautiful.'[38]

Muslim women were called on not only to heed modern fashion norms but also to use cosmetics and visit hair salons. This was closely connected with the purely visual aspect, the un-covering dimension, of the clothing reform ideals: the bodies and faces of Muslim women would now be visible to all in Bulgarian society and would conform to urban-based Bulgarian socialist aesthetics. An article in *Lada* in 1959 focused on the visibility and, hence, need for beautification of Muslim women's faces:

> Woman today has entered into our social, economic, and political life. She is an equal comrade and co-worker of men in science laboratories and in material production and public life. All prejudices, connected with her personal, public, and social situation have disappeared. The Pomak woman threw off the veil, but many women still have not thrown off the idea that taking care of one's face, the necessity of a nice complexion and the use of cosmetics is indulgent and vain. Exactly now, when the woman is constantly under everyone's gaze in the factory, in society, in enterprises, she should have a tidy, proper and beautiful appearance.[39]

Articles appeared regularly in the Turkish press too, that both instructed Muslim women how to dress and spoke of the necessity of visiting hair salons and using cosmetics.[40] Make-up and fancy hair-dos were deemed acceptable for builders of socialism, as long as beauty was couched in socialist terms. Fashion was re-fashioned as a modernizing, Europeanizing force that was an acceptable part of the socialist discourse. Traditional Muslim women's clothes, meanwhile, could not be justified in these terms or viewed through this lens. Instead, they remained a thorn in the side of the socialist regime.

According to reports from the Muslim districts, veils and *shalvari* persisted and continually re-surfaced on the streets of Muslim villages throughout the period. As noted earlier, since the beginning of the communist period the garments of Muslim women had carried a certain degree of political weight, linked directly to opposition sentiments. As early as 1951, Party cadres began to speak of the 're-veiling' of de-veiled women as a form of protest by the local Muslim population.[41] In the period following the 'cultural revolution', local officials continued to complain that Muslim women were wearing veils and *shalvari* in their districts.

Furthermore, as one communist cadre complained, in many cases, even when the 'transition to dresses' had been achieved, '*shalvari* were still being worn underneath the dresses of Muslim women in the villages'.[42] 'Re-veiling' and re-donning of *shalvari* among the Muslim masses were widely observed in this period, as were other manifestations of 'Islamic sentiment', generally conceived in connection with presumed resistance to the Party programme.[43] Furthermore, Turkish and Pomak Party members whose wives, sisters, and daughters refused to 'break with the old ways' and continued to wear veils were called to account for failing to set an example.[44] There were ongoing Party discussions about how 'many of our Turkish leaders say they are for de-veiling but don't set an example . . . their mothers, sisters and close ones don't follow the example of de-veiling.' A Party report from Razgrad duly denounced the Turkish president of the agricultural cooperative who reportedly 'did not convince his wife to wear a dress', and so raised the question of 'how to liquidate the *shalvari* which remain in their [Muslim women's] dressers'.[45] Women's wardrobes were clearly perceived as a reflection of their political-cum-national loyalties.

The battle over Muslim women's garb continued throughout the communist period on the sidelines of a bigger assimilation campaign in the 1960s and 1970s that targeted Pomaks (and Gypsies) for an attempted total Bulgarianization. In 1984 the BCP launched the hotly contested assimilation campaign against Turks, which came to be known euphemistically as the 'rebirth process'. The Turks of Bulgaria were now assumed to be Islamicized, Turkified Bulgarians, as Pomaks had been since the turn of the century. Hence, Zhivkov's famous assertion in 1985 that 'there are no Turks in Bulgaria'. The 1984 assimilation decree called for the wholesale illegalization of the veil, *shalvari*, and other 'Turkic' articles of clothing. As laid out in a decree passed down to the town of Gledka in 1984, 'Citizens are prohibited from wearing non-traditional Bulgarian clothes like *shalvari*, veils, and others.'[46] Other documents from the period explicitly banned any scarves that are 'veil-like' while also in slightly larger towns such as Ruse prohibited both 'immodest attire' and 'non-traditional clothes'.[47] These decrees make it clear that persons in such attire cannot be served at public establishments and 'no jobs shall be made available to those who wear baggy pants . . . in the streets'.[48]

The assimilation decree, and its attendant legislation on clothing, was reversed only in 1989 after the communist regime was toppled by popular resistance, both Bulgarian and Turkish. Whether consumer resistance and the visible display of Eastern (or Western) garb by the women of Bulgaria really played a role in eroding the edifice of communism is unknown. What is clear is that in the communist period the production and consumption of clothes, perhaps to a larger degree than other realms of material culture, constituted a battlefield where social and cultural change and continuity were negotiated.

Notes

1 Haskovo Okrûzhen Dûrzhaven Arkhiv (hereafter HODA) [Haskovo Regional State Archive] (F-675, O-1, E-112, L-71: 1951).
2 According to the Bulgarian Census of 1992, 800,052 or 9.43% of the population of Bulgaria claimed Turkish origin. See Petya Nitzova, 'Bulgaria: Minorities, Democratization and National Sentiments', *Nationalities Papers* vol. 25 (December 1997) pp. 729–40. While no information on Pomaks was included in this census, according to 1990 estimates there are 268,971 Pomaks in Bulgaria. The author is well aware of some of the recent controversy surrounding the term 'Pomak', which is not universally used by Bulgarian-Muslims to identify themselves and might imply a group unity that does not exist. Nevertheless, I will use the term here for simplicity's sake.
3 See for example Ruth Barnes and Joanne Eiche, *Dress and Gender: Making Meaning* (Oxford: Berg Publishers Inc., 1992); Ruth Rubinstein, *Dress Codes: Meanings and Messages in American Culture* (Boulder: Westview Press, 1995); Hildi Henderson, *Clothing and Difference: Embodied Identities in Colonial and Post-Colonial Africa* (Durham: Duke University Press, 1996); Anne Hollander, *Sex and Suits* (New York: Alfred Knopf, 1994); Grant McCracken, *Culture and Consumption: New Approaches to the Symbolic Character of Goods and Activities* (Bloomington: Indiana University Press, 1988).
4 McCracken, *Culture and Consumption*, p. 61.
5 Ibid., p. 61.
6 One of the few works that deals with consumerism and, in part, issues of clothing in the former Eastern bloc is the exceptional comparative article on East and West Germany, Ute Poiger, 'Rock 'n Roll, Female Sexuality and the Cold War Battle over German Identities', *The Journal of Modern History* vol. 68 (September 1996); See also the occasional discussion of clothes in Slavenka Drakulic, *How We Survived Communism and Even Laughed* (New York: W.W. Norton and Company, 1991). On Soviet Central Asia see Gregory Massel, *The Surrogate Proletariat: Moslem Women and Revolutionary Strategies in Soviet Central Asia, 1919–1929* (Princeton: Princeton University Press, 1974); on Muslim women in Azerbaijan see N. Tohidi, 'Soviet in Public, Azeri in Private: Gender, Islam, and Nationality in Soviet and Post-Soviet Azerbaijan,' *Women's Studies International Forum vol. 2* (1996) pp. 129–45.
7 Drakulic, *How We Survived Communism*, p. xiv.
8 See Poiger's comparison of West German criticism of American consumer culture with the East German critique of American culture in the 1950s. Poiger, 'Rock 'n Roll', p. 587.
9 For a useful overview of Bulgarian ethnography see Khristo Vakarelski, *Etnografia na Bûlgariya* (Sofia: Izdatelstvo na Nauka i Izkustvo, 1974).

10 See Ibid., and Stoyu Shishkov, *Pomatsi v Trite Bulgarski Oblasti: Trakia, Makedonia i Mizia* (Plovdiv: Pechatnitsa ìMakedoniaî, 1914).

11 Stoyu Shishkov, *Bûlgaro-Mokhamedanite (Pomatsi): Istoriko-Zemepisen i Narodoychen Pregled c Obrazi* (Plovdiv: Tûrgovska Pechatinitsa, 1936).

12 Stoyu Shishkov was the patriarch of Pomak studies. See works as listed above. The idea of the forcible conversion of Pomaks is virtually uncontested in Bulgarian literature on the topic, while non-Bulgarian scholarship questions the idea that Pomaks – in most cases – were forcibly converted to Islam. See for example Peter Sugar, *Southeastern Europe under Ottoman Rule 1354–1804* (Seattle: University of Washington Press, 1977) pp. 51–2.

13 Velichko Georgiev and Staiko Trifinov, *Pokrûstvaneto na Bûlgarite Mokhamedani 1912–1913: Dokumenti* (Sofia: Akademichno Izdatelstvo 'Prof. Marin Drinov', 1995) p. 8.

14 Ibid., p. 443.

15 Plovdiv Dûrzhaven Arkhiv (hereafter PDA) [Plovdiv State Archive] (F-959K, O-1, E-110, L-56: 1958).

16 Tsentralen Istoricheski Dûrzhaven Arkhiv (TsIDA) [Central Historical State Archive] (F-264, O-1, E-440, L-9: 1941).

17 See for example Vera Bil'shai, *Reshenie zhenskogo voprosa v SSSR* (Moscow: Gosudarstvennoe izdatelstvo politicheskoi literatury, 1956).

18 On Soviet Muslim women see Dilorum Alimova, *Reshenie zhenskogo voprosa v Uzbekistane, 1917–1941* (Tashkent: Izdatelstvo 'FAN' 1987), or Massel for an English-language interpretation of the phenomenon. On Bulgarian Muslim women see for example Binka Mileva, *Zheni ot Rodopi*, (Sofia: Izdatelsvo na Natsionalniya Sûvet na Otechestven Front, 1960).

19 See, for example, the Bulgarian women's magazine *Zhenata Dnes*, August 1954, p. 8. Here the emulation of Soviet 'socialist realism' in fashion is described as a process of integrating national textile themes into modern fashion. In addition, *Zhenata Dnes*, April 1961, 19, features a fashion layout of clothes that 'show that our national clothes can be a rich source of beautiful elements for the decoration of modern women's clothing.'

20 D.C. Bloomer, *The Life and Writings of Amelia Bloomer* (New York: Schocken Books, 1975).

21 TsIDA (F-214, O-1, E-716, L-19: 1947).

22 TsIDA (F-1B, O-12, E-222, L-53: 1946).

23 HODA (F-182K, O-1, E-92, L-20: 1946).

24 HODA (F-675, O-1, E-112, L-3-8: 1951).

25 TsIDA (F-28, O-16, E-49, L-1: 1960).

26 TsIDA (F-28, O-16, E-49, L-10: 1959).

27 TsIDA (F-28, O-16, E-49, L-106: 1960).

28 TsIDA (F-28, O-16, E-49, L-16: 1960).

29 TsIDA (F-747, O-1, E-19, L-165: 1965).

30 TsIDA (F-28, O-16, E-49, L-125: 1960).

31 TsIDA (F-28, O-16, E-49, L-16,23: 1960).

32 TsIDA (F-28, O-16, E-49, L-21: 1960).

33 Maria Los, ed., *The Second Economy in Marxist States* (New York: St. Martin's Press, 1990), 5.

34 See for example Sharon Wolchik and Alfred Meyer, *Women, State, and Party in Eastern Europe* (Durham: Duke University Press, 1985) pp. 183-184.

35 From inside cover of *Lada,* summer, 1959.

36 TsIDA (F-28, O-16, E-49, L-36: 1960).

37 TsDA (F-1B, O-509, E-5, L-116: 1962).

38 *Yeni Isik* 13 December 1971, p. 3.

39 *Lada* (Summer 1959).

40 *Yeni Isik,* 19 July 1975, p. 3.

41 HODA (F-675, O-1, E-112, L-73: 1951); TsDA (F-28, O-16, E-49, L-23: 1955).

42 TsIDA (F-28, O-16, E-49, L-16: 1960).

43 TsIDA (F-1B, O-5, E-509, L-90: 1962).

44 HODA (F-675, O-1, E-112, L-71: 1951).

45 TsIDA (F-28, O-16, E-49, L-21: 1960).

46 *The Tragedy of the Turkish Minority in Bulgaria* (Ankara: Foreign Policy Institute, 1989) p. 56.

47 Ibid., p. 64.

48 Ibid., p. 55.

All You Need is Lovebeads: Latvia's Hippies Undress for Success

Mark Allen Svede

In 1971, composer Uno Naissoo, a relatively liberal member of Soviet Estonia's musical establishment, offered this observation in a Tallinn cultural weekly:

> If a hippie naked above the waist and with a cross around his neck, plays a violin . . . this does not mean the music is bound to be bad. Let us remember that in fact we have always sanctioned (tacitly or even officially) everything that has acquired international circulation; only we have been late by up to ten years.[1]

His time estimate notwithstanding, this sounds like a modest, reasonable statement to Western, post-Soviet ears. But contemporary readers would have heard, loud and clear, the impressive range of broken taboos that Naissoo was pardoning. The generosity of his view of social nonconformism, with its acknowledgement of hippies, their habitual state of undress and the iconography of the 'Jesus freak', was exceptional enough. Readers also knew perfectly well that, below the waist, the violinist was likely to be wearing something more provocative than the stodgy Soviet approximation of blue jeans sporadically available at GUM and other fine department stores. He was probably not fiddling away at some folk melody exalted by state censors as a palatable expression of youthful identity but, rather, sawing through a jazz improvization or, worse, a rock riff, riddled with alienation. And if any of the readers had recently visited Riga, capital of the adjacent republic of Latvia, they would realize that the hippie wasn't necessarily a he, but more likely a bare-breasted young woman named Inta Grinberga, a trained classical violinist in the midst of what is now regarded as a classic generational revolt (Figure 10.1).

The possibility that a particularly vibrant youth subculture might exist in the Baltic region of the USSR was discernible to foreign observers of Soviet society as early as 1961, when Vasilii Aksenov published *Zvezdnyi bilet* (Starry Ticket).[2] In his novel, three Russian *stiliaga* protagonists, aping American fashion fads and affecting the ennui of Western teenaged hoodlums, flee their dull Moscow surroundings and head to Estonia, where the youthful eccentricities in their dress and behaviour that drew constant reproach in Russia are scarcely remarked upon

Figure 10.1 Inta Grinberga and Andris Grinbergs, 24 August 1972. (Documentation of Latvia's first Happening, *The Wedding of Jesus Christ*.) Photo credit: Māra Brašmane.

once they find themselves on the exotic, Western-looking streets of Tallinn. This state of tolerance may have come as some surprise, however, to Americans who were reading the translation of Aksenov's book at the same moment as an article appeared in the American press, written by a Chicago youth who travelled roughly the same route as these aspiring hipsters, but who characterized life in the Baltics only a few years before as anything but free spirited.

So the Russkys flung a Youth Festival [in 1957] and plastered their major cities with pasteboard doves of peace burdened with banners proclaiming "Peace and Friendship." It was a mite depressing in Riga for instance, where the town was still closed to visitors because nobody had bothered to clean up the wartime rubble. And where the home folks still cussed the Russians every time they got out of earshot.

We sneaked into Riga, mostly because the airport gendarmes seemed a little sleepy, and looked around. It was a 'closed city', so the Russkys hadn't bothered to plaster those phoney doves anywhere. And there wasn't 'peace and friendship' slogans, either. Those were strictly for tourists and Riga wasn't having tourists that year.[3]

While the flippant recollections of a Midwestern youth travelling through unfamiliar territory and fiction penned by the son of a Moscow dissident can hardly be expected to corroborate as historical fact, these two accounts are useful for plotting a certain liberalization that occurred in the Baltic states during the 1960s. Whereas Riga was bereft of 'peace and friendship' slogans on the eve of the 1957 World Youth Festival in Moscow, less than ten years later exterior walls in the medieval section of Riga would be covered with peace signs and graffiti proclaiming 'Long live hippys!' 'Hippy street', 'All you need is love' and 'LSD/LSD/hipi/hipi'.[4] Not long after that, and not far away, an establishment composer would publicly excuse the physical trappings of a hippie musician as being irrelevant to the quality of his performance.

Nevertheless, one's physical trappings often constitute a type of performance, and this became especially true as hippie culture developed and spread worldwide during the 1960s. Of course, for much of the duration of Soviet commodity culture, merely obtaining one's physical trappings proved to be an epic, sometimes inventive, performance for consumers of any persuasion. But because hippies were particularly ill-served by the state-planned economy, their performance was more improvisational than most. Despite the fact that a great deal of the performance had been scripted by peers in the West, hippies in the USSR were forced to research their *mise-en-scène* from afar and to fabricate most of it from scratch, resulting in a high degree of originality and, therefore, complete concordance with the international hippie ethos.

It would be inaccurate, however, to consider the material culture of Soviet hippies simply as an import product or an exercise in replication. Just as certain American or British hippie fashions evolved from earlier counter-cultural styles within those respective societies, some of what was seen on the bodies and within the environments of Soviet hippies had domestic origins. And just as one would do well to examine the material culture of Western hippies nation by nation – if not commune by commune – while maintaining constant watch over those characteristics that enjoyed international currency, this examination of Soviet hippie material culture will concentrate on the phenomenon as it evolved in Latvia, refocusing occasionally on the larger picture.

It is a historiographic commonplace that Stalin's death ushered in a period of profound liberalization. Residents of the Baltic republics also benefited from the Thaw, but their comparatively recent, forced entry into Soviet society ensured that the benefits would be more erratically dispensed than elsewhere, often to be repealed. Even when local officials managed to overcome their paranoia of heightened monitoring by the Kremlin, quite often the liberalization measures they had taken were construed by central authorities as evidence of 'bourgeois nationalism' among those newcomers to the Soviet fold and thus overturned. While Aksenov's *stiliagi* cavorted on the beaches around Tallinn, numerous Soviet Latvian officials were readjusting to life in the Russian interior, where they had been deported only a year or so earlier during a purge of their too-liberal government.[5] Among the purged were the First and Second secretaries of the Latvian Komsomol, blamed for subverting Latvian youth's fraternal (pan-Soviet) instincts, as well as lesser party functionaries like Pēteris Kampars, who remained in Latvia on the condition that he report to the KGB any subversion he witnessed within Riga's young bohemian community. He was in a unique position to do so, because he was romantically involved with, and later married to, the nonconformist painter Birute Delle, an inspirational figure for local hippies. This political episode underscores how remarkable it was that a closely watched segment of Latvian society chose to become *bitņieki* [beatniks] and others, a few years later, *hipiji* [hippies]. Admittedly, these terms are somewhat unreliable nominations. While certain individuals were clearly affiliated with one or the other sensibility (at least as we understand these sensibilities from Western experience), other individuals resist easy categorization, especially in terms of material practice. Nonetheless, the terms 'beatnik' and 'hippie' describe rather distinct communities that dominated Latvian public spectacle and debate in different halves of the decade (and in the 'hippies' case, long thereafter).

Both constituencies would eventually merge, more in popular memory than in reality, as the *kazisti*, so named because both groups frequented the café *Kaza*, which opened in September 1962 on Vaļņu Street in the medieval quarter. *Kaza,* which means 'goat' in Latvian, actually adopted its name from Riga's first automated coffee dispenser – brand name, *Casino* – an imported machine that was installed in the small room behind one of the city's main worker cafeterias.[6] Habitués liked the latent foreignness of the name; it suggested not only gambling on the Riviera but also, homonymically, *casa* (as in *mi casa es su casa*).[7] Inside, *Kaza* was neither exotic nor homey. It opened sporting the typical Soviet low-end cafeteria décor, which is to say none whatsoever, and, contrary to standard expectations for an establishment frequented primarily by artists and writers over the course of a decade, it acquired no spontaneous décor in the form of graffiti or donated artworks.[8] Its clientele consisted of a close circle of twenty or so *kazisti* who, in turn, attracted their own circle of friends. The vast majority were in their twenties – indeed, within a five year range of each other – and the men and women were a mix of Latvians and Russians, with the addition of two elderly Jewish men. According to Juris Zvirgzdiņš, whom many consider to be the beatniks' ringleader, the *kazisti* spent their time reading not only *samizdat* literature, but also banned publications from the first Latvian Republic era and Polish- and German-language journals, especially issues devoted to America or Britain.[9] American Beat poetry, for example, arrived in Latvia by way of Poland, where it had been translated in the journal *Przekrój* (Profile).[10] Another Polish publication, *Szpilki,* introduced the singular illustration styles of Saul Steinberg and Slavomir

Mrožek, whose influences are clearly evident in the *kazisti*'s numerous, whimsical drawings from this time.[11] There wasn't much else to do at *Kaza* besides drink coffee, read, doodle and converse; if one wanted to smoke the preferred *Šipka* and *Slnci* filterless cigarettes or drink wine, the patron needed to repair to the adjacent stairwell, nicknamed café *Kariete* ('carriage').[12] But it was all about mobility anyway: after *Kaza* closed at 7pm, the crowd moved to the open-air café *Putnu dārzs* ('bird garden') until its closing at nine, and then onto *Skapis* ('cupboard' or, fittingly, 'wardrobe'), which remained open until eleven.[13]

This circuit allowed for a certain amount of promenading in their mildly idiosyncratic clothing. Though attentive to matters of dress, Riga's beatniks scorned the *stiliaga*'s ostentation and crass materialism, particularly that of Russian *stiliagi* who sometimes vacationed at Jūrmala, a nearby resort. Indeed, even Latvian-born *stiliagi* had avoided the flashy suits and wide, gaudy ties of their peers. Whether trips to nearby Estonia afforded them the chance to watch Finnish television broadcasts or they saw snapshots of close relatives who formed part of the sizeable Latvian diaspora in the West, Latvian youths occasionally glimpsed how their Western kindred dressed. They certainly understood the discrepancies between *stiliagi* and 'stylish'. Correspondingly, the equivalent Latvian term *stilīgais* ('stylish one') resonates with an acute sense of self-irony that the average *stilīaga* lacked.[14] Hanging around Jūrmala's popular café *Līdo,* the native dandies-manqué favoured simple wool or cotton jackets with zippers and padded shoulders, narrow trousers and caps not unlike the one worn by their American literary hero Holden Caulfield.[15]

Riga's beatniks, on the other hand, weren't particularly infatuated with authentic Western clothing. In fact, they despised the numerous sailors stationed at the city's naval base who sold jeans on the black market, and they refused to patronize these profiteers. Although the rather affordable prices of 4–5 rubles for a blue pair and 10 for a white caused Rigans to regard jeans as little better than workwear during the early 1960s,[16] local beatniks romanticized poverty and dressed even more thriftily (Figure 10.2). When they hand-knitted the nearly knee-length, dark blue or black pullover sweaters that anchored their sombre uniform of untailored jackets, casual pants and sneakers, it was less a matter of making something stylish than simply making something conspicuously unSoviet.[17] That male and female beatnik alike wore these sweaters distinguished them from most fashion-conscious youth elsewhere in the USSR, where, as *stiliagi* gave way to zoot-suited, flat-topped *shtatniki,* their female counterparts, *chuvikhi,* evolved into 'ingenues'. The ingenue, according to one Soviet fashion text, was 'characterized by a childlike hairstyle, a round, turndown collar, a slight décolleté, a naïve gaze (achieved by outlining the eyes to make them round and wide), light pastel hues in makeup, a miniskirt, clothes that outlined the figure, and the mannerisms of a capricious child'.[18] Given its burgeoning population of Russian-speaking immigrants, Riga has its share of ingenues and *shtatniki,* too, but the restrained, unisex nature of the Latvian beatniks' sartorial revolt is worthier of note, mainly because their hippie successors would inherit many of their methods of self-education and fabrication, though almost none of their discretion.

Conversely, other Soviet cities had *beatniki,* looking much like Latvian *Bitņieki,* but with the requisite addition of jeans. Public ridicule also became integral to the look. Just as *stiliagi* originated as a journalist's pejorative, *beatniki* were assailed by *Sovetskaia kul'tura* in 1963 as *kurinye bogi,* or 'chicken gods'. According to the style critic, they grew 'beards and strange haircuts', wore sweaters that made them look like Americans, swaggered in the style of warriors from the film *The Seven Samurai*, and listened to 'contemporary music on miniature Japanese radios. [. . .] The highest style is three fellows and one fully collectivized female sputnik.'[19] Authorities seemed not to understand that such vitriolic, vividly detailed editorials were less effective at dissuading young minds than at enticing them, especially the more independent, intelligent ones that had learned to read against the grain of propaganda. Indeed, several *kazisti* credit official texts with both stimulating their curiosity about foreign 'decadence' and providing clear instructions on how to effect it.[20] Given that the USSR's first portable transistor radio, the VEF 'Gauja,' had been manufactured and sold in Riga since 1960,[21] a beatnik could accessorize his or her outfit well before the next issue of *Sovetskaia kul'tura* hit the kiosk.

No doubt Latvia's beatniks also viewed Kurosawa's samurai film, though not necessarily for perfecting their gait. As musician Jānis Vanadziņš recently recalled, early in the 1960s 'the *fashion* was to be clever: read good literature, see good films, study all philosophies'.[22] In fact, Rigans had exceptional opportunities to see good films, and films from abroad served as incidental primers of personal style for both beatnik and hippie. While residents and visitors of Moscow had that city's International Film festival for significant artistic and sartorial inspiration, cinephiles in Riga benefited from semi-private screenings held by the Latvian Cinematographers Union.[23] Local movie-goers saw not only Fellini's *8-1/2,* so infamous and galvanizing in Moscow in 1963, but also seminal, visually hip works by Antonioni, Bertolucci, Godard and others, some of which came quietly via official distribution channels, others arriving through other means. Eižens Valpēters, an artist affiliated with both camps of *kazisti,* recalls another, earlier film that captivated local audiences with its sympathetic views of American culture. On the occasion of de Gaulle's 1966 visit to Moscow, François Reichenbach's documentary *L'Amerique vue par un français* (1960) was screened in several Soviet cities, Riga included. The first extended footage of ordinary Americans in quotidian situations seen by their contemporaries in Latvia, this film was utterly revelatory, especially a scene showing prisoners staging a rodeo for their own entertainment, visual evidence that American convicts enjoyed clothing and furniture of manifestly better quality than what was available in the USSR. The film inventoried material culture fads, such as hula hoops, and devoted much attention to teenagers in general.[24] Though Valpēters does not specifically mention them, the film's images of multi-racial communities, San Francisco street life, Disneyland, commercial advertising and New York City architecture probably equally bedazzled audience members, and may have sited many of their American fantasies (especially powerful later, when Latvian hippies felt themselves participating in a global, urban culture they could never visit in person).

Obviously, music also transmitted international youth sensibility; BBC, Voice of America and Radio Luxembourg broadcasts reliably provided jazz and rock soundtracks for Latvian parties. Juris Zvirgzdiņš recalls, 'We listened to Elvis Presley, Jim Morrison, Jimmy Hendrix, Janis Joplin, Bob Dylan, and Joan Baez'.[25] This playlist was evident even to my émigré grandparents when, in the mid-1960s, they received a letter from a young relative in Riga requesting a gift of blue suede shoes. Biruta Delle, who once painted a work titled *Joan Baez Sings of Peace* and called her unofficial painting studio 'Submarine' after the famous yellow one, claims that Latvian listeners heard the Beatles as early as the average Londoner did[26] and indeed Rigans started wearing half-frame wire-rimmed eyeglasses shortly after John Lennon himself adopted the look from the Byrds.

Long before this eastern flank of the British Invasion landed, sailors had smuggled jazz recordings into Riga, where an underground *Roentgenizdat* industry in the late 1950s dubbed the music onto used x-ray plates, easily obtainable and suitable for the primitive recordings that commanded premium prices on the black market.[27] With the proliferation of tape recorders in the 1960s – again, *Made in Latvian SSR* – *roentgenizdat* gave way to *magnetizdat,* the reel-to-reel duplication of rock albums either smuggled from the West or, increasingly, brought by visiting émigré relatives. The beatniks' scruples regarding the purchase of American consumer goods tended to disappear when the merchandise was contraband music. How could they resist, when faced with *Komsomolskaia pravda* headlines that virtually dared them to buy contraband, headlines like 'Those Who Love Jazz Today Will Sell the Soviet Motherland Tomorrow' and '[There's] One Step from Jazz to the Finnish Knife'?[28] Given such truncated Nordic geography, Rigans had little trouble at all getting to the USSR's first jazz festival, held just across the Latvian-Estonian border in Tartu in 1964.

If jazz was treacherous, rock was something unspeakable (and, its rabid critics might add, dangerously unhummable). According to the foremost authority on Soviet Rock, Artemy Troitsky, 'Extensive research has convinced me that the first genuine rock group surfaced in Riga'.[29] Pits Andersons, who began his music career by translating English lyrics from *magnetizdat* for the vocalist of the pioneering rock band The Revengers, recalls, 'The Revengers began playing in 1961; electric guitars from Czechoslovakia were already in the stores, but the bass was home-made, using piano wires for strings. The wires were so hard that the bass player had to wrap his fingers in tape in order to play'.[30] They played Elvis, Bill Haley and Little Richard covers plus black r'n'b numbers. For instance, The Revengers played 'Love Potion Number Nine' before The Searchers made it a pop hit.[31] After a stint as The Revengers' lead singer, Andersons formed his own band, Melody Makers. In April 1965, a scheduled Melody Makers performance was cancelled, and hundreds of fans stood for six hours outside the Riga concert venue, the former Orthodox cathedral located four blocks from *Kaza*. Fans carried banners that exhorted 'Free the Guitars!' and passers by joined the demonstration, 'but the militia stood by in bewilderment until the onset of nightfall finally dispersed the crowd'.[32] Latvian youth counterculture had finally experienced solidarity.

Party ideologues who posited a cause-and-effect relationship between modern Western music and juvenile delinquency no doubt felt vindicated by the timing of the hippies' debut in Riga. Less than two months after the Melody Makers fiasco, the youthquake struck Latvia. In the summer of 1965, a small group of hippies began congregating in *Doma laukums* (Dome Square), located alongside the medieval cathedral (Figure 10.3). They made conspicuous display of long hair and customized jeans, painted each other's bodies with Flower Power symbols, played guitars, danced to their own kind of music (as they would, in due time, to that of the Mamas and Papas) and, in general, revelled in an eroticized version of

Figure 10.2 Riga's hippies gather in Dome Square, 30 June 1968, wearing clothing of their own design. Andris Grinbergs seated in centre. Photo credit: Māra Brašmane.

the All-Union 'fraternalism' that deposed Komsomol secretaries had supposedly rendered unachievable in Latvia. These youths banded around a nineteen-year-old clothing-design student named Andris Grinbergs, and by his estimation there were, at first, seven true hippies: two girls and five boys who would initially meet on Saturdays and Sundays, joined by sympathetic youth of various ethnic backgrounds: Latvians, of course, but also Estonians, Lithuanians, Russians and Ukrainians who had recently immigrated to Riga.[33] As it has since been hypo-thesized about the relatively advanced state of a queer community in Riga, the fact that so many young people attracted by job opportunities and the residual Western atmosphere of the major Baltic cities had relocated to the western Soviet republics made it possible for this new generation to explore alternative lifestyles at a safe remove from vigilant, censorious families who stayed behind in the Soviet interior.

According to hippie musician Jānis Vandadziņš, hippiedom was an almost instantaneous phenomenon, at least in its visual manifestation.[34] This was largely attributable to Grinberg's acute eye and even sharper methods of locating sources of inspiration. For instance, the fashions of Mary Quant and the spectacles of Twiggy and Jean Shrimpton were surreptitiously gleaned from copies of *Vogue* held in the restricted collection of the Latvian Academy of Sciences' Fondamentāla bibliotēka, to which Eižens Valpēters finagled unauthorized access.[35] Valpēters also translated dispatches about Western youth fashion from copies of *Przekrój,* which Grinbergs notoriously filched from the mail.[36] Even without translation skills, aspiring hippies could acquire plenty of nontextual information from these sources. Careful scrutiny of photographs gave them their first indication of how new dance styles from the West looked, Whereas most *kazisti* enjoyed the Twist (Figure 1.3), hippies danced the Madison and the Hully-Gully. Naturally, extrapolating move-ment from a still image was problematic, but recently restored film footage of a party held in one of their flats proves that their dance moves conformed fully with dances popular in the West – given that the original movements were improv-isational anyway.[37]

The same mastery could be claimed for their dress, and, again, the more improvisational the better. Hippies delighted in the Russian slang term *samostrok,* meaning 'sartorial *samizdat'* or 'self-published' clothing.[38] Because they had heard that many hip Westerners in the mid-1960s sewed their own outfits, they never regarded *samostrok* as being downmarket or inauthentic. Indeed, once the sewing began, they experienced the mainstream commercial validation common to creators of street fashion everywhere. Riga's black market responded to their innovation of making bell-bottomed jeans from blue-dyed canvas and then transplanting labels from the readily available straight-legged American variety. The price of contraband jeans, unchanged for years, suddenly and rapidly escalated.[39] For other articles of clothing, fabrics, usually synthetic, were painted with psychedelic designs similar

Mark Allen Svede

to those popularized by Emilio Pucci, and then sewn into garments. Standard patterned fabrics manufactured in Soviet mills were sometimes suitable for *samostrok,* given the right density of figure (for example, a tight paisley) and its inspired combination with other patterned fabrics (say, a light-paisley-on-dark-ground juxtaposed with a dark-on-light variation). Even an insipid machine-printed floral fabric, the stuff of unremarkable sundresses, delivered more visual impact when it was sewn into pants, combined with a plain muslin shirt with voluminous, lacey cuffs and collar, and then worn by a man. Beatniks may have been innovative regarding the unisex nature of their pullover sweaters, but hippie fashion further confounded traditional clothing-based notions of gender identity by dressing men in delicate, intricate fripperies and women in elementary shapes and comparatively sober materials.

Because not everybody who may have been so inclined had access to Andris Grinberg's original clothing designs, alternative means arose for dressing as a hippie. Though not strictly a youth-oriented phenomenon, an unofficial design realm developed about this time in Riga,[40] its small ateliers shadowing but out-manoeuvering the state's centralized garment industry in terms of meeting consumers' changing tastes. Ready-made clothing – even the dreariest Soviet *prêt-à-porter* – could be adorned with hand-drawn or embroidered peace signs, hearts, butterflies and flowers.[41] Or store-bought items were recut to form more modish silhouettes. Or, simply, they were cut. Finished cuffs, sleeves and vest bottoms were often coarsely fringed, forming a kineticized counterpart to the beaded headbands, necklaces and long tresses of hair that conspired to keep the hippies' upper bodies in constant motion. The rather austere look of the beatnik was supplanted by an ensemble animated in its coloration, patterning and structure.

The Latvian hippie look involved the complex layering of many garments and accessories, say, a neckchain worn over a scarf over a vest over a shirt. But then, the same observation could be made about Latvian traditional ethnic costume, and this is where hippie style in Riga became less obviously an indiscriminate import from the West. Photographs that show Grinbergs and friends wearing coronals of daisies (Figure 10.3) may seem indistinguishable from mass-media images of Flower Children in Haight-Ashbury, but the stylistic ontogeny is more complicated. Just as American hippies appropriated elements of ethnic traditional dress at a time when racial minorities and native peoples were gaining political visibility in North America, Latvian hippies revived elements of indigenous folk attire at the very moment when the prohibition was lifted against celebrating the Latvian summer solstice festival *Jāņi.*[42] First Secretary of the Latvian Communist Party Arvīds Pelše had regarded the *Jāņi* rituals of singing ancient songs, wearing oak-leaf wreaths and so forth to be pernicious displays of bourgeois nationalism, so this holiday, which had long served as an implicit (hetero)sexual rite of passage for youth, was outlawed from 1959 to 1966. However, Pelše was promoted to the

Figure 10.3 Hippies in Riga's Dome Square, 30 June 1968. Photo credit: Māra Brašmane.

Politburo in Moscow shortly before San Francisco's Flower Children began their Summer of Love, and soon the incipient Flower Children of Riga resurrected elements of *Jāņi,* ranging from the floral coronals to sexual license.

While one cannot wholly ascribe the hippies' blossoming headgear and sexuality to an ethnographic revival, poet Uldis Bērziņš does credit the 1960s generation with the explosion of interest in Latvian folklore.[43] In fact, several images of an early hippie gathering show a woman dressed in an outfit analogous to the regional costume of the Valmiera district (Figure 10.4). Her skirt is virtually identical to the traditional satin-weave skirt bearing a narrow vertical pattern of light multi-colored stripes against a dark background; she wears a checkered vest similar in cut to the short *Valmieras jaka* (jacket), which tended to be colourfully decorated; a utilitarian-looking dark sweater substitutes for the traditional plain shirt; and her hair is encircled by a beaded, fringed headband functioning much like the embroidered hair ribbons once worn by Valmiera's unmarried women.[44] This adaptation of a costume traditionally reserved for communal celebrations such as song and dance festivals was fully in keeping with the carnivalesque atmosphere created by hippies.

On the other hand, certain elements of Latvian ethnographic style that seem most visually akin to mod Western fashion never appeared on the bodies of Riga's

Figure 10.4 Latvian hippies and friends near café *Kaza*, late 1960s. Woman at left is wearing an outfit derived from a regional folk costume, while male seated in centre sports the pointy shoes popular among *stiliagi*. Photo credit: Māra Brašmane.

hippies. The popular Op Art-patterned fabrics of designers such as John Bates have uncanny visual equivalents in traditional Latvian fabric designs, such as the two- and three-block overshot weave patterns *divdaļīgs pārstaipu drellis* (known to most weavers as 'Monk's Belt') and *divdaļīgs četrnīšu drellis* ('Summer/ Winter').[45] The subtler colouration of the traditional versions evidently rendered them unsuitable as psychedelica, and to replicate such complex patterns in higher chroma paints would have been nearly impossible. (And for some reason, the skills of sympathetic weavers were never enlisted to reinterpret these designs with brighter yarns.)

Also absent from the Latvian hippies' wardrobe were the components of military uniforms that American hippies often incorporated into their surreal ensembles as an affront to what they regarded as an overdecorated institution of violence. This absence is unsurprising, given that the Red Army was a *de facto* occupational force in Latvia, and one not nearly as compelled to protect freedom of speech and wardrobe choice as its Western counterpart. As susceptible to arrest as the hippies might haven been had they worn Soviet military garb in less than official capacity, they were subject to harsh criticism from academic folklorists for not maintaining idealized ethnographic standards. Any interpretive latitude with folk dress was distrusted as a betrayal of the Latvian national soul.

But then, hippies couldn't please everyone. Understandably, their imaginative adaptation of folk costuming curried favour with neither purists nor officials who excused ethnography as one of the few acceptable means of expressing personal identity. Less foreseeable, however, was the tremendous resistance they encountered from their fellow *kazisti,* the beatniks. When hippies began frequenting *Kaza,* the café's previous regulars did not welcome them. Beatniks suspected that the hippies' drug use was either a KGB provocation or, if self-motivated, a likely reason for KGB intervention into what had been their completely open environment.[46] In sharp contrast to their American namesakes, Latvian beatniks did not take drugs, an abstinence palpable in Juris Zvirgzdiņš's dismissive remark that the hippie phenomenon began as 'pill-popping'.[47] Others more intimately acquainted with these newcomers insist that the hippies' interests only gradually expanded from the sartorial to the pharmaceutical (and from the musical to the sexual). Even so, their pharmacopœia was relatively limited. Because LSD was typically unavailable, they took illegally obtained prescription drugs, mainly barbiturates, sniffed glue or smoked Central Asian opiates.[48] Eventually, other *kazisti* did experience guilt by association. Standing in the doorway of *Kaza,* Eižens Valpēters was captured on film for a television news critique of the youth phenomenon and misrepresented in the commentary as a drug dealer.[49] In the public imagination, 'hippie' and 'drug addict' became synonymous.

Nevertheless, the hippies of Riga exerted a powerful and not entirely negative impression on the public. Vacationers who came to 'Riga de Janeiro' from the Soviet interior, intending only to enjoy the beaches on the Gulf of Riga, found instead a spectacular group of hippies parading seductively in front of the city's tourist attractions. And because this public included disaffected youths, the scene in Latvia predictably attracted recruits from Leningrad, Moscow and elsewhere. Some remained within this peripheral, libertine community – recalling the migration of American youth to the Bay Area a few years earlier – while others exported hippie culture to their hometowns. Before long, a hippie network existed in the USSR, concentrated in the western centres of L'viv, Riga, Tallinn and Vilnius.[50] Smaller provincial cities, like Liepaja, also hosted this phenomenon. When progressive theatre director Ināra Eglīte visited renowned hippie Ieva Brašmane (aka Clinger) at the Liepaja Latvian Drama Theater, one of the few places a hippie might find employment, she noticed tell-tale grafitti on the houses: flowers, 'Beatles' and 'Make Love, Not War',[51] an apt slogan for one of the USSR's most militarized cities.

In Russian, this expanding informal network was soon called the *sistema;* a member of their extended community, a *sistemnyi;* and someone sympatico to hippies, *okolosistemnyi.*[52] The use of Russian as the hippies' *lingua franca* underscores the multi-ethnic composition of this subculture, but more linguistically revealing, their clothing terms derived predominantly from English. These range from the metonymies *baton* (from *button*), which meant a shirt constructed of sleek fabric with, as a rule, floral patterning and many buttons, and *leybl* (label) signifying both jeans and the all-important foreign label conferring authenticity and status; to simple transliterations: *beg* (bag or rucksack), *būtsi* (boots), *klouz* (clothes), *shuzy* (shoes), *tayukha* (tie) and *truzera* or *trauzers* (trousers). Clothing qualities were also anglicized: *brandovyi* (brand-new) or *sayz* (size), as were hippie accoutrements: *chik-faer* ('chik!'-fire, an onomatopœic cigarette lighter), *draga* (drugs), *posteri* (poster) and *smok* (tobacco products). Their Soviet surroundings were exoticized: *dragstor* (drugstore), *flets* (flat), *pīpl* or *pīpli* (people), *saunds* (sound), *sinema* (cinema), *šops* (shop) and *treins* (train). Perhaps most revealing – as it were – the body and its recreational possibilities took on a foreign flavor: *aizy* (eyes), *beksayd* (backside), *fak-seyshchn* (fuck session), *feys* (face), *frilav* (free-love), *khendy* (hand), *khayr* (long hair), *khich* (hitchhike), *kis* (kiss), *mustasha* (moustache), *penis, prik (*prick) and *tok* (rap).

Some of this argot might seem immaterial to a study of hippie material culture, but the paradox remains that much of the hippies' energy went into *dematerializing* culture. While beatniks embraced poverty through well-worn dress, the hippies preferred to embrace each other while fully undressed. By the early 1970s, nudity became the uniform at a camp called – like that first Soviet portable transistor radio – 'Gauja.' Located north of Riga where the river Gauja meets the sea, the site attracted hippies from throughout the USSR.[53] In early Happenings organized by performance artists Andris and Inta Grinbergi their specially designed costumes were especially prone to come off. But contrary to scathing, sexphobic editorials about the hippies' lifestyle, all was not a *fak-seyshchn.* Like the beatniks, hippies were greatly interested in the metaphysical issues, and, alas, this interest was often facilitated by material things. For example, Indira Gandhi's state visit to Moscow occasioned special limited-edition publication of the *Bhagavad Gita* and a translation of Mahatma Gandhi's *An Autobiography* – to demonstrate Soviet 'freedom of religion' – and these coveted texts became important metaphysical influences in Latvia.[54] According to Sandrs Rīga, later jailed in a psychiatric hospital for stewarding the nascent ecumenical movement, hippies in Tallinn and Moscow shared the Riga community's tolerant spiritual tendencies.[55]

Their spiritual outlook, like that of many Western hippies, was an amalgam of world religious and secular humanist ideologies. The Buddhist goal of Walking the One True Path translated, in everyday experience, as avoiding all complicity with the Soviet system. The doctrine of passive resistance preached by Gandhi meant this avoidance was to be non-confrontational, as in the hippies' preference for the marginal social status and minimal mainstream social interaction afforded by jobs like that of a building superintendent or guard, whose once-a-week, 24-hour shifts largely freed hippie-employees from daily drudgery, and whose more or less secluded, unsupervised working environment allowed for long meditative silences, long philosophical discussions and, not unimportantly, long hair. In matters of compassion, the Beatles were not the only preachers of 'All You Need Is Love'; the Roman Catholic example of Francis of Assisi held tremendous appeal. While this elective universe of moral values and models might seem overly convenient, the hypocrisies of institutional religion were more avoidable this way. For instance, Catholicism's pervasive sexism was remedied by the adoption of proto-feminist strategies, though it must also be stressed that gender equality was not entirely achieved by the hippies' ideological syntheses. Just as the long, dark sweaters of the male beatniks were invariably knitted by their girlfriends, wives or grandmothers, hippie household duties were usually performed by the female members of these heterosexual couples. To their credit, however, hippies so radically devalued patterns of bourgeois domesticity and so simplified their material-based routines that the rudimentary issue of women taking sole responsibility for cooking, cleaning and child-rearing was ameliorated. Feminist poet Liāna Langa recalls from a childhood spent in hippie households that the adults' relationships were remarkably unexploitative for that time and place, just as the premium they placed on meditative silence rendered these homes unusually peaceful, particularly in contrast to the din of collectivized life in communal flats down the hall.[56]

Although, in the end, much of Soviet hippie culture focused on immaterialities such as love and mutual respect, the phenomenon transpired in very real, very hateful surroundings. Good vibes and common values may have connected the hippies of Riga's café *Kaza* with those frequenting Tallinn's café *Pegasus*, but physical interactions were increasingly subjected to interference, first from zealous gangs of Komsomol members[57] and then, as the international student movement gained in strength at the end of the decade, from the increasingly vigilant KGB. Even the basic hope for student internationalism was fragile: the *kazisti* followed the course of the Prague Spring via VOA and BBC broadcasts with great excitement, but upon learning about the Warsaw Pact invasion of Czechoslovakia, they drank heavily and bitterly.[58] One of the hippies, a boy named Rips, lodged a public protest by setting himself afire at the base of the pre-Soviet Freedom Movement in the centre of Riga. Accordingly, youthful optimism about improvement of the domestic situation waned as the Brezhnev era bore onward. Uldis Leinerts, the charismatic poet of the *kazisti* died mysteriously – murdered, it's believed, by the KGB.[59] Grinbergs and others were conscripted into the military, temporarily interrupting their hippiedom. When director Modris Tenisons organized Riga's premiere of *Jesus Christ Superstar,* the production was suppressed after one performance. Pressured to relocate, he moved to Lithuania and founded a movement group at the Kaunas Drama Theater. On 14 May 1972, when the Kaunas hippies gathered at the town's central fountain to give a performance of the musical *Hair!,* another hippie, Romas Kalantas, self-immolated in protest against the Soviet system. In response, hippies rioted alongside other activists on 18–19 May, drawing inter-national attention to Baltic nationalism. Tenisons, the editor of the Lithuanian journal *Jaunystë* (Youth) and the theatre's chief director, were somehow held responsible for the unrest and were punished.[60]

Despite their personal tragedies, the hippies of Latvia revolutionalized aspects of Soviet society – and in ways that even they might not have anticipated. The recent recovery of Imants Bril's 1972 film *Sejas (Faces),* a suppressed Goskino Latvija documentary about the ostensible evils of international youth culture, reveals hippie culture's pervasive influences. Unscreened because the director's sympathies effectively rendered this film a guide to where in Riga one might dance to Iron Butterfly's 'In-a-Gadda-da-Vida' or how to decorate one's flat with assemblages of Marlboro wrappers and retired record albums 'made gray'[61] from incessant playing on bad equipment, *Sejas* revealed just how widespread Jimi Hendrix t-shirts, marijuana smoking and open sexuality had become. To judge by its sheer number of photogenic subjects, the streets and parks of Riga were overrun by tuned-in, turned-on youths. Representations of this vibrant counterculture were not always suppressed. Appearing in numerous publications at this time, a painting titled *Cry,* by Janis Osis, shows Jane Fonda at a microphone, flanked by a go-go dancer in a green afro, a policeman in riot-gear and another woman wearing hotpants and platform shoes. Purportedly a critique of American culture, this appealing tableau would be reproduced in a survey of new Latvian painting as an exemplary realist work, though *Cry's* unreal colours were made even more lurid by inferior Soviet presswork.[62] No similar technical excuse explains the appearance, in an utterly pedestrian handbook on women's hairstyling from 1974, of the option of requesting a cyan-dyed shag cut from one's comrade beautician.[63] Perhaps the most damning evidence of the hippies' influence on the mainstream youth of Latvia, guitarist and erstwhile hippie Jānis Vanadziņš recently recollected playing a gig in the early 1970s at the Pioneer Palace, looking down from the band's position on the balcony and watching the twirling masses in their white shirts and red neckerchiefs.[64] By hippie standards, they were seriously overdressed. And yet, they were missing lovebeads.

Notes

1 Quoted in *Sirp ja vasar* (29 October 1971).

2 Originally appearing in *Iunost'*, nos. 6–7 (1961), it was translated for a British edition in 1962 and an American edition in 1963.

3 Tony Weitzel, 'A Taste of Russia in '57, Last Good Year for Slogans', *Chicago Daily News* (19 October 1963).

4 These English-language slogans are visible in Imants Bril's 1972 documentary film *Sejas* (Faces) and photographs by Māra Brašmane.

5 Regarding this neo-*Zhdanovschina* against Latvian culture, see Romuald J. Misiunas and Rein Taagepera, *The Baltic States: Years of Dependence 1940– 1980* (Berkeley and LA: University of California Press, 1983), pp. 134–41, 155–9. Additional information about the personalities involved comes from interviews with Biruta Delle and her associates in Riga, mid-February 1998.

6 Pauls Bankovskis, '*Kaza* ir vēsture [is history]', *Rīgas laiks*. vol. 1 (Jan 1994), p. 33. According to key regulars' recollections, the true *kasists* was a beatnik, not a hippie. Hippies, however, remember this differently.

7 Interview with Biruta Delle, Riga, 15 February 1998.

8 Interview with former dissident Sandrs Rīga, Riga, 15 February 1998.

9 Bankovskis, '*Kaza* ir vēsture', p. 34.

10 Interview with artist Eižens Valpēters, Riga, 17 February 1998. Both Valpēters and Zvirgzdiņš recall significant inspiration from reading Kerouac.

11 In particular, drawings by Valpēters, now in the Norton and Nancy Dodge Collection of Nonconformist Art at Rutgers University's Zimmerli Art Museum, possess the surreal intelligence and wit of Steinberg.

12 Juris Zvirgzdiņš, 'Mēs pasmaidīsim un atbildisim vienkarši un nemelojot: – Mēs dzīvojām! Kādas kompānijas portreta skice (We will chuckle and answer simply and not lie: – We lived! Portrait sketch of one crowd)', *FF* (November– December 1997), p. 37.

13 Recalled by poet Andris Bergmanis in Bankovskis, '*Kaza* ir vēsture', p. 36.

14 Delle and Valpēters interviews.

15 Valpēters, for example, recalls the impact of Salinger's character upon his own maturation.

16 Jānis Vanadziņš, 'No hipijiem Latvijai ir daudz gaišu cilvēku . . . (From the hippies, Latvia has many bright people . . . ' *FF* (November-December 1997),

p. 28. In later years, a pair of jeans could command 100 rubles in certain markets (see below).

17 Delle interview.

18 V.A. Kruichkova, 'Moda kak forma potrebleniia' *Moda za i protiv* (Moscow: Iskusstvo, 1973), p. 248, quoted by Ol'ga Vainshtein in 'Female Fashion, Soviet Style: Bodies of Ideology,' *Russia – Women – Culture,* Helena Goscilo and Beth Holmgren, eds (Bloomington: Indiana University Press, 1996), p. 65.

19 From an unnamed articled in *Sovetskaia kul'tura* (24 Aug 1963), cited in Peter J. Babris, *Baltic Youth under Communism* (Arlington Hts, IL: Research Publishers, 1967), p. 55. The commentator's decision to avoid the female form of the noun *sputnik – sputnitsa* may indicate that the female beatnik was regarded less as a fellow traveller or life companion, conventional translations of that word, than as a satellite, with its newer, space-age connotation with the attendant, chauvinist implications that she revolved around a primary (male) body, led a flighty existence, and so forth.

20 Delle interview.

21 Imants Eglītis, 'Latvijas radiodizains'*, Latvijas dizains*, M. Lacis ed. (Riga: Liesma, 1984), p. 98.

22 Vanadziņš, 'No hipijiem Latvijai', p. 28.

23 For a brief discussion of the exceptionally liberal Latvian film community, see Val S. Golovsky, *Behind the Soviet Screen: The Motion Picture Industry in the USSR, 1972–82* (Ann Arbor: Ardis, 1986), pp. 44–5.

24 Valpēters interview. The impact of new contacts with Western material culture is difficult to overestimate. For example, everyone in the room during my interview with Sandrs Rīga could name 1955 as the year chewing gum debuted in Latvia.

25 Zvirgzdiņš, 'Mēs pasmaidīsim un atbildisim', p. 37.

26 Delle interview.

27 The persistence of this phenomenon was described by Māris Krusts, a defecting Latvian sailor, in an émigré newspaper interview: 'Melodies in Short Supply', *Laiks* (Time) (Brooklyn NY, 5 December 1962).

28 Rīga interview. Again, a roomful of interviewees could remember these headlines verbatim.

29 Artemy Troitsky. *Back in the USSR: The True Story of Rock in Russia* (London and Boston: Faber & Faber, 1988), p. 21.

30 Ibid. Troitsky adds that bass guitars first appeared in stores in 1967.

31 Ibid.

32 Ibid., pp. 22, 26

33 Much of the detailed information that follows has been gleaned from a seven-year correspondence and many casual discussions with Grinbergs, making it now as much an act of recollection on my part as it was on his. Visual

information is taken from photographic archives of Grinbergs and *kaziste* Māra Brašmane, as well as a series of underground films that have recently come to light.

34 Vanadziņš, p. 28. Valpeters, while acknowledging Grinberg's singular stylistic initiative in Riga, noted in his interview that hippie fashion was generated elsewhere almost simultaneously.

35 Sandrs Rīga interview.

36 Andris Bergmanis, quoted in Bankovskis, '*Kaza* ir vēsture', p. 36.

37 This film is Andris Grindberg's *Pašportrets* (Self-Portrait) (1972; restored 1996).

38 Interview with Valpēters, Sandrs Rīga and poet Liāna Langa, Riga, 15 February 1998.

39 This process was described by Valpēters who credits Grinbergs with the best tailoring skills and most inventive designs among the hippies. The price increase is mentioned in Vanadziņš, p. 28, along with the charming fact that rulers, for rigorous scientific verification of whose bell-bottoms were widest, were a common hippie wardrobe accessory.

40 Delle interview.

41 Interview with Māra Brašmane, Riga, 19 February 1998.

42 This prohibition was one aspect of the cultural purge of 1959.

43 Bankovskis, '*Kaza* ir vēsture', p. 40.

44 For a detailed description of folk attire, consult Velta Rozenberga's commentary in *Latviešu tautas tērpi* (Latvian Folk Costume). *I. Vidzeme* (Riga: Jāņa sēta, 1995), pp. 64–5

45 Examples can be seen in Anita Apinis-Herman, *Latvian Weaving Techniques* (Kenthurst NSW: Kangaroo Press, 1993), pp. 77–9.

46 Unless otherwise noted, information about drug culture was taken from interviews with Delle and Valpēters.

47 Bankovskis, '*Kaza* ir vēsture', p. 34.

48 Although his account suffers from the fact that he mistakes his belated participation in the Riga scene (mostly during the 1970s) for the evolution of the whole, Mark Yoffe effectively catalogues local drug culture in 'Hippies in the Baltic. The Rock-And-Roll Era', *Cross Currents: A Yearbook of Central European Culture,* vol. 7 (1988), p. 161.

49 On a more positive note, legendary videographer Andris Slapiņš once used an image of Valpēters and a female hippie to secure admission to the Moscow film school, banking on its Occidentalist attraction.

50 Sandrs Rīga interview.

51 'Es biju gandrīz hipijs' ('I was almost a hippie'), *JA (Jaunā āvize*'s Saturday supplement) (10 Jan 1999) p. 8.

52 A compilation of the hippies' argot can be found, intermixed with slang from subsequent Soviet youth subcultures, in F.I. Riozhanskii, *Sleng khippi: materialy k slovariu*. (St. Petersburg: Evropeiskogo doma, 1992). Additional information about Latvian-language slang was provided by filmmaker Haralds Elceris via private e-mail correspondence.

53 Sandrs Rīga interview.

54 Ibid. *Moia zhizn'* was published in 1959 by Izdatel'stvo vostochnoi literatury, Moscow.

55 Ibid.

56 Phone interview with Liāna Langa, 15 November 1999, Columbus, Ohio.

57 Vanadziņš, 'No hipijiem Latvijai', p. 29.

58 Valpēters interview.

59 Langa interview, 15 February 1998.

60 Information taken from conversations with Tenisons, his remarks in 'Es biju gandrīz hipijs', p. 8, and Rokas M. Tracevskis, 'Remembering the flower power of Kaunas', *Baltic Times* (21–27 May 1998) p. 17.

61 Vanadziņš, 'No hipijiem Latvijai', p. 28.

62 Aija Nodieva. *Latviešu jaunākā glezniecība* (The New Latvian Painting) (Riga: Liesma, 1974) p. 176ff.

63 A Kļimoviča *et al., Friziera darba meistarība* [Mastery of the hairdresser's craft], (Riga: Zvaigzne, 1974) p. 128ff.

64 Vanadziņš, 'No hipijiem Latvijai', p. 28.

Index

Index